CW00919780

THE COUNTRY HOUSE AND THE GREAT WAR

The Country House and the Great War

Irish and British experiences

Terence Dooley & Christopher Ridgway

EDITORS

FOUR COURTS PRESS

Typeset in 10.5 pt on 12.5 pt Ehrhardt by
Carrigboy Typesetting Services
FOUR COURTS PRESS LTD
7 Malpas Street, Dublin 8, Ireland
www.fourcourtspress.ie
and in North America for
FOUR COURTS PRESS
c/o ISBS, 920 NE 58th Avenue, Suite 300, Portland, OR 97213.

© The various contributors and Four Courts Press 2016

A catalogue record for this title is available
from the British Library.

ISBN 978–1–84682–617–7

All rights reserved.
No part of this publication may be reproduced, stored in or introduced
into a retrieval system, or transmitted, in any form or by any means
(electronic, mechanical, photocopying, recording or otherwise),
without the prior written permission of both the copyright
owner and publisher of this book.

Printed in England
by TJ International, Padstow, Cornwall.

Contents

Contributors

FERGAL BROWNE is originally from Belgooly, Co. Cork and is a graduate of University College Cork. He has published a number of articles and co-edited *Tracton: where the abbey lies low* (Tracton, 2007). He now lives in Monasterevin with his wife Katherine.

EDWARD BUJAK is senior lecturer in British studies and history at Harlaxton College. He is a fellow of the Royal Historical Society, Royal Society of Arts and the Higher Education Academy. He is the author of *Reckless fellows: the gentlemen of the Royal Flying Corps* (London, 2015) and *England's rural realms: landholding and the agricultural revolution* (London, 2007).

PHILIP BULL is an adjunct professor in history at La Trobe University, Melbourne and a visiting professor with the Centre for the Study of Historic Houses and Estates at Maynooth University. The author of *Land, politics and Irish nationalism: a study of the Irish land question* (Dublin, 1996), he has also written numerous articles on nineteenth- and twentieth-century Irish history. He is currently organizing and cataloguing the large archive of papers at Monksgrange, Co. Wexford.

FIDELMA BYRNE is an Irish Research Council postgraduate scholar. Her research interests include nineteenth- and twentieth-century social history, landed estates and assisted emigration. She is currently completing her doctoral thesis entitled 'Estate management practices on the Wentworth-Fitzwilliam estates in Yorkshire and Ireland, 1815–65: a transnational comparative analysis' under the supervision of Prof. Terence Dooley at Maynooth University.

CAROLINE CARR-WHITWORTH is collections curator, art, for the north region of English Heritage. She was appointed in 1991 as a core member of the team which conserved and opened Brodsworth Hall near Doncaster to the public in 1995 and has been involved in several exhibition and conservation projects there. She is the author of its guidebook, *Brodsworth Hall and gardens* (English Heritage, 2009), and with Virginia Arrowsmith of 'Emerging from the shadows: maids & mistresses at Brodsworth Hall' in Ruth Larsen (ed.), *Maids & mistresses: celebrating 300 years of women and the Yorkshire country house* (York, 2004).

IAN d'ALTON has written extensively on southern Irish Protestantism from the eighteenth to the twentieth centuries, and is the author of *Protestant society and politics in Cork, 1812–1844*. He was an editorial advisor and contributor to the Royal Irish Academy/Cambridge University Press' *Dictionary of Irish biography* (2009). He is currently working on the fascicle for Naas, Co. Kildare in the RIA's

Irish Historic Town Atlas series, and a book on the Royal Historical Society's Alexander Prize (he was a recipient in 1972). He is currently a visiting research fellow at Trinity College Dublin, 2014–16.

TERENCE DOOLEY is director of the Centre for the Study of Historic Irish Houses and Estates at Maynooth University where he also lectures in nineteenth- and twentieth-century Irish history. His latest book is *The decline and fall of the dukes of Leinster, 1872–1948: love, war, debt and madness* (Dublin, 2014).

RONAN FOLEY is a lecturer in the Department of Geography at Maynooth University where he teaches and researches on GIS and health geographies. He is the current editor of *Irish Geography* and has written on a range of topics associated with therapeutic landscapes, healthy blue space and medical histories. His current work explores historic and contemporary social and cultural histories of swimming in Ireland. He is also a director of the Oral History Network of Ireland and a committee member of the Society for the Study of Nineteenth-Century Ireland.

DONAL HALL is a PhD graduate of Maynooth University (2011). He is the author of *World War I and nationalist politics in Co. Louth, 1914–20* (Dublin, 2005); *The unreturned army: County Louth dead in the Great War, 1914–1918* (Dundalk, 2005). He is currently working on the Co. Louth volume in the Irish Revolution, 1912–23 series (edited by Marian Lyons and Daithí Ó Corráin).

PAUL HOLDEN, FSA, is house and collections manager for the National Trust at Lanhydrock in Cornwall. He has published widely, and his most recent books include *The Lanhydrock atlas* (Fowey, Cornwall, 2010), *The London letters of Samuel Molyneux, 1712–13* (London, 2011) and *The Cornish country house* (in preparation). He is chairman of the Cornish Buildings Group, editor for *Architectural Historian* and a reviewer for the Society of Antiquaries of London, the Society of Architectural Historians of Great Britain and the Royal Society.

CHRISTOPHER HUNWICK read Literae Humaniores at Lincoln College, Oxford, before spending a year as archives assistant at the Oxford University Archives in the Bodleian Library. He qualified as Master of Archives and Records Management from Liverpool University. For four years he was Manchester Cathedral's archivist, working closely with Chetham's Library. In 2007, he took up his present position as archivist to the duke of Northumberland at Alnwick Castle. From 2010 to 2015 he served as the honorary secretary of the Historic Houses Archivists' Group.

BRETT IRWIN has been working in archives and records management at the Public Record Office of Northern Ireland since 2010. He has worked on the cataloguing and the promotion of the Londonderry Papers since 2013. He has published articles in *ARC, History Ireland* and in the Archives and Records

Association newsletter. He is currently studying for a Master's degree in archive management at the University of Dundee.

COLM MCQUINN is a graduate of English and history from University College Cork and also holds a Higher Diploma in archival studies. He is archivist for Fingal County Council and has published numerous articles on the various collections under his curatorship in historical journals. In 2014, Colm curated an exhibition on the experience and correspondence of a prominent Dublin family, the Hely-Hutchinsons, during the Great War, based on the family papers donated to the Fingal Archives in 2009.

IDA MILNE is currently the holder of an Irish Research Council Marie Curie Elevate Postdoctoral Fellowship, shared between Maynooth University and Queen's University, Belfast, looking at the changing landscape of childhood disease in Ireland during the twentieth century. She was awarded a PhD by Trinity College Dublin in 2011 for a dissertation on the Irish experience of the 1918–19 influenza epidemic, and has published widely on this topic, including most recently a chapter in Lisa Marie Griffith and Ciarán Wallace (eds), *Grave matters: death and dying in Dublin* (Dublin, 2016). She specializes in the social history of medicine and disease in twentieth-century Ireland, and often uses oral history to develop her research. She is a director of the Oral History Network of Ireland.

DAVID MURPHY is a graduate of University College Dublin and Trinity College Dublin. He has taught at both of these institutions, teaching electives on European and Irish history as well as military history and the history of polar exploration. He has lectured abroad at various institutions including the Dutch Military Academy, Breda, the United States Military Academy West Point, and the US Command and General Staff College, Fort Leavenworth. His publications include *Breaking point of the French Army: the Nivelle Offensive of 1917* (2015) and *Lawrence of Arabia* (2011). He is a member of the Royal United Services Institute.

CIARÁN REILLY is a PhD graduate of the History Department at Maynooth University. He specializes in nineteenth- and twentieth-century Irish history, with a particular interest in the Great Famine, country houses and landed estates, as well as the revolutionary period 1916–23. He is the author of *The Irish land agent: the case of King's County, 1830–1860* (Dublin, 2014); *Strokestown and the Great Irish Famine* (Dublin, 2014) and *John Plunket Joly and the Great Famine in King's County* (Dublin, 2012).

CHRISTOPHER RIDGWAY is curator at Castle Howard in North Yorkshire, where he has lectured and published extensively on the history of its collections, architecture and landscape. He is chair of the Yorkshire Country House

Partnership, a collaborative research project between the University of York and the country houses of Yorkshire, and is also adjunct professor attached to the Centre for the Study of Historic Irish Houses and Estates at Maynooth University. His most recent publications include *The Morpeth Roll: Ireland identified in 1841* (Dublin 2013), and *Duty calls: Castle Howard and the Great War* (2014).

DAWN WEBSTER studied at Trinity College Dublin and in 1987, she graduated with an MA in Museum Studies from University College London. Since 2000, she has been curator at Kiplin in North Yorkshire. In collaboration with the Yorkshire Country House Partnership, Dawn has worked on projects including 'Duty calls: the country house in time of war'. This culminated in an exhibition in 2013–14 at Kiplin using estate archives and collections dating from the English Civil War to World War Two.

Introduction

TERENCE DOOLEY & CHRISTOPHER RIDGWAY

The Great War continues to be debated endlessly: there are countless publications on the causes, the military conduct, the key participants, the fighting and home fronts, and the manifold consequences of the conflict – social, political, cultural, economic and so on. The commemorative window 2014–18 has seen a flood of new contributions to these debates, many from professional historians. These remind us that the First World War was a war of many things: politicians, commanders, soldiers and civilians; guns, shells and ships; towns and villages; and of course countless individual lives. The conflict was also a great war of words in the form of official documents, military directives, government circulars, press coverage and propaganda campaigns, as well as personal records – letters, poems, journals and memoirs. No war before had ever been so assiduously recorded.

A century on from this cataclysmic event, in the UK and Ireland there has been a renewed interest in those who lived through the war. Researchers and local and family historians have either set out to discover for the first time ancestral histories, or have re-evaluated heirlooms from that generation. This has been particularly significant in an Irish context. Whereas for many years much has been written on the contribution of Ulster unionists and members of the Ulster Volunteer Force (UVF) to the war, it is only recently that there has been an upsurge of interest in the role of the war in the area that became the Irish Republic. New research on the experiences of ordinary soldiers who fought and died, civilian responses at home to the war effort, as well as the impact of the conflict on wider Irish politics and society, has begun to fill a major gap in Irish historiography. For a good part of the twentieth century the coincidence of the European war with the Easter Rising of 1916 and the subsequent struggle for independence has been viewed in binary terms. This engendered a collective amnesia, and a denial of the complex role this huge conflict played in reshaping the political, socio-economic and cultural landscapes of the island of Ireland as a whole.

The mass of first-hand narratives and mementos in the UK and Ireland, whether uncovered in institutional archives or retrieved from an obscure corner of a drawer, may not radically alter our general understanding of the war but these testimonies represent, at the very least, an opportunity for many more individual voices to be heard.

While the wealth of published material increases, and the level of scholarly debate is set to continue to grow, the primary archive remains something of a fixed resource. The words on paper, either contemporary or retrospective, set down by that generation who fought or lived through the war at home, will not grow any bigger. An enormous amount of material has been retrieved from obscurity as people respond to calls for more information from bodies such as the Imperial War Museum, and the national repositories in Kew, Dublin, Belfast, Aberystwyth and Edinburgh, as well as local record offices all over the UK and Ireland. But as a body of documentation – known, half-known or yet to be properly investigated – this is an archive that is essentially frozen in time, belonging to what has been called 'the 1914 Generation'.

With this impetus to look back a century has come a new willingness to map the extent of this archive, and also to explore and comprehend what was recorded by those who were alive 100 years ago. But as more and more material is identified there comes a desire to make sense of these voices, especially those that are being heard for the first time. Do these accounts start to coalesce into a vast singular experience? Was the war more or less the same for every man and woman, combatant and civilian, adult and child, urban and rural dweller? Do these new voices merely serve to thicken and enrich an accepted understanding of the war, or do they reveal a myriad of subtle and individual differences, as each individual set down their thoughts *in extremis*? The answer must tend towards the latter.

In presenting a volume devoted to the country house and the First World War, there is an obligation to balance both of these perspectives; will there be too much country house and not enough war? Or will the military viewpoint eclipse the lives of landowners, servants and tenants whether at the front or at home? This collection of essays draws on landed family and estate papers across the UK and Ireland, many of them still in private family collections. Most of these narratives have never been heard before; the authors have mined single collections of papers, or records from various sources, including local and oral testimony, to present the fate of houses and families during the 1914–18 period. In Ireland, there are particular reasons why the 1914–18 archive has been under-recognized, under-valued, and under-explored, but the fact remains that the breadth and depth of the personal record still offers enormous potential for fresh narratives in the first instance followed, in due course, by analysis and deeper comprehension.

Fergal Browne reveals an extraordinary record of endurance and survival in the case of Robert Heard, who seemed to live a binary life between the Western Front and his family home in Kinsale: each was equally real and precious to him. Heard's fate is also an example of that cruel irony – someone who lived through the entire conflict only to die of influenza during the global pandemic that claimed more lives than the war.

Edward Bujak's account of the lives of fighter pilots narrates the crossover from a warrior class of the past to a new kind of technocratic combatant. But the rise of aerial warfare could never shed an earlier chivalric ethos, nor could the new airmen entirely escape the social hierarchies of Edwardian Britain.

For Philip Bull the wartime correspondence between Edward Richards-Orpen and his wife, Margaret, is both a portrait of a marriage, and a record of an ambitious soldier keen to receive recognition for his ingenuity in keeping forces on the move. His work on the fleets of motorized transport remind us that the attritional world of the trenches was far from static, even if the internal combustion engine was ultimately dedicated to provisioning and reinforcing the fixed line of the Western Front.

Fidelma Byrne's work at the Centre for the Study of Historic Irish Houses and Estates (CSHIHE) on a pioneering prosopographical database of combatants from the landed classes in Ireland is much more than a statistical analysis. While the data she has collated enables all sorts of patterns and trends to be identified, either in terms of shared backgrounds (school, academy and regiment), or with regard to casualty figures, behind this empirical data there always lie intense human stories, as exemplified by the Acton and French families.

The bigger picture that emerges from the Maynooth database is complemented by the kind of microhistory of an estate presented by Caroline Carr-Whitworth. Research for the 'Duty calls' exhibition in Yorkshire in 2013 led to an astonishing response by local families. Such was the volume of material uncovered, loaned or donated that the narratives of the workers and families linked to Brodsworth Hall and the locality virtually eclipsed the wartime records of their employers, the Thellusson and Grant-Dalton families.

For Ian d'Alton, the life of Norman Leslie is a reminder that many of these figures from the war had colourful, dramatic and complex lives before 1914. The war may have claimed his life but it was clear that for Leslie these years represented an intense fulfilment of expectations and desires.

Ronan Foley chronicles the specialized transformation of Mount Stuart on the Isle of Bute into a convalescent home. While hundreds of miles away from the scene of fighting, the conversion of the nineteenth-century mansion is a reminder how country houses pressed into medical use were linked to the front by an umbilical cord of suffering that stretched from casualty-clearing station, to base camp, to port and distribution point in Britain and eventually to a centre for healing.

Donal Hall reveals how the life of Roger Bellingham, like that of Norman Leslie, ended early in the war, in the spring of 1915. He did not live to witness the Easter Rising in 1916. The Bellinghams of Co. Louth were an example of a Catholic landed family totally involved in the war effort, with Edward's brother seeing action through to 1918, and his parents instrumental in local recruiting and welfare campaigns.

Paul Holden's account of Tommy Agar Robartes weaves the loss of the heir to Lanhydrock with the deaths of other parish members commemorated on the local war memorial. This is a story typical of many communities across Britain and Ireland, one of a devastating impact upon family lives and ultimately the local population and economy.

For Christopher Hunwick, the impact of the war at Alnwick Castle in Northumberland falls into two divisions. There is the well-documented life of Lord William Percy, whose hazardous pre-war adventures in Siberia were considered more extreme than his time in the trenches; Percy's voice is rare among those of the combatants in recognizing that there were places more perilous than the Western Front. But the Alnwick exhibition is also an example of how to recover a host of other identities belonging to those who did not leave records like Percy. Using complementary archival sources, the project has excavated real lives, personalities and occupations behind the names on the Alnwick memorial; and more moving still is how research discovered names of people who were missing from it. This has enabled a new Roll of Honour to be created, supplemented by the names of those who were not included in 1919.

For Brett Irwin, the work of Lady Londonderry is a reminder of the role that communities in Northern Ireland played during the war, as well as the work of women who were tireless in their efforts on the home front. The network of correspondence that survives in PRONI also reveals just how easy it was to exchange information and news during the war. Regardless of local or temporary disruptions, the mail continued to get through.

Colm McQuinn shows how for the Hely-Hutchinson family news from the front was regularly relayed through the letters of brothers Coote and Dick, back to their parents and siblings in Ireland. Importantly, we are reminded that the graphic descriptions of the destructive universe of the trenches, so familiar to readers today, were once very new and shocking, and hard for those at home to grasp, let alone visualize. The brothers' story is also clouded by family injustice, with Dick disinherited by his father following an unsuitable marriage. While Coote would play a prominent role in public life after the war, his younger brother was forced to stay in the army until 1926.

Ida Milne provides a deeply personal memoir of growing up in the aftermath of the war, in the shadow of lost uncles. This account serves to emphasize how long the memory of the war was, even for children who were too young to comprehend it, or who were born just after 1918.

David Murphy explores an intriguing connection between T.E. Lawrence and Pierce Joyce. The latter was a professional soldier while Lawrence joined up for intelligence work in 1914; the two men encountered one another in 1916, when the scruffy young Lawrence made a poor first impression on Joyce. In spite of their shared experiences in the desert, Joyce remains a largely forgotten figure, even though Lawrence referred to him in his celebrated *Seven pillars of wisdom*.

What is less known is that the Irish worlds of both men closely overlapped, particularly among their parents' generation.

Ciarán Reilly examines the wartime experiences of William Tyrrell of Ballindoolin, who eventually escaped the nightmare of the trenches with a commission in the Royal Flying Corps. Tyrrell's interests always tended towards the skies, often choosing to describe his war through the idiom of shooting; more than once he likened the enemy to snipe, a comparison fresh in his mind after spending some of his leave shooting at Rathmoyle, Co. Roscommon. His experiences show, as with many soldiers, that while they could be taken away from home it was virtually impossible to take the reassuring familiarities and vocabularies of home away from them.

Dawn Webster's account of the Talbot family of Kiplin Hall in North Yorkshire chronicles how four siblings did their duty. Bridget Talbot worked for the Red Cross in Italy, where she endured conditions and hazards every bit as dangerous as those on the Western Front. Her diaries are vivid testimony of a world that could shift from the dangerous to the normal in an extraordinarily short space of time: thus after coming under shellfire one afternoon she had only to travel a short distance from the danger zone to hear an opera recital in a nearby house.

The publication of this volume, with its focus on Ireland and Britain, is timely because 2016 is the 100th anniversary of the 1916 Rising, one of the most defining events of modern Irish history. This year also marks the centenary of the battle of the Somme, which opened on 1 July 1916. Aside from the horrendous casualty figures of the first day, this five-month campaign left thousands of young Irishmen killed, wounded or missing. The executed leaders of the Rising were swiftly enshrined in Irish memory, but those soldiers who saw themselves as Irish, and who fought and died at the Somme, were for decades consigned to relative obscurity, in general remembered only privately by their families or by low-key commemorative committees. The leaders of the 1916 Rising have been appropriately commemorated in this centenary year. Those who fought at the Somme have also been recognized during the course of 2016; the commemorations for the critical naval engagement of the war – the battle of Jutland in May 1916 – marked the important part played by Irish sailors. Recognition of the intertwined nature of these once-opposing perspectives means that the 1916 Rising and its aftermath can now be discussed more comprehensively within a broader framework of European history from 1914 to 1918; it is no longer viewed as an isolated occurrence in a peculiar Irish vacuum.

Moreover, the official launch of the 1916–2016 Centenary Programme in Ireland emphasized that the commemorative process needed to be informed by a full acknowledgment of the complexity of historical events and their legacy – that due recognition ought to be made of the multiple readings of history, and of the multiple identities and traditions that make up the Irish historical experience.

Some of the essays in this volume pick up this challenge by ventriloquizing forgotten voices and offering a reassessment of what the Great War meant to the country house. In Ireland, the contribution of the country house community to the war was especially disproportionate to its demography.[1]

This volume aims to draw together original research by people in Ireland and the UK working in a variety of fields, and to provide a focus for non-institutional scholars to participate in the wider historical debate, entirely in keeping with the ethos of popular, contemporary re-engagement with the Great War during the 2014–18 commemorative period.

The editors are grateful to the authors for their contributions to this volume, which first saw the light of day at the Twelfth Annual Historic Houses of Ireland Conference organized by the Centre for the Study of Historic Irish Houses and Estates in 2014, part of Maynooth University's contribution to the decade of commemorative events. The editors would also like to record their deep gratitude to Fred and Kay Krehbiel, for their generous sponsorship, which made that conference possible; and also for their wider support of the work of the CSHIHE. We would like to thank the Ireland Funds (and Kieran McLaughlin) for its invaluable support in 2015–16. As ever, without the support of the Office of Public Works, research, annual conferences and publications such as this would not be possible. We would like to acknowledge the support of the Maynooth University Publications Grants Scheme, with a special word of thanks to Prof. Bernard Mahon, vice president for research. Without the indefatigable efforts of Catherine Murphy, the administration for the conference, and the many and varied tasks related to this publication would not have been accomplished; she carried all of them out with her customary professionalism and good humour. Our thanks go also to Laura Servilan Browne, Fidelma Byrne, David Gahan and Dr Ciarán Reilly for the work completed thus far on the Irish country house and war database. We are grateful too to Den Stubbs for his design work, to Robert Williams for editorial assistance and to the staff at Four Courts Press.

The stories in this volume are aimed at the general reader, but have plenty of detail and colour to satisfy the specialist too, and are illustrated with a remarkable range of largely unknown images. They are a powerful reminder of the experiences common to many during the 1914–18 period, as well as a record of how each individual life was shaped by personality and unique circumstances. These accounts increase our understanding of the war through their individuality: whether a land agent in Yorkshire, a soldier in France, an airman in the skies, a patient on the Isle of Bute, a widow at home in Ireland or England or a nurse in Italy. Their personal trajectories through the war may differ but

---

1 In Ireland, the term 'big house' is commonly used to refer to the country house and thus the interchangeability of these terms in some of the Irish-related essays in this volume.

most of these individuals came from a common background, that of the country house and landed estate. The authors of these first-hand accounts have long left the world, but their presence endures through their written words in letters, diaries, reports or articles, the majority of them of course never destined for publication. These narratives confirm how the vast array of personal papers relating to the Great War, whether professionally indexed and stored in specialist repositories, or cherished by descendants in the family home today, provide an extraordinary testimony that has still to be explored fully.

This volume has excavated a series of unknown histories pertaining to the family in the country house, and also to their staff, tenants and neighbourhoods. These essays have reached beyond the façade of the memorial cross or the archive index and, for want of a better phrase, re-humanized many of the names found therein. We now have a stronger sense of how behind each name there lie intricate narratives that identify the individual in question, situating him or her in local communities, whether at home or away, while also establishing their role in the greatest cataclysm the modern world had known.

The death of the Pallastown heir: Lt Robert Heard, Irish Guards

FERGAL BROWNE

Cork and County Cork in the twentieth century is a difficult book to find nowadays. Published in 1911, it is a veritable who's who of Cork society at the time. However, there is a look of considerable pathos about the photo of one of the youngest people in the 'Contemporary biographies' section. Aged just sixteen at the time the photo was taken, Robert Henry Warren Heard of Pallastown House, Belgooly, Co. Cork, was among the largest landowners in Munster, having inherited his estates at the age of two on the death of his father (fig. 1.1).[1]

The Heard family's origins can be traced back to Cork, when in 1579 John Heard from Wiltshire arrived in Ireland with Sir Walter Raleigh and was granted lands in Bandon.[2] In 1834, his descendant, John Isaac Heard, purchased the freehold of much of the town of Kinsale from the estate of the late Edward Southwell, 21st Baron De Clifford.[3] Using profit from the rent of the family's urban properties, John Isaac Heard's son, Captain Robert Heard, purchased Pallastown House from the Townsend family c.1864.[4] The Townsends had built Pallastown in the late eighteenth century. Local folklore maintained that the interior ceilings had been plastered by the 'Kinsale Giant', Patrick Cotter O'Brien, without using a ladder.[5] On his purchase of the house Captain Heard immediately began making improvements. An advertisement appeared in the *Cork Examiner* on 27 April 1864 soliciting tenders for the enlargement of Pallastown House.[6] As a result of the work, the house was almost doubled in size, leading it to be described as a '2-storey house in a mild Tudor revival style, but with a classical portico' (fig. 1.2).[7]

From 1876, properties in Kinsale town were sold to finance the purchase of more land, increasing the size of the Pallastown estate.[8] By 1878, the Heards' holdings comprised 2,005 acres in Cork and 8,846 acres in Tipperary, where the

Sincere thanks to the late Stawell St Leger Heard; Margaret O'Neill, Pallastown; John Hamblin, Lancing College; Nicholas Cook and Dr Ian d'Alton. **1** Richard Hodges, *Cork and County Cork in the twentieth century* (Brighton, 1911), p. 217. **2** Sir Bernard Burke, *A genealogical and heraldic history of the landed gentry of Ireland* (London, 1904), p. 255. **3** Ian d'Alton, *Protestant society and politics in Cork, 1812–1844* (Cork, 1980), pp 108–9. **4** Paul John Ryan, 'Property, business and power: a study of proprietorship in Kinsale, 1851–1951' (PhD, UCC, 1997). **5** *Connaught Telegraph*, 25 July 1896. **6** *Cork Examiner*, 27 Apr. 1864. **7** Mark Bence-Jones, *A guide to Irish country houses* (London, 1988), p. 230. **8** Ryan, 'Property, business and power', p. 35.

1.1 Robert Henry Warren Heard, photographed in 1911 for inclusion in Richard M. Hodges' *Cork and County Cork in the twentieth century.*

family owned another house, Lackamore Lodge.[9] Recalling Kinsale in the 1890s, the playwright Lennox Robinson noted that 'Country society was represented by families such as the Heards of Pallastown ... These were our aristocracy; they mingled to some extent with the gentry of the town, but only to some extent.'[10]

Despite spending large amounts of money improving Pallastown as well as ordering a yacht to be built at the Thuillier family boatyard in Kinsale in 1894,[11] Captain Heard spent the last years of his life on his estate in Tipperary, dying there in 1896.[12] The estates passed to his son, Robert Wilkes Heard, with Henry Thomas Daunt appointed as the second executor.[13] Robert Wilkes Heard had married Charlotte Amyand Powys of Wynters in Essex in 1888. In 1895, after three daughters, the longed-for son – Robert Henry Warren Heard – was born and the family's future seemed secure.[14]

Robert Wilkes Heard died in 1897, aged only forty-five. The following year his widow married Richard Charles Pratt. The Pratts were another prominent family in Kinsale. The new Mr and Mrs Pratt, together with the Heard children, moved into the Heard family town-house, 10 Fisher Street, Kinsale.[15] On 2 October 1899, the contents of Pallastown House were sold at auction on the

9 U.H. Hussey De Burgh, *The landowners of Ireland* (Dublin, 1878), p. 213.   10 Lennox Robinson et al., *Three homes* (London, 1938), p. 86.   11 John Thuillier, *Kinsale harbour* (Cork, 2014), pp 211–12.   12 *Southern Star*, 19 Sept. 1896.   13 *Cork Examiner*, 5 Feb. 1897. 14 Burke, *Landed gentry of Ireland*, pp 254–5.   15 Hodges, *Cork and County Cork*, p. 217.

1.2 Pallastown House, near Belgooly, *c.*1930, painted by Bertie Gallagher. Reproduced by
kind permission of Mrs Margaret O'Neill, Pallastown.

instructions of the trustee Henry Daunt.[16] The house was leased, first to John
Kingston and from 1908 to Major Isaac William Burns-Lindow, a career soldier,
serving with the 8th Hussars. In 1897, he had commanded the massed bands of
the Hussars brigade in Queen Victoria's Diamond Jubilee Procession in
London.[17]

Robert Henry Warren Heard – for whom the estate was held in trust – was
sent to school in England. He first attended Streete Court School in Westgate-
on-Sea before being sent to Lancing College, a private school in West Sussex.
While at Lancing he joined the school's Officer Training Corps, serving as a
private until April 1912.

Following the outbreak of war, Robert Heard was commissioned on 15 August
1914 as a 2nd Lieutenant in the Irish Guards (fig. 1.3). At his medical
examination it was recorded that he was 5ft 8in. tall and weighed 130lbs. He was
posted to the regiment's 1st Battalion.[18] Clearly, being an officer led to greater

16 *Southern Star*, 30 Sept. 1899.   17 Census of Ireland 1901; *British hunts and huntsmen*, vol. 4:
England North, Scotland & Ireland (London, 1911), p. 582.   18 www.hambo.org/lancing
(accessed 2 Dec. 2015); Rudyard Kipling, *The Irish Guards in the Great War*, vol. 1: *the First*

expenses. On 25 November he applied to the Master of the Rolls to have his annual allowance from the estate increased to £1,000. The trustee, Henry Daunt, did not oppose the application. An order was made by the court that £800 a year be paid to his mother, on her undertaking to pay him a personal allowance and also to maintain Pallastown House and demesne.[19] By this time, the Pallastown tenant – Major Burns-Lindow – had rejoined the South Irish Horse and was himself preparing to serve in France.

Having completed his training, Robert Heard embarked for France on 1 May 1915, joining his battalion the following day. In May 1915 the Irish Guards was one of the British regiments in action at the battle of Festubert. This was a coordinated attack with the French 10th Army to relieve pressure on the French by attracting German divisions to the British line. On 18 May, the 1st Battalion Irish Guards attacked German trenches at Cour l'Avoine Farm near Festubert. Heard was not in this assault, but on 19 May he joined No. 1 Company to replace officers killed. He was promoted to lieutenant on 20 September. The following month the Irish Guards took part in the battle of Loos, which was an attempt by the Allies to end the current stalemate by breaking through the German defences at Artois and Champagne. On 7 October, during this battle, Heard was shot in the right shoulder and the left thigh, while supervising work in the trenches near Vermelles. Three other men were also wounded. Removed first to Rouen, on 16 October he was evacuated to Southampton on the hospital ship SS *St Andrew*. A medical board was convened at Caxton Hall, London, on 21 October and reported on his condition:

> The Board finds that he received two wounds from rifle bullets. 1. The first one entering the top of the R shoulder above the clavicle, passing through and emerging above the scapula. Both punctures healed. 2. The second entering the region of the groin … & making its exit through the centre of the left buttock injuring no structures of importance in its course, puncture wounds both healed.[20]

Despite his injuries, Heard seems to have been eager to return to the front. In November 1915, he applied for a permanent commission in the Irish Guards, as his initial commission had been as a special reserve officer, which would only exist for the duration of the war. He received his permanent commission two months later on 4 January.[21]

Robert Heard returned to Kinsale during his recuperation. On 6 March 1916, he turned 21 years of age and became sole owner of Pallastown and the Heard estates. A celebration was held at the courthouse (now Kinsale Museum), where the tenants of the Heard estate presented him with a silver salver and his

Battalion (London, 1923), p. 95.   **19** *Cork Examiner*, 25 Nov. 1914.   **20** TNA, WO 339/44346; www.hambo.org/lancing; Kipling, *Irish Guards*, p. 119.   **21** www.hambo.org/lancing.

1.3 Lieutenant Robert
H.W. Heard, Irish Guards.
Photo courtesy John
Hamblin, Lancing College.

employees an old-Irish 'Loving Cup'. There was also an illuminated address, which read:

> Dear Mr Heard – We the undersigned, representing the tenants and purchased tenants of the Heard Estate, tender to you, on the auspicious occasion of your attaining your majority, our cordial greeting and congratulations. We also congratulate you on your pluck and courage in entering the Army and fighting for your country in the trenches in Flanders before reaching your majority, and are thankful to providence that you have recovered from the serious wounds you received. Your family has been long and favourably known as indulgent landlords, large employers of labour, and liberal supporters of every movement for improving the position of your tenants. They have always been foremost in promoting and encouraging shows and sports and every charitable and benevolent undertaking in this town and district. We wish you a bright and happy future, and pray that you may be spared to enjoy your large inheritance, and when the war is over that you will return home with honours, and settle down in Kinsale among the people who thoroughly appreciate your many good qualities and generous disposition, and uphold the traditions of your illustrious ancestors.[22]

22 *Cork Constitution*, 8 Mar. 1916.

The trustee of the estate, Henry Daunt, was the first signatory of the illuminated address. In his speech of thanks, Heard responded:

> I thank you most heartily for the silver loving cup which you have so kindly presented to me today and also for your expressions of regard. I need not tell you how highly I appreciate both. It has been my privilege to be wounded in the service of my country and it is with feelings of great thankfulness that my mother and I have come here today to meet so many friends and to celebrate my coming of age. I share with you the hope that I may be spared to fight to the end of this terrible war …[23]

The hope was also expressed by some townspeople that Robert Heard would someday be returned as an MP to the House of Commons.[24]

Given that he was now in full control of the Heard estate, Robert became involved in the management of Pallastown and also began taking a role in the community. At the Kinsale Show in July 1916 both he and his former tenant, Major Burns-Lindow, presented prizes for horses. Advertisements also appeared in the papers throughout the following months seeking ploughmen and stockmen for the Pallastown farm.[25] However, his military service was not yet over. At a medical board convened at the military hospital in Cork he was found to be fit for general service. He did not return to the Western Front until 30 September, when he was posted to the 2nd Battalion, joining them at Trones Wood on the Somme.[26]

The battalion had just been relieved by the 1st Coldstream Guards, after having sustained shelling for three days 'sitting and suffering … while parapets flew up and fell down on them'. Lt Heard was attached to No. 4 Company, and later gained command of it. During October the whole battalion was involved in intensive training behind the lines. Two weeks later they returned to the front. From then on, in the words of Rudyard Kipling, whose son John had fought and died with the 2nd Battalion in September 1915 and who wrote a two-volume history of the regiment as a memorial: 'Mud, filth, cold, exposure and the murderous hard work necessary to mere existence, were their daily and nightly fare.' Kipling goes on to describe the area in which they were based:

> You followed a duckboard track of sorts through Trones Wood, between ghastly Delville and the black ruins of Ginchy, and across the Ginchy ridge … where, if you were not very careful, the engulfing mud would add you to its increasing and matured collection of 'officers and other ranks'. These accidents overcome, you would discover that the front line was mud with holes in it.[27]

23 Ibid.   24 *Irish Independent*, 8 Mar. 1916.   25 *Cork Examiner*, 25 Nov. 1916, 22 Mar. 1917. 26 TNA, WO 339/44346; www.hambo.org/lancing.   27 Kipling, *Irish Guards*, p. 101.

Heard and his battalion endured these conditions until 22 November, when they were relieved by the Australian Division. They were put to work on road-building for the next ten days and returned to the front on 11 December. By 23 December, only seven were fit for duty.[28] Heard was one of them, but by 30 December he too was ill due to the atrocious conditions, and he left the battalion on New Year's Day. He was evacuated on 23 January from Rouen for Southampton. His case was reviewed by a medical board on 1 February:

> He has served in France several months & was wounded by G.S.Ws [gun shot wounds] in 2 places at Loos. Towards the end of December 1916 he began to have a bad cough for which he went sick on Dec 30th & was seen by the M.O. who sent him to hosp & then home. Present state, all signs of bronchitis have cleared up but he is very debilitated.[29]

Robert Heard again returned to Kinsale to recuperate, and, as he recovered, continued to run his estate. In January 1917, he contributed £10 to the Kinsale Flag Day subscription for the Red Cross. Farm produce from Pallastown was also donated.[30] On 21 February, he again found himself in a field. The Ballymartle ploughing match was taking place and Heard presented two prizes – available to local ploughmen only, for the best opening and the best closing of the sod. His own ploughmen won the prize for best turned-out team for the day.[31]

A medical board held at the military hospital in Cork on 26 March passed him fit for light duty and he was passed fit for general service on 31 May.[32] In October 1917 he took part in the battle of Passchendaele. In the course of it, on 9 October, the Irish Guards were obliged to cross a river – 'the abominable Broembeck … more of a sluit than a river'.[33] In doing so, they came under fire. A military citation relating to Heard reports that:

> During the attack on the Broembeck on the 9th of October 1917, this officer was in command of a company of the leading wave. He led his men with conspicuous ability and throughout the action displayed the greatest bravery and initiative. This officer's splendid courage and fearlessness in face of danger had been a great example to all.[34]

In the month of October the Irish Guards lost 14 officers and 252 other ranks killed or wounded in just sixteen days. Later in 1917 the regiment returned to the Somme.

---

28 Ibid.   **29** TNA, WO 339/44346; www.hambo.org/lancing.   **30** *Cork Examiner*, 1 Jan. 1917.   **31** Ibid., 16 Feb. 1917.   **32** TNA, WO 339/44346; www.hambo.org/lancing. **33** Kipling, *Irish Guards*, p. 145.   **34** TNA, WO 339/44346; www.hambo.org/lancing.

1.4 Irish Guards, Ypres, August 1917. Photo from Fr Frank Browne SJ Collection, reproduced by courtesy of the Irish Picture Library.

In March 1918, the Irish Guards were on the defensive from the Germans' spring offensive, which was an attempt to overwhelm the Allies before the vast military resources of the US could be put to use. Robert Heard was in the thick of heavy fighting at Ervillers. While relieving another unit in the line, the Germans attacked and broke through on his right, leaving the flank of his company exposed. He deployed his men while under heavy machine-gun fire to form a defensive flank. He was awarded an MC for this action.[35]

On 12 April, the Irish Guards took part in the battle of the Lys, in which the Germans again tried to push the British out of Ypres and back to the Channel ports. If the allies lost the important supply depot of Hazebrouck, then the road to the ports would be open to the German armies. The 4th Guards Division, of which the Irish Guards were part, was deployed to fill gaps in the Allied line. The battle took place in open country: there was little cover and the Guards were

35 Kipling, *Irish Guards*, p. 202.

constantly sprayed by German machine-gun fire. The battalion HQ moved to
the village of Caudescure and Heard was ordered to deploy No. 4 Company in
the orchards to the east of the village. A trench mortar battery was sent up to
support him and his men. The following day the Australian Division was
deployed in support, bringing the German advance to a halt. The Irish Guards
were placed in reserve, and dug in around Hazebrouck. On 19 April, they
relieved two companies of the Australian Division on the east edge of the forest
of Nieppe. The Germans shelled the forest with chlorine gas on 21 April 1918.
Rudyard Kipling, writing in 1923, commented that 'nothing … will make men
put on their masks without direct pressure, and new hands cannot see that the
innocent projectile that lands like a "dud" and lies softly hissing to itself, carries
death or slow disablement'.[36] While Heard was not a 'new hand', he was severely
injured, suffering significant lung damage. He was evacuated once more, the
third time in his military career, from Rouen on 29 April. A medical board
reported that he had conjunctivitis, vomiting, cough and bronchitis. His eyes
were blistered and irritable and there was 'irritation of the nasal mucous
membrane'.[37]

While recuperating, in June 1918 Heard was awarded a bar to his MC, for his
action at Broembeck on 9 October of the previous year.[38] He again returned to
Kinsale during his recuperation. At the Cork Show in July 1918, three of his
ponies – Pallastown Prince, Pallastown Beauty and Lady Torchfire – won prizes.
He also won second and third prizes for his pure-bred Aberdeen Angus heifers.[39]
In October a board passed him fit for service and he was ordered to report to the
London Command Depot at Shoreham.[40] By this time the Irish Guards were
based in Cambrai, but it was becoming clear that the war could not continue for
long. Robert Heard does not seem to have rejoined his regiment in France, and
although he was in England, he continued to run the Pallastown estate. In
December a large auction was held at Pallastown under the auspices of Robert
Acton – Kinsale's auctioneer – of most of the cattle and sheep from the estate.
The auctioneer announced that Heard was reducing his livestock numbers in
order to increase the acreage under tillage. It seems clear that he had plans for
the Pallastown estate and he also stated his intention of constructing further
housing for the tenants on his land in Kinsale.[41]

However, none of this was to be. In early 1919 Heard contracted influenza, his
lungs having been severely weakened from the effects of the gas attack. He was
removed to the military hospital at Purfleet, Essex. By late February he
developed septic pneumonia. He died on 3 March, three days before his 24th
birthday. When the *Irish Independent* announced his death, it noted that the

36 Ibid., p. 179.   37 TNA, WO 339/44346; www.hambo.org/lancing.   38 Ibid.   39 *Skibbereen Eagle*, 13 July 1918.   40 TNA, WO 339/44346; www.hambo.org/lancing.   41 *Skibbereen Eagle*, 7 Dec. 1918; *Cork Constitution*, 5 Mar. 1919.

influenza epidemic was such that over seventy policemen of the Dublin force were off duty owing to illness and that seventy-three people had been buried in Glasnevin Cemetery on 4 March.[42]

In its obituary for Robert Heard, the *Cork Constitution* stated:

> News of the death of Lt Robert H.W. Heard, 2nd Batt. Irish Guards, which occurred on last Monday evening was received in Kinsale and the surrounding area with profound regret. The deceased took a very keen and practical interest in all charitable and humane work connected with the late war and to the various associations and branches for that object contributed substantial sums. As owner of a large portion of the town of Kinsale and landed property in the surrounding districts, and with a genuine desire for the general welfare and prosperity of the locality, much was expected of him in the future ... and his very sad and early demise is the cause of much grief.[43]

Heard was buried alongside his father and a sister, Amayand, who had died in 1918, in St Multose Cemetery, Kinsale. In April 1920 his mother applied to the War Office for his medals.[44]

Following his death, the trustees once again took control of the estate. In December 1920, a series of auctions were held in which Pallastown House and farm and all the livestock and farm implements were sold. Pallastown House was purchased by John Jagoe, owner of Jagoes Mills near Kinsale.[45] The Heard family retained ownership of the urban properties in Kinsale, with fixed rent payments being paid to the four remaining sisters, who all left Ireland. A legal covenant established in 1926 prevented any further break-up of the estate and by the 1950s much of the freehold of Kinsale town was still in the possession of the family, although by then rent payments seem to have petered out.[46]

Despite technically not being a casualty of war, having died of influenza – though the damage to his lungs from the gas attack would have been a contributory factor – Robert Heard was commemorated on the war memorials at Lancing College and in St Finbarr's cathedral, Cork.[47] He was also named on a plaque in St Multose church, Kinsale. Pallastown House later become the property of the Clarke family, from whom it passed to the Cattell family.[48] The condition of the house had deteriorated significantly by the 1960s, and the main house was eventually

42 TNA, WO 339/44346; www.hambo.org/lancing; *Irish Independent*, 5 Mar. 1919.   43 *Cork Constitution*, 5 Mar. 1919.   44 TNA, WO 339/44346; www.hambo.org/lancing.   45 *Cork Examiner*, 27 Nov. 1920, 18 Dec. 1920.   46 Terry Connolly, 'Fisher Street', *Kinsale Record*, 23 (2015), pp 37–52.   47 http://cork.anglican.org/our-story/world-war-i-centenary/the-war-memorial-heroes-column-st-fin-barres-cathedral-cork (accessed 29 Dec. 2015); www.hambo.org/lancing; Karen Healy, 'Roll of Honour', *Kinsale Record*, 22 (2014), 115–24. 48 Bence-Jones, *Guide to Irish country houses*, p. 230.

demolished, with the servants' quarters being converted into a new residence. The farm is now the property of Dan and Margaret O'Neill.

What would have happened had Robert Heard lived is a matter of conjecture. The only certainty is that his death contributed significantly to the breaking of a family connection with Kinsale and the surrounding district which had lasted over 300 years.

A winged aristocracy: air power and the country house elite

EDWARD BUJAK

In November 1918, there were 401 operational aerodromes in Britain housing a host of training squadrons.[1] These training squadrons and aerodromes were part of the new Royal Air Force formed in April 1918 by amalgamating the Royal Navy Air Service and the far larger Royal Flying Corps. The RAF's training aerodromes were concentrated in the rural south and east of England and each covered several hundred acres. These aerodromes intruded into a countryside still owned by an aristocracy living in ancestral seats exuding hereditary authority, tradition and continuity. This intrusion resulted in country houses being rivalled by the great hangars housing the aeroplanes that now buzzed over the rooftops of England's stately homes.

If the rural elite of Edwardian England was 'doomed by modernity',[2] then the aeroplane and the Air Ministry, and its predecessor the War Office, were its heralds. But, as David Edgerton points out, 'the new technologies of the twentieth century ... were already established in Edwardian England'.[3] Lady Victoria Pery, daughter of the earl of Limerick, the countess of Dudley, and Lady Diana Manners, daughter of the duke of Rutland, for example, had all been up in an aeroplane before the war.[4] Subsequently, during the war itself, the aristocracy welcomed the appearance of aerodromes in the countryside because the aeroplane allowed the aristocracy to meld together modernity and the aristocratic military tradition.

In the Great War, a flying officer in the RFC was both a qualified pilot and an officer with a wartime commission in the army. As a temporary officer a pilot was also, if temporarily, a gentleman. By contrast, the original cadre of pilots were already officers and gentlemen by birth.[5] The pre-war RFC reflected the social system of Edwardian England. Flying was equated with good horsemanship.

---

1 Centre for Air Power Studies, 'Synopsis of British air effort during the war, 1914–1918', *Air Power Review*, special ed. (Spring 2013), 196. See also 'Civilian flying', *The Times*, 25 Apr. 1919, which puts the number of aerodromes and landing grounds in Britain and Ireland on 11 Nov. 1918 at 337.   2 David Edgerton, *England and the aeroplane: militarism, modernity and machines* (London, 2013), p. 18.   3 Ibid., p. 19.   4 Mark Bostridge, *The fateful year: England 1914* (London, 2014), p. 106.   5 See George Robb, *British culture and the First World War* (London, 2002), pp 86–7. But, it was also possible to become a gentleman through personal effort: see Christine Berbereich, *The image of the English gentleman in twentieth-century literature: Englishness and nostalgia* (Aldershot, 2007), p. 8.

2.1 Belvoir Castle, Leicestershire. T608051-056. Harlaxton-Russia Prints. Reproduced
with the kind permission of the Trustees of the Royal Air Force Museum.

Consequently, its original pilots and officers were drawn from among the elite,
socially exclusive, cavalry regiments of the British Army. The result was that the
RFC never became, as Edgerton argues, 'a corps of flying civilian or military
engineers: it represented the bringing together of technology with the
aristocratic martial spirit. The association of piloting with horsemanship was an
obvious manifestation of this combination'.[6] In 1915, in France, the officers of
No. 7 Squadron RFC were 'immaculately dressed ex-cavalry officers, with …
servants … to ensure they remained polished … . Nearly all of them bore a
proud family association with the British cavalry and they had put away
regimental saddles and spurs reluctantly'. Even so, for most RFC squadrons,
'several horses were kept for the recreational use of officers … thundering
around the fields of France'.[7] The cavalrymen in question were country
gentlemen and foxhunters who in France hunted hares behind the gun lines
'beautifully mounted on their first chargers'.[8] In so doing, they were replicating

6 Edgerton, *England and the aeroplane*, p. 81.   7 Elizabeth O'Kiely, *Gentleman air ace: the
Duncan Bell-Irving story* (Madeira Park, 1992), p. 63; Edward Bujak, *Reckless fellows: the
gentlemen of the Royal Flying Corps* (London, 2015), p. 9.   8 Joshua Levine, *Fighter heroes of*

2.2 Belton House, Lincolnshire. Aerial view. T608051-160. Reproduced with the kind permission of the Trustees of the Royal Air Force Museum.

the scene in England, where foxhunting continued throughout the war. The justification for doing so in wartime was explained by *Country Life* in 1914 in suitably patriotic terms:

> If the hunting field is the school for our cavalry, so also it is the playground [on leave] of many both cavalry and infantry officers, and if they who are fighting our battles for us could be asked, one and all would say, 'Keep hunting going … till we come back.' Alas! already we know of many who we shall never meet … again, but we will [do our duty and] … keep going the sport they loved, and which helped to make them … the finest soldiers in the world.[9]

WWI: the extraordinary story of the pioneering airmen of the Great War (London, 2009), p. 186.
9 'G.', 'Cub hunting and the war', *Country Life*, 3 Oct. 1914, p. 463.

Four years later, in the same magazine, William Ogilvie reviewed hunting's contribution to the nation's war effort: 'In the cavalry, in the Air Force, with the infantry and the guns the hunting man has proved again and again his worth.'[10] Ogilvie's assumption that aircrew were automatically foxhunters is problematic given that by 1917 the RFC was no longer the preserve of the aristocratic ex-cavalry officer. The pre-war theory that the good 'seat', natural equilibrium and sensitive hands of a capable horseman equated to being a good pilot remained unquestioned throughout the war,[11] and analogies between the two were frequently made, but in practice more and more recruits were joining the RFC having never ridden a horse cross-country.

In November 1918, the new-formed RAF was the world's most powerful air force, with 30,000 flying officers.[12] This number could only be attained by abandoning the socially exclusive model of the Edwardian RFC. Initially, the RFC had turned to the public schools in its efforts to find more pilots and as a consequence its squadrons remained 'at least initially ... elite establishments in which grammar-school, lower middle and, most emphatically, working-class applicants found scant welcome'.[13] This, too, was an unsustainable model and necessitated a more egalitarian approach with adverts making their appearance in local newspapers. On 20 August 1917, the *Derby Daily Telegraph* published the following:

> Many boys in Derbyshire would welcome the chance of becoming pilots and observers in the Royal Flying Corps, for there is no branch of the service which has so tempted the adventurous youth of England. No boy desirous of helping to beat the Germans in the air is to be denied his ambition, for the War Office are developing the Flying Service, and require large numbers of youths who are willing to devote themselves to this end. 'Pluck, intelligence and initiative are the three requirements,' said a prominent recruiting officer in an interview. 'Every lad possessed of these has an ideal chance of making a name for himself.' Boys wishing to train as officers in the Flying Corps must be at least 17 years and 8 months of age. No one over the age of 25 years can be taken. At the age of 18 years the suitable candidate will be admitted into the officer cadet wing.[14]

Those who succeeded in becoming flying officers did so on their own merit and temperament 'even though their accents were not refined'.[15] This transformation was noted in *The Lancet*: 'Flying is not now confined to the public school boy,

---

10 Will B. Ogilvie, 'The future of fox hunting', *Country Life*, 7 Dec. 1918, pp 516–17.
11 Ralph Barker, *A brief history of the Royal Flying Corps in WWI* (London, 2002), p. 21.
12 Centre for Air Power Studies, 'Synopsis', p. 196.   13 Ian Mackersey, *No empty chairs: the short and heroic lives of the young aviators who fought and died in the First World War* (London, 2012), p. 58.   14 'The Royal Flying Corps', *Derby Daily Telegraph*, 20 Aug. 1917.   15 Robb, *British culture*, p. 86.

the cavalry officer, or the athlete. We take many of our pilots at present from the lower middle classes and the artisan class.'[16] The air service, according to Patrick Bishop, was 'a machine of social transformation, elevating likely young men from the lower classes and making them officers'.[17] As a result, the training squadrons in England became social melting pots, supplying the operational squadrons with an increasing variety of individuals, encouraging its growing cosmopolitanism.[18] What brought together this increasingly eclectic military organization was the common identity of pilots selected for their pluck, temperament and technical skill, but in this new techno-driven meritocracy there was still a role for the aristocracy, the foxhunter and the country house.

Titled aristocrats were already prominent individuals in society. When their social standing was combined with the supposed glamour of the air war they became celebrated in both their success and tragedy.[19] In 1914 the *Newcastle Journal* reported: 'Countess Annesley has been officially informed that Lord Annesley, of the Royal Flying Corps who left England by aeroplane for France, is missing.'[20] In 1916, the *Dundee Courier* informed its readers that Lord Doune, the heir of the earl of Moray, had won the MC for his:

> distinguished and meritorious service. A few weeks ago in France, Lord Doune, while flying over the enemy lines, brought down a German Prince under circumstances reflecting great credit on the young Scotsman. Lord Doune, who left the Scottish Horse last October for more exciting work, was home on leave last week. He flew back on a new machine.[21]

The fate of Captain Lord Lucas was likewise the subject of press speculation in the same year. The son of the Hon. Auberon Herbert, a younger son of the earl of Carnarvon, Lucas had lost a leg while reporting on the South African War. Subsequently, in 1914 he joined the Cabinet, but in May 1915 he resigned and, despite having only one leg, 'at once … joined the Royal Flying Corps, though he was many years over the standard age for this arm. Proving a skilful pilot, he soon gained his [flying] certificate and went out to Egypt, where he saw a good deal of service. On his return to England he was engaged for some months in instructing recruits for the Flying Corps.'[22]

The RFC's training system relied on the rotation of operational pilots through its training squadrons. The efficacy of this arrangement is open to

---

16 Lee Kennett, *The first air war, 1914–1918* (New York, 1991), p. 119.   17 Patrick Bishop, *Wings: the RAF at war, 1912–2012* (London, 2012), p. 30.   18 See ibid., p. 110 and Kennett, *Air war*, p. 136.   19 A combination memorably satirized by the character of Lord Flashheart. The fact that it still works as satire is itself a reminder of the potency of this combination. See Ben Elton and Richard Curtis, 'Plan D: private plane', *Blackadder goes forth*, episode 4 (1989). 20 'Titled airman missing', *Newcastle Journal*, 10 Nov. 1914.   21 'Lord Doune's gallantry rewarded', *Dundee Courier*, 25 May 1916.   22 'Death of Lord Lucas', *The Times*, 4 Dec. 1916, p. 11.

question given that it was justified on the grounds of giving experienced pilots a period in which to rest and recuperate. Instruction work may have removed the attentions of the enemy, but it did not remove the risk of death or serious injury. In 1916, the *Daily Mirror* informed its readers that Lord Lucas had had a 'narrow escape in an aeroplane accident'.[23] The risks inherent in instructing young pilots in the English countryside was an experience Lord Lucas shared with Lord George Dundas, the younger son of the marquess of Zetland, who became an instructor at the Central Flying School in 1916, having been made a flight commander that same year.[24] Similarly, Captain John Leighton, the son and heir of Sir Bryan Leighton, who became a flight commander in 1915 following his secondment to the RFC from the Scots Guards, 'returned to England for a rest',[25] doing so by becoming an instructor at Brooklands. Leighton's father had been lieutenant-colonel of the Westmorland and Cumberland Yeomanry but also 'resigned to go to the front with the Royal Flying Corps'.[26] His son returned to France where he died as a result of wounds received in 1917. The risks of flying in France were, however, equal to those of flying in England. Of the 14,166 RFC/RAF pilots killed in the war, over half were killed in training.[27] Among them was William FitzRoy, Viscount Ipswich, heir to the duke of Grafton. He had transferred into the RFC from the Coldstream Guards only to be killed in a flying accident with No. 17 Training Squadron when flying an RE8 machine at Yatesbury in Wiltshire on 23 April 1918.[28]

In 1916, Lord Lucas was offered command of a squadron in France but deferred his promotion 'until he had gained experience on the Western Front'.[29] Unfortunately, shortly after arriving in France he failed to return from a flight over the German lines on 3 November. One week later *The Times* reported that 'so far nothing has been heard of him or his machine'.[30] On 4 December the same newspaper confirmed that he had been killed. He had gone to France, 'for the life of greater activity which he preferred'.[31] J.M.B. was Maurice Baring, the son of Lord Revelstoke, a close friend of Lord Lucas and a fellow officer serving in the RFC. Baring was deeply affected by his death and wrote an elegy entitled 'In memoriam Auberon Herbert, Captain Lord Lucas, Royal Flying Corps killed November 3rd, 1916':

23 'Lord Lucas' escape', *Daily Mirror*, 19 May 1916; see also 'Death of Lord Lucas', *The Times*, 4 Dec. 1916, p. 11. **24** Gerald Gliddon, *The aristocracy and the Great War* (Norwich, 2002), p. 432. **25** Ibid., p. 310. **26** G.B., 'What Shropshire has done for the war, I', *Country Life*, 11 Mar. 1916, p. 347. **27** Joshua Levine, *On a wing and a prayer: the untold story of the pioneering aviation heroes of WWI, in their own words* (London, 2008), p. 63. **28** Glidden, *Aristocracy*, p. 350. **29** 'Death of Lord Lucas', *The Times*, 4 Dec. 1916, p. 11. **30** 'Lord Lucas missing', *The Times*, 10 Nov. 1916, p. 8 and 'Death of Lord Lucas', *The Times*, 4 Dec. 1916, p. 11. **31** 'Lord Lucas Missing', *The Times*, 10 Nov. 1916, p. 8.

You had died fighting …
Such fighting as blind Homer never sung,
Nor Hector nor Achilles never knew,
High in the empty blue.
High, high, above the clouds, against the setting sun …[32]

This elegy echoes W.B. Yeats' 'An Irish airman foresees his death',[33] written in memory of Major Robert Gregory, son of Lady Augusta Gregory. Homeric allusions were a prominent part of the discourse of an air war in which the one-on-one combat between fighting scouts outshone the vital work of the machines undertaking artillery spotting and photographic reconnaissance. In the House of Lords in May 1916, Lord Curzon of Kedleston Hall spoke of the:

> daily series of almost Homeric combats … going on in the air, each one of which deserves almost a chapter in an epic. In these combats our men are showing that the mastery of the air – a phrase which I particularly dislike, and which I shall use as little as possible – that the mastery of the air is a thing that oscillates from side to side, and if it expresses anything at all, rests as often, if not oftener, with our men as with the enemy.[34]

Lord Curzon was responding to a motion tabled by Lord Montagu of Beaulieu on the subject of how best to coordinate efforts between the War Office (responsible for the RFC, or the military wing of the original RFC established in April 1912) and the Admiralty (responsible for the RNAS, which superseded the naval wing of the original RFC). Lord Curzon presided over a new Air Board that superseded the Joint War Air Committee chaired by Lord Derby,[35] but it was still far short of the new air department advocated by Lord Montagu, one of the great pre-war advocates of airpower.[36]

With Lords Montagu and Curzon debating the structure of the air service in the House of Lords, Lord Hugh Cecil, a younger son of the marquess of Salisbury, who became a lieutenant in the RFC in 1915, was celebrating the

---

32 Maurice Baring, *In memoriam. Auberon Herbert, Captain Lord Lucas, Royal Flying Corps, killed November 3rd, 1916* (Oxford, 1917), p. 10. See also Piers Paul Read, 'What's become of Baring?', *The Spectator*, 10 Oct. 2007, www.spectator.co.uk/2007/10/whats-become-of-baring/; David Cannadine, *The decline and fall of the British aristocracy* (London, 1990), p. 75; and Mark Girouard, *The return to Camelot: chivalry and the English gentleman* (London, 1981), p. 287. **33** W.B. Yeats, 'An Irish airman foresees his death' in *The wild swans at Coole* (New York, 1919). **34** 'House of Lords: the air debate. Lord Curzon's position', *The Times*, 25 May 1916. **35** Malcolm Cooper, 'Blueprint for confusion: the administrative background to the formation of the Royal Air Force, 1912–1919', *Journal of Contemporary History*, 22:3 (1987), 439. **36** During the war his neighbours at RFC Beaulieu were the instructors and pupils of No. 16 Training Squadron equipped BE2c, Avro 504 and Curtiss JN4 machines. See 'WWI East Boldre airfield photos go on display', www.bbc.co.uk/news/uk-england-hampshire-32848671 and 'Royal Flying Corps, Beaulieu', www.thenewforestguide.co.uk/history/forest-

2.3 Stoke Rochford Hall, Lincolnshire. T608051-084. Harlaxton-Russia Prints.
Reproduced with the kind permission of the Trustees of the Royal Air Force Museum.

achievements of the air service. In so doing, he contributed to the corps' efforts
to encourage a common identity among its pilots that went beyond pluck and the
heroic to encompass the chivalric, thereby uniting the 'qualities of ancient and
of the most modern warfare'.[37] In Lord Cecil's opinion: 'The officers of the
Flying Corps ... remind us of the knights of old; and certainly since the days of
the knights there has been no such opportunity in war for the display of the
personal qualities of the individual ... [when] we see our knights-errant of the
air go forth in an aeroplane.'[38] David Lloyd George described pilots in similar
terms: 'The heavens are their battlefield; they are the cavalry of the clouds. High
above the squalor and the mud ... They are the knighthood of this war ... They
recall the old legends of chivalry ... let us think of the chivalry of the air.'[39] As
Mark Girouard points out, 'the language which depicted the war as glorious,

airfields/beaulieu/royal-flying-corps-beaulieu/#.   **37** Lord Hugh Cecil, 'The Royal Flying
Corps: the work and training of the Royal Flying Corps', *London Illustrated News* (London,
1918), p. 4. See also Maryam Philpott, *Air and sea power in World War I: combat experience in
the Royal Flying Corps and the Royal Navy* (London, 2013), p. 182.   **38** Cecil, 'Royal Flying
Corps', p. 4.   **39** David Lloyd George, *War memoirs of David Lloyd George*, vol. ii (London,

heroic or chivalrous … became increasingly hard to apply … to war in the trenches'. Significantly, he goes on to suggest there were 'other aspects of fighting which bore (or could be made to bear) more resemblance to the war in story-books. The activities of the Royal Flying Corps were one of them'.[40]

Unlike the ground war the air war was idealized, 'however, inaccurately, as resembling pre-industrial chivalric contests';[41] it restored individual heroism to the war and gave Britain a 'heroic alternative to the squalid and anonymous war in the trenches'.[42] Airmen were described by Cecil Lewis, as the 'devil-may-care young bloods of England [and the Empire], the fast-livers, the furious drivers – men who were not happy unless they were taking risks'.[43] According to Arthur Gould Lee they were a new 'winged aristocracy of warriors'.[44] They were not born aristocrats, but they now embodied a melding of modernity and the aristocratic martial spirit; a combination that had until recently been associated exclusively with the pilot-aristocrat. The country house elite were open to this social intrusion because they recognized in these non-aristocratic pilots the same dash, vigour and reckless valour of the foxhunting originals. As *Country Life* explained in 1916, foxhunting 'cannot be too highly extolled as a sport which tends to promote valour and to cultivate those virtues which go to making of good cavalrymen'.[45] Tactically, cavalry was now redundant, but the virtues of the cavalryman were still exhibited by the airman, as Ogilvie stated in 1918: 'The old sport will be rejuvenated and given fresh life by the dash and vigour of our cavalry and yeomanry officers, and by the reckless valour of the flying men returned.'[46]

The exploits of these airmen were described in *Country Life* in 1917 by 'Contact', who reminded his readers: 'if, as a reaction against the nerve-edging job of war flying, they are apt to run wild during periods of leave, there are surely extenuating circumstances … remember that those same wild youths are they whose flying life is reckoned not in years, nor even in months, but in hours'.[47] Given the poignancy of being in the cavalry of the air, the social elite of the English countryside welcomed the increasingly cosmopolitan pilots of the neighbouring training aerodromes into their stately homes. In Lincolnshire, Sir Charles Welby of Denton Manor (fig. 2.4) as 'the owner of the Manor House with its extensive lawns, ponds, woodlands and private golf course, and as the possessor of some 17,000 acres … was in a good position to entertain, and he extended hospitality widely to the young [flying] officers in the neighbourhood'.[48]

1933), p. 1115.   **40** Girouard, *The return to Camelot*, p. 291.   **41** George Robb, *British culture and the First World War* (London, 2002), p. 202; see also John H. Morrow, *The Great War in the air: military aviation from 1909 to 1921* (Shrewsbury, 1993), p. 241.   **42** Michael Paris, 'The rise of the airman: the origins of air force elitism, *c.*1890–1918', *Journal of Contemporary History*, 28:1 (1993), 24, and Robb, *British culture*, p. 202.   **43** Patrick Bishop, *Wings: one hundred years of British aerial warfare* (London, 2012), p. 111.   **44** Morrow, *War in the air*, p. 241. **45** 'Shropshire, I', p. 346.   **46** Ogilvie, 'Future', p. 517.   **47** 'Contact', 'The remarkable in war flying', *Country Life*, 3 Nov. 1917, p. 416; see also Jack Brownlow, *Melton Mowbray, queen of the shires* (Wymondham, 1980), pp 257–61.   **48** Denis Richards, *Portal of Hungerford: the*

2.4 Denton Manor, Lincolnshire. T608051-137. Harlaxton-Russia Prints. Reproduced with the kind permission of the Trustees of the Royal Air Force Museum.

The neighbouring houses of Harlaxton Manor (fig. 2.5) and Belvoir Castle were similarly opened to the pilots and instructors at RAF Harlaxton, who were even invited to go foxhunting, much to the consternation of pilots who choose instead to watch all 'the bustle and activity in the bright frosty morning ... and the stamping of the horses ... [followed by] the Hunt Ball ... [with] the local gentry ... in their little red coats'.[49] In 1919, Lady Diana Manners had also 'hoped to entertain the boys before they left'.[50] A similar pattern can be observed in Hampshire where the pupils and instructors who were being encouraged by Robert Smith Barry to fly with greater skill and recklessness were always considered *persona grata* in the surrounding country houses.[51]

Training amid the country estates of rural England, pupils were able to both achieve the social transformation highlighted by Bishop and transform their self-identity into something more than that of a temporary officer and gentlemen.

life of Marshal of the Royal Air Force Viscount Portal of Hungerford (London, 1977), p. 71.
49 Edward Bujak, *Reckless fellows: the gentlemen of the Royal Flying Corps* (London, 2015), p. 127.   **50** Howard Wallace (ed.), *Parti patter: being serious and smiling chatter about a number of globe trotters awaiting the word to race for home* (Grantham, 1919), p. 21.   **51** F.D. Tredrey, *Pioneer pilot: the great Smith Barry who taught the world how to fly* (London, 1976), p. 99.

2.5 Harlaxton Manor, Lincolnshire. T608051-116. Harlaxton-Russia Prints. Reproduced with the kind permission of the Trustees of the Royal Air Force Museum.

This new elite of air officers and gentlemen were surrounded by the heraldry of their knightly antecedents, reinforcing a 'chivalric self-image'.[52] In an aeroplane they could loop and spin their machines above the roofs and battlements of some of the greatest houses in England. The owners of these homes could, in turn, look up and see the heirs to the aristocratic originals, a new winged aristocracy with whom they could identify, flying overhead. As Charles Masterman observed in *England after the war* (1922): 'In the retreat from Mons and the first battle of Ypres [in 1914] perished the flower of the British Aristocracy ... They did not form part of the armies that won the war. They were of a totally different character and temper ... Their tradition was only carried on by the chivalry of the air.'[53]

52 Robb, *British culture*, p. 202.   **53** Gerald Gliddon, *The aristocracy and the Great War* (London, 2002), p. xvii.

Behind the front in France: the story of the heir to Monksgrange

PHILIP BULL

Edward Richards-Orpen was the son of Adela Orpen, landlord of Monksgrange in Co. Wexford, and the medieval historian Goddard Orpen; he graduated from Cambridge in 1906, and in April 1914 married Margaret Tomalin, daughter of the owner of the Jaeger clothing company. From his marriage until 1916 he preoccupied himself with building a new wing at Monksgrange to be his family's residence, he and Margaret having their first child in 1915. In this he was using the mathematical, engineering and practical skills derived both from his mathematics degree at Cambridge and his interest in the theory and practice of engineering and construction. It was these skills he brought to bear on the war effort after his enlistment in late 1916 in the army's Motor Transport School of Instruction.

After initial training in the Grove Park Cadet School he was posted to the British Expeditionary Force in France as part of the Army Service Corps, arriving there on 6 February 1917. While in France, and until his demobilization in February 1919, he corresponded almost daily with his wife who was living in London with their son John and daughters Virginia born in 1916 and Charmian born in 1918. Of the correspondence so far located in the archive at Monksgrange there are over 330 of Edward's letters written from France to Margaret and more than 240 from her to him.[1] This essay is based principally on the insights into his wartime activities and experiences as revealed in the couple's correspondence.

While Edward's letters are very informative, Margaret contributes to this exchange significantly by questioning him about the details of his work and activities (fig. 3.2). Often there are numbered lists of questions in her letters and she was persistent in demanding answers. Thus we have a record of many things that might otherwise never have been put to paper. In one letter in late February 1917, less than a month after Edward's arrival in France, Margaret listed twenty-two questions for him to answer.[2] His reply revealed that he was already the 'boss' of a workshop, with all the vehicles under his charge; the nearest town to

---

1 Unless otherwise stated all references in this chapter are to this correspondence in the Monksgrange Archive. This archive is in progress of organization and cataloguing and so no numbered locations of individual documents are yet available. 2 Margaret Richards-Orpen [hereafter MR-O] to Edward Richards-Orpen [hereafter ERR-O], 26 Feb. 1916.

3.2 (*above*) Margaret Richards-Orpen (née Tomalin). Photographer, Ethel Barker of Putney (1873–1936). All images are from the Monksgrange Archive and are reproduced by kind permission of Jeremy Hill.

3.1 (*left*) Edward Richards-Orpen in uniform.

where he was located, only a small one, was seven miles away; and he answered 'Yes', he could hear the gunfire, but the line of battle was at least six miles away. 'Food quite good & plenty of it' he wrote: for breakfast, bacon and eggs or sausages, with tea, toast, butter and jam; for lunch, meat and tinned fruit; for tea, tea, toast, jam and cake; and for dinner soup, meat and vegetables, sometimes including potatoes, followed by fruit or savoury and coffee. His only complaint was that the 'meat is rather tough'. Another of her questions was about the men under his control, to which he replied that they had usually been employed in workshops and had experience of managing small works.[3]

Edward was highly intelligent and very talented and had significant engineering, practical and theoretical abilities; Margaret was determined to assure herself that these were being properly recognized and used in the army. She also knew from experience of their relationship that there was a certain fecklessness in Edward's character, a propensity to put things off, to neglect important matters and to fail to look after his own interests; she constantly urged him to be more forceful in his own interests and 'do all the clever push things you hate & aren't at all good at.'[4] Later in the war, when he had assumed a much more responsible position, she wanted to know what a typical day was like for him; his reply included a full-page list of daily activities (fig. 3.3).[5] Their

3 ERR-O to MR-O, 3 Mar. 1917. 4 MR-O to ERR-O, 27 June 1917. 5 ERR-O to MRO, 29 Aug. 1918.

3.3 A typical day for Edward Richards-Orpen, August 1918.

correspondence is also rich in another facet of his talents, namely drawing. His letters often included pencil drawings, many of them intended for the amusement of his son John (fig. 3.4).[6] In parallel to Edward's experiences in France, Margaret was also doing her bit for the war effort by volunteering three or four days a week at a 'canteen' near Victoria Station for the support and

6 ERR-O to MRO, 27 June 1918.

'D Stands for daddy the children will say,
But it dos'nt for what we get every old day'

accommodation of soldiers, mostly those from the Australian Imperial Force.[7] She also had her own social imperatives, urging him to 'tell me all about all the men with you … as that seems to be a great topic of conversation with wives to see who is with who, & who's met who …'[8]

On his arrival in France Edward was examined on his knowledge of motor engines and for the whole of his service he was in charge of maintenance, repair and management of the motor vehicles, principally lorries and staff cars, for the units in which he was serving. He reported to Margaret on 7 February 1917 that 'they are going to test me for a workshop job' and that 'They are very particular about the workshop officers as they have a very responsible position.'[9] Within days he had been appointed workshop officer, with responsibility for a large number of men. In this he was to demonstrate considerable skills and

7 MR-O to ERR-O, 16 Feb. 1917; ibid., 24 Feb. 1917.   8 MR-O to ERR-O, 11 Mar. 1917.
9 ERR-O to MR-O, 7 Feb. 1917.

INSIDE OF DADDYS
WORKSHOP.

3.5 Drawing by Edward Richards-Orpen of his workshop for his son.

professionalism, as well as a propensity for taking initiatives, some of which were not always entirely welcome to his superior officers. Initially he had found the workshops very small and badly fitted out,[10] but he devoted considerable energy and ingenuity to improving them. He became increasingly adept at this task and proud of his achievements, which he illustrated in a drawing sent back for his son John (fig. 3.5).[11]

Characteristic of Richards-Orpen's approach to his work was his response to the problems created by the frequent moves made by his unit. Very early he began working on a moveable workshop, which he had not quite finished in early July 1917 when he sent a drawing of it to Margaret (fig. 3.6), noting with pride that two other workshop officers had copied his idea.[12] Another problem at the front was getting lorries across ditches or disused trenches, so he devised and built what he called a 'trench bridge' (fig. 3.7). These were heavy objects (10 hundredweight each)[13] and as they had to be moved in pairs it was necessary to rig up a derrick in the lead lorry of a convoy to unload them. He tackled the problem of where to park lorries when they were not in use by making 'portable lorry standings' from logs of wood, to prevent them from sinking into mud or sand. These were designed 'to enable a park to be laid down in a few hours sufficient to hold 50 lorries, each lorry carrying 'its own standing on board when it moves'.[14] He also devised a crane for raising a lorry out of a ditch.[15] He

10 ERR-O to MR-O, 'Monday' [8 Feb. 1917].   11 ERR-O to MR-O, 21 July 1918.
12 ERR-O to MR-O, 8 July [1917].   13 i.e., 508 kilograms.   14 ERR-O to MR-O, 2 Aug.
1917.   15 ERR-O to MR-O, 8 Aug. 1917.

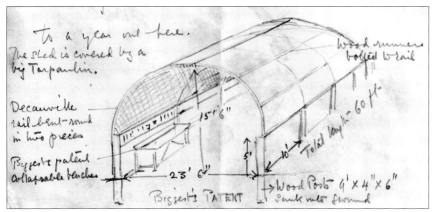

3.6 (*above*) Design by Edward Richards-Orpen for a moveable workshop.

3.7 (*right*) Design by Edward Richards-Orpen for a 'trench Bridge'.

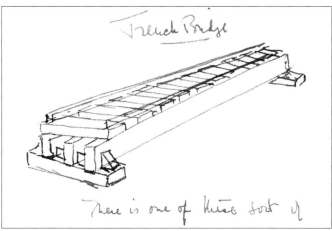

designed and made in his workshop a mounting for an anti-aircraft gun.[16] His letters reveal the constant application of his intellectual and practical faculties to the needs of these units, which were vital to support what was happening at the front. Margaret had asked him in a letter of 8 March 1917 'Have you done anything clever yet? And if so has anyone observed it yet.'[17] Within a short time she would be gratified on this score repeatedly as she received news of her husband's work with the Army Service Corps.

Supervising and managing the fleet of vehicles, as fundamental as that was, did not constitute what Richards-Orpen saw as the most challenging as well as the most creative part of his work. Increasingly important for him personally was instruction of officers in the driving, use and maintenance of vehicles and of the men under him in the technical knowledge required to repair and maintain them. Having no experience of teaching he set about understanding how information could be most meaningfully conveyed, whether to working-class men being

16 ERR-O to MR-O, 23 June 1917.   17 MR-O to ERR-O, 8 Mar. 1917.

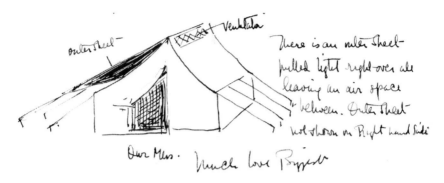

There is an inner sheet
pulled tight right over all
leaving an air space
between. Outer sheet
not shown on Right hand Side

Our Mess.   Much love Biggest

3.8 Mess tent designed by Edward Richards-Orpen to allow better ventilation.

instructed in manual and technical matters or officers, usually from the gentleman class, often significantly lacking in practical experience or technical knowledge. His inventiveness once again revealed itself. He recognized that lecturing from a lectern with the use of a blackboard was not the best way to engage interest nor to give a hands-on understanding of machines, so he cut up a Daimler engine and lit the crankcase with electric light to show better its internal working. With an eye to recognition of his work he was pleased to have completed this exercise as 'a surprise for the Colonel when he comes back off leave.'[18] This was to be the model for a number of such engines to be set on blocks, cooled through copper pipes bringing water from the sea and all to be constituted into what was essentially a teaching laboratory.[19] He soon became acquainted with the challenges and frustrations of teaching, writing to his mother in October 1918: 'I am still at the same job, teaching the young about motors, it means lectures & correcting numerous examination papers all worse than the ones that come before'.[20]

In his work he demonstrated his capacity as a scavenger, an art that put him in good stead for his later civilian life. In June 1918, he went to a large scrap heap in order to find fittings he could use for repair of engines as well as for the model engines he was constructing for teaching purposes.[21] He also set out to pick up some old aeroplane engines in order to demonstrate more modern practices than were possible with vehicle engines.[22] Always keen to acquire new knowledge that he could impart, he was constantly asking Margaret to send various magazines across to him, especially the *Automobile Engineer*, and books on electrical engineering. Using this knowledge he set up generators and lighting in some of the tents, in particular for the officers, thus enabling them to work at night. Some visiting Guards Officers expressed astonishment at this and the other comforts

18 ERR–O to MR–O, 'Monday' [?30 Sept. 1918].   19 ERR–O to MR–O, 1 June 1917.
20 ERR–O to Adela Orpen, 6 Oct. 1918.   21 ERR–O to MR–O, 'Monday' [10 June 1918].
22 ERR–O to MR–O, 'Sunday' [25 Aug. 1918].

3.9 Drawing by Edward Richards-Orpen of himself as officer in charge.

that were enjoyed in his mess.[23] He also designed a modification to the tents to improve ventilation and reduce the danger of rain getting in (fig. 3.8). So much had he achieved in improving living conditions that one of his colleagues jokingly suggested he contribute an article to *Country Life* in its series on lesser country houses, illustrating their mess tent with the excellent furniture Edward had managed to buy or scavenge locally.[24]

Working the army system was always an issue for Edward. On his arrival in France he observed that 'They have their own methods of doing everything here & of course don't like anyone else's way'.[25] This became a constant refrain. His cousin, the artist William Orpen, posted not far away, has described how he had to manipulate situations in order to get access to superiors and thus bypass those who, for reasons of jealousy or ignorance, frustrated what he needed to do as a war artist.[26] This was very much the same for Edward. He identified the superior officers that would be most likely to support his initiatives, and cultivated them accordingly. In the end, this was to pay off for him in terms of his advancement.

Very early Edward achieved promotion from first to second lieutenant. In the second half of 1918 he was made acting officer in charge of Instruction in place

23 ERR-O to MR-O, 24 May 1917.   24 ERR-O to MR-O, 9 June 1917.   25 ERR-O to MR-O, 6 Feb. [1917].   26 William Orpen, *An onlooker in France, 1917–1919* (London, 1921).

of a fellow officer, R.H. Eliot, who was on leave (fig. 3.9).[27] So successful was he that on his return Eliot – a permanent army officer – was extremely annoyed to find that Edward was kept in his position as officer in charge, thereby reducing his own role to teaching driving.[28] Had Edward been promoted to captain this would have further incensed Eliot and possibly led to appeals and other complications. Promotion to captaincy eluded Edward but his concern was not so much about status as money; paid at a higher rate while acting officer in charge, he knew that his post-war service gratuity would be determined on the basis of rank at the time of demobilization. He was, however, pessimistic as to his chances, writing that '[I] don't think the extra pip will be given me as all regulars only think by seniority, it's no good arguing with them their minds are so distorted they cannot think otherwise.'[29] But against all the odds (there had been a freeze on promotions for those not in the permanent army) Edward got his third pip after the Armistice; he owed this to the colonel who had been his most avid supporter throughout his time in France, and who had appreciated his talents and the importance of his work. The report on his performance as an officer read:

> An excellent officer in every way. Has a variety of attainments, & is a first class engineer though that is not his profession. He has been under my command for about 8 months acting as an instructor & has carried out his duties to my entire satisfaction.[30]

Dealing with the mind-set of the army and the inept application of authority was something Edward seemed to be able to manage relatively well, while retaining a deep commitment to doing a good job and applying his initiative to improving methods and results.

What was life like for those serving behind the front line? It is possible to read this correspondence and to imagine that it was easy and pleasurable for those performing this type of work as distinct from the horrors faced by those in the trenches. Certainly there was a lot of fun, with occasional dances when neighbouring WRAACs were brought into the camp and plenty of camaraderie and entertainments. Music was a particular pleasure, with great attention paid to the state of the gramophone on which they played records, and there was a wish for new records to be sent out. Reading matter was important, Margaret sending him magazines and papers including *Country Life*, *Connoisseur*, *The Times*, *English Review*, *Commercial Motor*, *Blackwoods*, and *Nineteenth Century*, as well as various other automobile and engineering journals.[31] *Country Life* with its illustrated articles on architecture and furniture was a particular favourite

27 ERR-O to MR-O, 3 Sept. 1918.   28 ERR-O to MR-O, 3 Sept. 1918; [?10 Sept. 1918].
29 ERR-O to MR-O, 'Tuesday' [?10 Sept. 1918].   30 Army 'Recommendation Form', 1 Jan. 1919, signed by Colonel Fitzherbert.   31 MR-O to ERR-O, 14 Mar. 1917.

with Edward and something that his fellow officers became more interested in through his contagious enthusiasm.

What did he make of his fellow officers? To begin with he thought them 'quite decent fellows though not very friendly rather reserved and keep much to themselves & don't talk much', but he noted and found remarkable that they had good taste in music, with very little of what he called 'lower class music hall stuff'.[32] Initially, however, he kept to himself in the evenings reading, wanting to avoid getting caught up in the bridge-playing set in what was 'rather an expensive mess'.[33] By the middle of 1918 he was playing tennis regularly, with his wife sending out the balls that were needed.[34] He had also built himself a sand yacht in which he went 'sailing'; Margaret feared that he might drown or be hit by a torpedo until being told 'it only goes on land'.[35] The letters to his wife and parents were relatively free of negative or dangerous aspects of his army life, but that may have been due to a concern to save them worry; he later wrote that 'Dante's Hell was only in the halfpenny seats' compared with their conditions after the Somme.[36] At a personal level in the mess he encountered hostility to Ireland and Sinn Féin but he responded with criticism of British failure to understand the Irish point of view; when asked then why he was 'fighting for England' his reply was that he was not but against Germany.[37] He later reflected on the psychology of men, like himself, near to the front but not in the trenches:

> At the front I think we seldom complained, except at the mud & wet weather, we tended to understand the difficulties of others & in conse-quence were satisfied to put up with things that in other circumstances would be regarded as intolerable. We always had in the back of our mind that so many millions [were] so much worse off & exposed to both risks & discomforts infinitely greater that any form of grumbling on our part was not done.[38]

He contrasted this with those in 'the real back areas' at the Motor Transport School at Wissaut on the French coast, of whom he said 'all grumbled like hell!'[39]

Edward was generally intrigued by class distinctions, rather amused by having to instruct and correct exam papers for a 'real live Duke' on one occasion, but also noting as time went on that more newly arrived officers were being drawn from lower social classes and did not share the tastes he preferred. He also put up a defence of the class basis of the officer cohorts, referring to 'a definite attempt … made to keep as far as possible the officer personnel more or less to those having the same background in civilian life':

32 ERR-O to MR-O, 21 Feb. 1917.   **33** Ibid.   **34** Correspondence between ERR-O and MR-O during June 1918.   **35** Ibid.   **36** 'The Somme in early 1917'.   **37** Ibid.   **38** ERR-O, 'Somme 1917'.   **39** Ibid.

At first sight one might think this was merely being snobish [*sic*]. I think myself it is something quite different, an efficient unit is a happy unit, & men with much the same upbringing & outlook are more apt to all pull together, than mixtures in which differences & jealousies are prone to develop.[40]

He qualified this, however, by referring to a 'temporary gent' who was promoted and who caused divisions and tensions in the unit until they moved north for the Messines offensive in which the real dangers they faced showed that 'differences of outlook vanish in times of stress.'[41] On the other hand discussion of 'Oxbridge memories or even your school was dangerous [and] better be avoided' on account of sensitivities relating to inglorious rowing or other performance.[42] His conclusions, however, accord largely with subsequent literature, namely that there were very positive outcomes from the mixing of social classes in the theatre of war.[43]

A particular concern for Edward was what was happening at Monksgrange. His parents were getting old, and his mother in particular was responsible for the upkeep of the property and running the farm. Because of increasing government concern about food shortages a system of agricultural leave was introduced to enable servicemen from farming communities to assist at critical times like ploughing and harvesting. Edward constantly sought such leave and was finally granted it from August 1917, initially until the following February, but then

3.10 Construction of the new wing at Monksgrange.

40 Ibid.   41 Ibid.   42 Ibid.   43 Ibid.

extended to May 1918. As well as managing harvesting and sowing for the following season he continued with rebuilding the wing of the house which had been demolished in the 1820s, which was intended as his and Margaret's home (fig. 3.10). Two significances followed from this period of leave. He missed the campaign in the Passchendaele mud from which his own division suffered heavily; and Margaret became pregnant, giving birth in September 1918 to their third child, a daughter Charmian.

The state of affairs at Monksgrange presented considerable difficulties for Edward, for not only did he have to manage the estate *in absentia*, dealing with matters like a new tractor for the farm, but there were awkward personal issues too. By January 1919, he had still not been demobilized despite the war being formally over and problems at Monksgrange were reaching crisis point. Margaret's attempt to live there with their children, the new wing still not habitable, led to problems with Edward's mother. A letter to his mother indicates the nature and scale of the problem:

> The first thing to realize is, that every married woman requires a house of her own, where she rules, and arranges things to her way of thinking, etc.
>
> Secondly that no two people have the same ideas of how things should be done, it's not a question of the right or wrong way.
>
> Thirdly that it is out of the question expecting people to be able to accommodate themselves so as not to interfere with others.[44]

Edward attributed these problems partly, and no doubt rightly, to the very fact of war, but also to his mother and him not having reached a clear enough agreement. He had now also to deal with Margaret giving free vent to her anger with him, she being now more able to do so since he no longer faced the hazards of war. She criticized him for not being more direct with his mother, but more seriously for his inability to give her an answer as to where they were to live when he returned from France. Clearly they had to be in Ireland for him to complete the building that was to be their home, but in the meantime they had nowhere to live and Margaret's impatience led her into outbursts of sarcasm.

The correspondence between the couple reveals the robust nature of their relationship and provides a background to what was to be an effective, if sometimes turbulent, shared management of Monksgrange after Edward inherited from his mother in 1927. As well as opening up a window into the experience of those who provided support from behind the trenches, the particular case of Edward Richards-Orpen provides an insight into the development of attitudes and skills that need to be understood if we are to appreciate the role he later played as the owner of an Irish country house.

---

44 ERR–O to Adela Orpen, 23 Jan. 1919.

Edward put behind him the resentments and disappointments of his class at political developments in Ireland and threw himself into practical activities contributing to the development of the independent state, eventually becoming a senator in the Republic of Ireland. In the early months of 1919, a critical time both for his demobilization and the future governance of Ireland, Margaret pressed him in the more progressive direction being marked out by the earl of Midleton, who unsuccessfully attempted to draw the Irish Unionist Alliance into support of a new measure of Home Rule. Margaret wrote:

> I am convinced that the game is up for the die-hards. I never thought that before, tho I was always against them … If there were any good in last stands I might see some sense in it. But when it's a lost cause, what good can you do yourself or Ireland or Monksgrange or your family by sticking to it.[45]

Margaret was a product of the English manufacturing and commercial middle classes, inherently distrustful of and hostile to the old landed elites. Edward too had lived all his life and gone to school and university in England and thus been exposed to similar attitudes and assumptions while himself a product of that old elite. In Margaret's attitudes, forcefully expressed, we can see how he was being drawn away from what she called 'staying behind with the old ideas'[46] to adopting positive attitudes to the changes occurring in the Irish polity.

The striking evidence of Edward's capacity for innovative initiatives in the Army Service Corps, his practical and technical skills, and his ability at getting around bureaucratic and hierarchical obstacles tells us something about the temperament and character that contributed to his later positive and constructive roles in Irish society, economic life and politics. More generally though his war experiences demonstrate the professionalism and skill of men like him in providing support for the fighting men, and the contribution they made to turning the fortunes of the allied powers in the last year or so of the war. If, as has sometimes been suggested, a particular British military strength arose from the aptitude of individuals for initiative, innovation and spontaneity, then the record that Edward and Margaret Richards-Orpen have left in their correspondence highlights these attributes among one set of servicemen in their support role during the Great War.

45 MR–O to ERR–O, 23 Feb. [1919].   46 Ibid.

'Not another son': the impact of the Great War on two Irish families

FIDELMA BYRNE

In June 2013, the Centre for the Study of Historic Irish Houses and Estates (CSHIHE) began compiling a prosopographical database to record the level of participation and casualty rates among the Irish landed class in the Great War, together with brief biographical details of those killed in action. The research has yielded remarkable stories of service and loss. This is evident not simply in human terms but also social standing, as houses once the symbol of wealth and status succumbed to the imposition of death duties. The Acton family of Kilmacurragh House near Rathdrum in Co. Wicklow exemplify this point. Between 1908 and 1916 the estate suffered the loss of three landlords, two as a consequence of war. Thus, a triple set of death duties were levied against the estate and the financial burden became too much for a young widow. Equally moving is the case of the French family of French Park in Co. Roscommon: six sons served in the war but four never returned home. Aside from the human narrative, analysis of the wider data offers historical insight into the attitudes, tendencies, connections and instability underpinning a class in one of the defining moments of the twentieth century.

In December 2014, a letter from Joan Moore to this author enclosed a copy of her maternal family history. Her daughter, Johanna, felt this book might assist the CSHIHE in shedding light on a number of family members she presumed listed within the database. The book did, indeed, prove extremely helpful in identifying the named, yet in many instances faceless, individuals; however, a single sentence in Joan's letter was very revealing of how the horrors of two world wars had tormented her family: 'neither my mother or father ever spoke of their memories of the war, it was a subject not be talked about, and neither of my two brothers spoke about the Second World War and their time fighting in it.'[1] A generation removed, and a century after the onset of the conflict, it appears the events of 1914–18 had a profound effect on the collective consciousness of successive generations of her family. This stance is hardly surprising given that two out of three paternal, and four out of six maternal uncles fought on the battlefields of Europe and became casualties of the bloody conflict.[2]

___

1 Letter from Joan Moore, 15 Dec. 2014. I am deeply indebted to Joan and Johanna Moore of Mooresfort, Lattin, Co. Tipperary, for their kindness and support in sharing their incredible family history and for allowing me to retell it. I would also like to thank Joan's cousin, Maurice, for publishing the family history in 1999, which enabled me to connect the various generations.   2 Joan's mother was Eileen Agnes French of Frenchpark, Roscommon, who

53

The French family's primary seat of residence since the seventeenth century was Frenchpark near Boyle, Co. Roscommon, though the family's property portfolio also extended into Galway and Sligo. In 1851, they were conferred with the title Barons de Freyne of Coolavin in the peerage of the United Kingdom. By the turn of the century, the Frenchs were one of a dwindling number of families that comprised the Irish landed class. Landlord-indebtedness over successive generations and the introduction of the various land acts, most notably the Wyndham land act of 1903, had systematically eroded their economic and social prestige to the point that many were indiscernible from the lesser gentry apart from hereditary titles and their associated palatial dwellings.[3]

The political landscape of 1914 was no less reassuring: the thorny issue of Home Rule appeared to be reaching a conclusion within the confines of Westminster, despite the best efforts of Ulster unionists and, ultimately, the House of Lords to veto the legislation. The once-powerful upper chamber had virtually been rendered powerless as a consequence of the implementation of the Parliament Act of 1911. The passage of the third Home Rule Bill in May 1914 threatened to plunge the country into a state of civil war.[4] Therefore, in many respects, the assassination of Archduke Franz Ferdinand in Sarajevo in June 1914, and Britain's subsequent decision to declare war on Germany in August, offered the Irish landed classes a stay of execution. In Ireland, the prospect of civil unrest arguably offered a far less favourable outcome for the Protestant gentry and aristocracy than to take up arms for king and country. While some were imbued by a sense of necessity in the face of rising democracy, others were instilled by a sense of duty or obligation, as they were the sons, grandsons and great-grandsons of military men who had fought for their country during previous conflicts. When one examines the numbers who served in relation to the size of the cohort that existed in Ireland, the contribution of the landed class is significant.

While the loss of a loved one is always difficult to bear, some families encountered unimaginable loss and were thrown into a state of flux. The Kilmacurragh estate near Rathdrum in Co. Wicklow epitomizes in many respects the fragility of life and class during the early twentieth century (fig. 4.1). It belonged to the Acton family who had been resident in Co. Wicklow since the

married Major John William Fitzherbert-Brockholes on 19 Nov. 1917. Major Fitzherbert-Brockholes fought in the Great War together with his two brothers, Thomas Joseph (b.1887) and Roger Hubert (1891). Thomas was killed in action on 14 Mar. 1915. Two years later, in July 1917, Roger, a lieutenant in the Royal Navy, was also killed in action. See Charles Mosley (ed.), *Burke's peerage, baronetage and knightage*, 107th edition (Wilmington, 2003), vol. i, pp 822, 1069. This article is concerned solely with the maternal side of the family. 3 For a fuller discussion on landlord decline see Terence Dooley, *The decline of the big house in Ireland* (Dublin, 2001); Peter Martin, '"Dulce et decorum": Irish nobles and the Great War, 1914–19' in Adrian Gregory and Senia Pašeta (eds), *Ireland and the Great War: 'a war to unite us all'?* (Manchester, 2002), p. 28. 4 Alan O'Day, *Irish Home Rule, 1867–1921* (Manchester, 1998), pp 247–61.

4.1 Kilmacurragh House today.

reign of Charles I. Thomas Acton inherited the estate in 1854. He remained a bachelor, and, thus, on his death in 1908, the estate passed to his nephew, Charles Annesley Acton. Charles, then aged thirty-two, was the eldest surviving son of Col. Charles Ball-Acton and his wife, Georgina Cecilia Annesley.[5] He had been born in Peshawar, India, in 1876 where his father was stationed while serving with the 51st King's Own Yorkshire Light Infantry.[6] In keeping with strong family tradition all of the boys were educated at Rugby School, Warwickshire, and trained at the prestigious Royal Military Academy at Sandhurst. They were all destined for a life in the military.

Charles joined the Royal Welch Fusiliers in 1896, thereafter fighting in numerous theatres of war throughout the Mediterranean and Asia. In 1900, he led an expedition to China to suppress the anti-imperialist Boxer Rebellion, a role that earned him a promotion to the rank of captain. Reginald Thomas, one year Charles' junior, had followed in his father's footsteps and was gazetted to the 1st King's Own Yorkshire Light Infantry in 1897. He subsequently joined the 2nd Battalion, while the youngest son, Vere, became a 2nd lieutenant with the Oxford Light Infantry. Reginald and Vere were deployed to South Africa to fight

5 The eldest son, William Parsons, was born in 1871 but died in 1883 at the age of twelve from meningitis contracted at school. The couple also had three daughters, see L.G. Pine (ed.), *Burke's genealogical and heraldic history of the landed gentry of Ireland* (4th ed., London, 1958), pp 1–2.   6 See Revd J. Gelson Gregson, *Biography of Colonel Charles Ball-Acton, C.B.*, ch. x, available at www.parsonsfamily.co.uk/acton/india4.php (accessed 28 Aug. 2015).

in the Boer War. On 18 February 1900, at Paardeburg, Vere was killed in action; he was aged twenty.[7] On inheriting his uncle's estate in 1908, Charles resigned his commission and settled down to life in Co. Wicklow, where he became a JP, and in 1913 was appointed to the position of high sheriff of the county.[8] However, the outbreak of war in 1914 forever altered the fortunes of the family and the estate. Charles applied for a commission with his old regiment and was subsequently posted to France as captain of D Company in the 9th Battalion. Thirteen members of staff on the estate also enlisted, leaving 'just the head gardener and a boy to look after Kilmacurragh'.[9] All thirteen lost their lives during the conflict.

As his brother Charles did, Reginald resigned his commission following the end of the Boer War. However, he found himself drawn back into military life and in 1912 he joined the Special Reserves. In April of the following year he married Isabel Richmond of Rockhampton, Gloucestershire, and twelve months later a son was born. At the outbreak of war Reginald left the Special Reserves and enlisted with his old regiment and was dispatched to the front. Writing to his sister Evelyn in December 1914 he provided a fleeting glimpse of conditions, stating 'the trenches I have been in are simply disgusting'.[10] Approximately one month later he was wounded at Lindenhoek and sent home to recuperate. By March 1915 he was deemed well enough to return to duty and was dispatched to Hull to rejoin the 3rd Battalion.[11] Though it appears luck was on his side on this occasion, his brother Charles was not so fortunate.

In July 1915, Charles was promoted to the rank of major. On 25 September that same year, allied forces launched a three-day offensive against Germany after four days of heavy shelling. The battle of Loos was a complete failure: by the end of the third day casualties amounted to 80,000. It was to be the last battle for Charles Annesley Acton. He was severely wounded by an explosion on the first day of fighting when he went to the assistance of a comrade. Though transported to the base hospital, his injuries were too extensive to recover from and he died a short time later while attempting to write a letter home.[12]

With Charles' death, Reginald inherited the Wicklow estate. In March 1916, he was deployed to the front as part of the 7th Battalion. Approximately two months later tragedy struck once again. On 22 May, he agreed to patrol with a number of his comrades near Ypres. On their return it was noted that two members of the group were missing. Believing the men to be stranded, Reginald went in search of them but came under severe fire. He sustained two wounds; the second, a shot to the head, killed him. His body was retrieved by 2nd Lieutenant

7 Turtle Bunbury, *The landed gentry and aristocracy of County Wicklow* (Dublin, 2005), pp 102–4. 8 *Freeman's Journal*, 18 Dec. 1913.   9 *Sunday Independent*, 7 Sept. 2014.   10 Tom Burnell and Seamus Burnell (eds), *The Wicklow war dead: a history of the casualties of the world wars* (Dublin, 2009), pp 14–15.   11 Anon., *Memorials of Rugbeians who fell in the Great War* (Warwickshire, 1917), vol. iii.   12 *Wicklow News-letter*, 2 Oct. 1915.

4.2 Frenchpark, Co. Roscommon.

Bond and Private Garnet, who without regard for themselves carried it 200 yards while under attack. They were subsequently decorated for their bravery, with Bond receiving the MC.[13] Thus, a little over three years after her marriage, Isabel Ball-Acton found herself widowed with a two-year-old son, Charles, and an estate encumbered with three sets of death duties as a consequence of the loss of three successive owners within eight years. Cumulatively, this equated to 120 per cent of the value of the estate. Unable to generate revenue and on the verge of bankruptcy, the young widow was left with few options but to lease the estate in an effort to ensure its, and indeed her family's, survival.[14] And so the Acton family moved out of Kilmacurragh House. In the 1930s Charles returned to his ancestral home, only to sell it in the 1940s. The estate never fully recovered from the Great War; the deaths of three males had profound human and economic consequences on the lives and finances of the people that remained. The quick

13 Anon., *The roll of honour: a biographical record of all members of His Majesty's naval and military forces who have fallen in the war* (London, 1916), vol. iii, p. 1, available at https://archive.org/stream/rollofhonourbiog02ruvi #page/n9/mode/2up (accessed 28 Aug. 2015). **14** *Sunday Independent*, 7 Sept. 2014.

succession of natural and unexpected deaths was not uncommon and a number of landed families experienced similar degrees of devastation, not least of whom were the Frenchs of Frenchpark in Co. Roscommon (fig. 4.2).[15]

In August 1914, the estate at Frenchpark was presided over by Arthur Reginald French, 5th Baron De Freyne, following the death of his father Arthur the previous year. It is fair to say the succession of this estate was far from conventional in many respects. The 4th Baron was the fourth son of Charles French and Catherine Maree and had inherited the estate in 1868 at the age of thirteen. This was despite the fact that his three older male siblings were alive and well. The reason for this was that the 3rd Baron, Charles, a Protestant, had married a Catholic girl, Catherine Maree, in a Catholic ceremony in 1851. Inter-denominational marriage, though socially acceptable by the mid-nineteenth century, was 'only considered legal if performed by a clergyman of the established church or by a registrar'.[16] However, when it became clear that the 2nd Baron was unlikely to marry, Charles became the likely successor to his brother, and as such the validity of his marriage was called into question. Accordingly, in 1854, the couple remarried in a Protestant ceremony in Kilnamanagh church, by which time they had three sons. The youngest, William, arrived just a few hours before the ceremony after an impromptu stop at Mullingar railway station. Hence, it was only with the birth of Arthur in 1855 that a legitimate heir could be declared.[17]

In 1877, the 4th Baron married Lady Laura Octavia Dundas, a sister of the first marquess of Zetland. They had two children, Gwendolen and Arthur Reginald; Laura died in 1881. The following year Arthur married twenty-six-year-old Marie Lamb, the daughter of Richard Westbrook Lamb and his wife Marie Eaton of West Denton. The second marriage produced a further eleven children (three girls and eight boys). By all accounts life was never dull in Frenchpark with so many children about the place, a situation the children appeared to exploit to both their advantage and amusement. Apparently, when guests would arrive at the house, the children would line up to be introduced. As the line was long, it provided ample time for each child at the front to rejoin the queue at the rear and begin the process again, much to their delight and the bewilderment of the guests. Along with the laughter, life was tinged with moments of sadness. In 1893 Gwendolen, Marie's step-daughter, died prematurely one day prior to her fifteenth birthday, while in September 1913 the 4th Baron died after a month-long illness at the age of fifty-eight, at which point Arthur Reginald, or Reggie as he was known, became the 5th Baron De Freyne.[18]

All the boys attended Oratory School in Reading. Fr Edward Pereira, the headmaster, was a trusted friend of Marie's and on occasion frequented Frenchpark and the family's town-house in London. When Bertram, the

15 See Dooley, *The decline of the big house*, pp 122–7.   16 Maurice French, *The Frenchs of French Park* (Warminster, 1999), p. 30.   17 Ibid.   18 Ibid., pp 34–6.

youngest, left the school in 1918, Fr Pereira felt compelled to write to Marie to express his sadness that no more French boys would frequent the corridors. In his letter he also described the calibre of the men they became:

> as they have come to us, one after the other, we have always known that we could rely on them, and they have never disappointed us: and it becomes almost a recognized thing that they should become Captains of the school, a clear proof that not the masters only, but the boys too realised their sterling worth.[19]

It is obvious the boys were born to lead. Reggie's military career began in 1899 when he was commissioned into the Royal Fusiliers, City of London Regiment, but it came to an abrupt halt in 1902 following a moment of recklessness, in which he married the daughter of a Scottish publican, much to the disdain of his family. Annabel Angus was a divorcee with a ten-year-old son at the time of her marriage to Reggie. Numerous fathers were suggested, though the child was called Ronnie True.[20] The marriage was short-lived, lasting only seven weeks. And it proved a costly experience: Reggie resigned his commission and duly disappeared, while the sorry episode continued to cost the estate £1,150 annually.[21] With time Reggie redeemed himself, serving with Company A of the 8th Infantry of the US Army and was reconciled with his father by the time of the 4th Baron's death in 1913.[22]

When the Great War began, Reggie returned home and gained a commission in the South Wales Borderers. All but three of his half-siblings joined the war effort too, including William (b.1885), Edward Fulke (b.1886), Louis (b.1888), George (b.1890) and Ernest (b.1894). Hubert and Bertram were too young to enlist, while the eldest son from the second marriage, Francis, was spared the trenches, perhaps as he was viewed as a likely successor to Reggie. The boys kept the family updated with their progress through regular correspondence. Though the realities of war were omnipresent in the letters, so too is the lighter side of life, as Reggie's letter of 1 December 1914 demonstrates. In it, he thanks his sister Muriel (or Moule as she was more affectionately known) for her correspondence before apologizing as he had only 'glanced through it' before losing the letter as there were 'some rather pressing things to attend to'. He makes numerous requests of Frank, mainly to sort out a subscription for *Punch* and the *Sporting Times* and also to send 'an electric torch' as his had been damaged by water.[23] A letter dated 27 April 1915 from George to Moule provides extensive details on military tactics. At that time, George's battalion was involved in

---

19 Ibid., Appendix C., p. 57. 20 Ibid., p. 41. In March 1922, Ronnie True murdered a London prostitute called Olive Young (real name Gertrude Yates). He was sentenced to death but this was commuted to life imprisonment by reason of insanity. He died in Broadmoor in 1951; see also *The Times*, 7 Mar. 1922. 21 Ibid., Appendix E., p. 61. 22 *Irish Independent*, 11 Sept. 1913. 23 French, *Frenchs of French Park*, Appendix F., p. 62.

constructing a 'new front line' which involved 'working till 2 and very often 3 in the morning from dark'. There was heavy fighting in the area south of his position and they were concerned the Germans were 'using asphyxiating gases again'. He then went on to describe how this was done and how a 'moist rag ... preferably dipped in a solution of bi-carbonate of soda' usually nullified any effect.[24]

Of the others, William gained the rank of lieutenant in the 6th Battalion, the Worcestershire Regiment. He fought in the war, returned unscathed and subsequently fought in the Second World War. Louis served as a lieutenant in the Royal Army Services Corps (Territorial Forces) and returned home after the conflict. The others were not so fortunate. On 9 May 1915 Reggie and George, who were serving side by side with the South Wales Borderers at the battle of Aubers Ridge on the Western Front, were both killed in action. Following Reggie's death at the age of thirty-five, Francis became the 6th Baron De Freyne. Ernest, while serving as a lieutenant with the 5th Battalion, South Wales Borderers, was wounded in action and soon after died on 16 August 1917. He was only twenty-three years old. Edward Fulke, a 2nd lieutenant in the Royal Field Artillery, had been captured by the Germans. He was the last of the French boys to die in the course of the Great War, for two days after peace had been declared on 13 November 1918 he died while still a prisoner of war in Germany. He was thirty-two years old.[25]

Their mother Marie French died on 20 February 1923, aged sixty-six. In a letter to her daughter Lily shortly after her death, Marie's long-time friend, Fr Edward Pereira, recorded those 'awful days of war', and Marie's pain at the loss of her sons:

> First Reggie, who had more than made good the slips of the past; and George, a life of singular promise – so straight, so unselfish, so strong. But there was much still to bear. Dear Little Ernest, one of the most winning characters I have ever met: and then the long drawn out agony when old Thomas [as Fulke was sometimes known] was missing, with no word of news; the short lived joy when it was known that he was alive and well; the expectation of his speedy return, all making the blow greater when the news came of his death.[26]

A short time after the death of Fulke, Pereira, in conversation with Marie, asked her 'how she managed to hide so successfully, except from the closest observers, the full weight' of the tragedy. She responded, as must have countless mothers and wives, that 'she must keep a smiling face to keep the family together', a family that was decimated by war; she was a remarkable woman.[27]

24 Ibid., Appendix F., pp 62–3. 25 Mosley (ed.), *Burke's peerage*, vol. i, pp 1068–9. 26 French, *Frenchs of French Park*, Appendix D., p. 60. 27 Ibid.

These case studies reveal the precarious nature of Irish estate management during the war years, and equally, the fragility of the Irish landed classes. However, in the majority of cases that appear in the CSHIHE database, country house owners and heirs apparent who enlisted returned home to their loved ones, though many were physically and emotionally scarred. For families such as the Actons, and, in particular, the Frenchs, the sense of loss for the sons who never returned home and who were buried in the numerous theatres of war across Europe was all pervasive. Charles Annesley Ball Acton is buried at Loos in France. Reginald Thomas Ball Acton has no known grave but is listed on special memorial 9 in White House Cemetery, Ypres, Belgium. Reggie and George French lie side by side at Cabaret-Rouge, Souchez, France. Ernest is buried at Plot 3, Row I-18 at Dozinghem, Belgium; Edward Fulke is buried at Niederzwehren, Kassel, Germany.[28] The Great War may not have eradicated the Irish landed class, but it certainly dealt them a severe blow.

28 Ibid., pp 43–4.

Captains and cowmen: Brodsworth Hall's community during the Great War

CAROLINE CARR-WHITWORTH

> Like all other estate owners, the labour problem through the war has presented itself in acute form at Brodsworth. His agent is an officer in the Army; his head gardener is just called up; three estate clerks have gone; the man in charge of the poultry is about to be superseded by a woman because the military claim him; and the squire told us he has not a chauffeur left. Quite a large number of the little army of men who find employment on the Brodsworth estate are now serving their king and country.[1]

As the author of this article in the *Live Stock Journal* for 21 July 1916 remarked, the relentless demand for manpower was one of the most strongly felt effects of the Great War on a country house estate like Brodsworth Hall in Yorkshire's West Riding. Research for the 'Duty Calls' exhibition at Brodsworth confirmed this assessment, exploring the experiences of many of the men who left for the war and of the community who continued to live and work at Brodsworth. Their stories give insights into both remarkable and more ordinary facets of individual lives and the workings of one estate. They may also, as the *Live Stock Journal* surmised, illustrate effects of the war commonly felt in rural communities.

Brodsworth Hall, an English Heritage property, took part in the Yorkshire Country House Partnership's joint project to explore the impact of war on the country house, culminating in the 'Duty Calls' exhibitions in 2013–14.[2] Brodsworth's project, supported by the Heritage Lottery Fund, tackled both world wars. It focused on personal experiences, revealing among other things how veterans of the Great War found themselves serving on the home front, often in the Home Guard, in the war of 1939–45. The starting point for the team of volunteer researchers and curator was the memorial window in Brodsworth church, inscribed with ten names from 1914–18 and six from 1939–45. The estate papers and, particularly, the land agent's correspondence held in Doncaster Archives were valuable primary sources as were school log-books, local newspapers and the military archives of various regiments and the holdings in The National Archives.[3] These were augmented by photographs from the Hall

---

1 Doncaster Archives [hereafter DA], DDBrod 18/3.   2 For further information on this project go to www.ychp.org.uk.   3 For agent's correspondence see DA, DDBrod 15, 16; school log-

5.1 The model dairy at Brodsworth's home farm in 1913, 'with ornaments in white' as cowman and later Captain Basil Waghorn described himself and fellow workers (private collection).

and from a number of families. While the project enabled a broad picture to be pieced together of Brodsworth's community during the Great War, some aspects and figures remain ill-defined; it can perhaps only ever be an incomplete picture.

The 'squire' mentioned by the *Live Stock Journal* was Charles Thellusson (1860–1919), third son of Charles Sabine Thellusson, who had remodelled the 8,000-acre Brodsworth estate in the 1860s. Inheriting the estate from his financier great-grandfather after it had been managed by trustees for over fifty years, Charles Sabine Thellusson had energetically turned Brodsworth into a model modern country seat. He built a new Italianate house set in formal gardens and parkland and rebuilt farms on more efficient lines. The woodlands were taken in hand and the number of gamekeepers increased so that Thellusson could indulge his passion for shooting and entertaining in the winter (as a leading yachtsman he often spent his summers on the south coast). The farm rents, however, were often inadequate to support this way of life, but after his

books (Brodsworth, DA SR58) (Hampole, DA SR64) and (Marr, DA SR66). A useful guide to the history of the estate is English Heritage, *Brodsworth Hall and gardens* (English Heritage, 2009).

third son Charles Thellusson inherited the estate in 1903 an additional income stream was found through leasing land to the Brodsworth Main Colliery Company to sink what was to become one of the most productive pits in the country. This enabled Charles to continue to enjoy the life of a country squire. At the home farm he built a model dairy for his pedigree Jersey herd, kept beef cattle and pigs, and also expanded a poultry farm that supplied both commercial birds and prizewinners for competitions from England to New York (fig. 5.1). His achievements in this field were the reason for *Live Stock Journal*'s article in 1916, which implies that his main aim during the war was to keep the estate and life at Brodsworth running as usual.

Charles Thellusson was aged fifty-four in 1914, too old for military service. He and his wife Constance had no children of their own, but had made Brodsworth a home for younger relations, particularly their two Grant-Dalton nephews who had been orphaned at a young age. Like all families during the war the Thellussons feared for those on active service. Charles, the older Grant-Dalton brother and potential heir to the estate, was a keen motorist and volunteered for the Army Service Corps. It welcomed drivers and those with estate management experience, also recruiting Brodsworth's land agent and at least one estate chauffeur. Charles served briefly in France, leaving the army at the end of the war as a captain.

Stuart Grant-Dalton, his younger brother, had a more eventful war (fig. 5.2). Commissioned into the Princess of Wales' Own Yorkshire Regiment in 1906, he went to France in April 1915 as a captain with the 5th Battalion and was wounded almost immediately in the second battle of Ypres. After a short convalescence at Brodsworth he trained – in a few days – to become a pilot in the RFC and then joined 14 Squadron in Egypt. He was awarded the DSO and bar in 1916 – the DSO for landing to rescue another pilot who had been shot down and managing to take off again with them both, and then the bar for fighting off an attack from three enemy planes, in which he was so badly wounded that he had to have a leg amputated. However, he continued to serve and helped to develop the New Zealand RAF between the wars, retiring with the rank of Wing Commander in 1940.[4]

Another cousin, Eustace Grant-Dalton, was also a professional soldier who left for France with the British Expeditionary Force in August 1914 as a captain in the Prince of Wales' Own Yorkshire Regiment. He was captured at the battle of the Aisne only a few weeks later and spent the rest of the war in prisoner-of-war-camps of Crefeld and Gütersloh. Later in life he married his cousin Charles' widow, Sylvia, and among the collections at Brodsworth is a fascinating

4 *Green Howard Gazette*, 1914–18, and *Green Howards in the air* at the Green Howards Museum, Richmond; Michael Napier, *Winged crusaders: the exploits of 14 Squadron RFC and RAF, 1915–1945* (Barnsley, 2013); Geoffrey Bentley and Maurice Conly, *Portrait of an air force, the Royal New Zealand Air Force, 1937–1987* (Wellington, 1987).

5.2 Captain Stuart Grant-Dalton in a BE2c in Egypt, 1916 (Brodsworth Hall).

play script from his time in captivity, entitled *A Jerry-built Genesis*, containing a photograph of the officer actors in costume, the 'Cercle Artistique de Gütersloh in 1916' (fig. 5.3). Organized activities such as dramatic societies, camp magazines and athletics were all ways in which imprisoned officers fended off boredom and depression, since unlike prisoners of other ranks they were not allowed to work.[5] Two of the Thellussons' nieces also became VAD nurses, and for Adeline Thellusson this brought her both an OBE and a role for the rest of her life as matron of the St Dunstan's hostel for war-blinded servicemen in Brighton.[6]

At the outbreak of the war Charles Thellusson was enjoying a salmon-fishing holiday in the Outer Hebrides. According to the recollections – and annoyance – of his cook, Caroline Palmer, Mr Thellusson was so apprehensive of the potential German naval threat that he immediately set sail for home in his steam yacht around the north of Scotland with hardly time to pack supplies.[7] Back at Brodsworth the land agent, John Mellor's, greatest worry was that the combination of military activity connected with recruiting around Doncaster and short-time working at the colliery would spell disruption to the pheasant shooting that season.[8]

5 *White Rose*, Nov. 1970, regimental magazine held at the Prince of Wales' Own Regiment of Yorkshire Museum, York.   6 *St Dunstan's Review*, Dec. 1937.   7 Information relating to Caroline Palmer and valet Alfred Edwards who married in 1916 by courtesy of the Edwards family.   8 John Mellor to Augustus Thellusson, 11 Aug. 1914 (DA, DDBrod 16/14).

5.3 Keeping up spirits in Eustace Grant-Dalton's prisoner of war camp in Gütersloh in 1916 (Brodsworth Hall).

John Mellor, aged thirty-four in 1914, immediately rejoined the regiment he had served with before coming to Brodsworth as agent in 1911, soon transferring to the Army Service Corps and serving in France. In the expectation of only a short-term absence by the agent and his clerks, temporary assistance was sought from a nearby estate until eventually a replacement agent, Mr McKee, was found for the duration of the war. One of the estate clerks, Allan Simpson, joined the 12th York & Lancaster Regiment (the 'Sheffield Pals'), and was killed with most of its men on the first day of the battle of the Somme, in the same month the *Live Stock Journal* article was being written.

Many young men from Brodsworth enlisted immediately, perhaps in the spirit of enthusiasm at the start of the war, although their motives may have been varied and complex. John Mellor's example, as a respected figure on the estate, must have been influential, and his promise of a weekly wage of ten shillings and safeguarded jobs on their return may have encouraged some to join up (fig. 5.4). However, correspondence in the estate archive reveals poignantly that McKee and Charles Thellusson had not initially been aware of this offer. Subsequently, they received a request for payment on behalf of the ailing and impoverished father of one of the young gardeners, Charles Hickman; although unsuccessful

5.4 Gamekeeper Walter Lamb, whose father, also a gamekeeper at Brodsworth, received his allowance of 10 shillings a week (private collection).

on his first attempt to enlist, he later joined up and was killed on the Somme in September 1916.[9] The estate honoured this request, and made similar payments on behalf of other employees for every week of their military service. Men on active service were also sent gifts from the estate such as a leather wallet at Christmas, and a shaving set on their return.

The King's Own Yorkshire Light Infantry recruited in nearby Doncaster, where its territorial battalion had been based. Footman James Hunt initially joined the regiment but within days was one of over 200 men transferred to the Royal Navy, which was receiving fewer recruits. Sent to the Dardanelles with the Royal Marine Light Infantry Plymouth Battalion, he was killed on Y Beach at the age of twenty-one in May 1915, and was probably Brodsworth's first casualty. Men from Brodsworth saw action with various battalions of the King's Own Yorkshire throughout the war, including at Loos, where gamekeeper Joseph Bufton was killed, as well as the Somme and Passchendaele. Gardener Harry French had been a signaller with 6th Battalion, but after being wounded became

9 For the agent's correspondence in Apr. 1917 with Mr Hickman, see DA, DDBrod 15/44.

5.5 Brodsworth's football team in 1910 with its captain, Richard Mason, sitting in front of Charles and Constance Thellusson (Brodsworth Hall).

a signals instructor at Welbeck, Nottinghamshire, returning briefly to Brodsworth after the war. The memorial plaque presented to the family of John Smeaton of 2/5th King's Own Yorkshire Light Infantry, who was killed in the German advance of March 1918, was a moving exhibit in the 'Duty Calls' exhibition. Possibly Brodsworth's last casualty was farm boy Joseph Poppleton of the 2nd Battalion, the youngest son of the bailiff at home farm, who had enlisted in September 1914 and died from wounds in the Somme area in June 1918.

Men like John Smeaton came from families who had worked on the Brodsworth estate for generations. But some estate and household workers before the war came from other parts of the country; positions like valet, footman, chauffeur, and gamekeeper were often filled in answer to advertisements. For such young men the war may have seemed a further opportunity for adventure or advancement. Two newcomers from the south were chauffeur Richard Mason and Basil Waghorn, the second cowman at the model dairy, who had grown up in a London workhouse. Both were keen sportsmen, and they were in the estate football team that Mason captained (fig. 5.5). Both enlisted in the Royal Munster Fusiliers, seeing service in the Dardanelles, Salonika and Egypt. Mason was awarded the DCM for conspicuous gallantry at Suvla Bay on 16 August 1915, and Waghorn was described as 'sober, honest, intelligent and trustworthy' on his

5.6 The wartime wedding at Brodsworth of the chauffeur, George Raper, and cook, Martha Lockey (Brodsworth Hall).

promotion from sergeant to 2nd lieutenant in 1918.[10] Both eventually achieved the rank of captain. However, neither returned to Brodsworth; it perhaps held less appeal as well as fewer opportunities for employment after the war. The last entries on their military records are police requests for references in 1926 for Waghorn to work as a conductor, and in 1930 for Mason as a driver on London 'carriages', perhaps an indication that work was hard to find for veterans, even of proven ability.

The 1916 *Live Stock Journal* article mentioned that the head gardener, Frederick Larner, had just been called up; after the initial wave of voluntary enlistment, older men from Brodsworth either volunteered under the Derby Scheme of late 1915 or were conscripted from 1916. This had an additional impact on the running of the estate by removing senior and experienced staff, including the head gamekeeper, William Colledge, and butler, William Marshall.

A vivid illustration of this point is provided by the wedding photograph of senior chauffeur George Raper and cook Martha Lockey in January 1916 (fig. 5.6). Raper, aged forty-three, joined the Army Service Corps and is in his new uniform, while his best man, valet Alfred Edwards, wears the Derby Scheme armband to show that he had attested but not yet been called up. Edwards was,

10 For Waghorn's full military service record, see TNA, WO374/70843.

5.7 Jim Woodward with his family at his estate cottage; he tore off his uniform on his return because of the lice (private collection).

in fact, turned down on medical grounds and remained at Brodsworth, taking on the work of chauffeur, butler and the duties of other men who had left the household. He died in 1919, worn down perhaps by both the work and his weak lungs.

Shooting provides a special prism through which to understand the effects of the war at Brodsworth. Gamekeepers were useful recruits for the army and Brodsworth keepers, William Colledge and George Webb, were recommended to the recruiting officer by General Copley of nearby Sprotbrough Hall as 'not only strong, hefty fellows but steady reliable men'. They were drafted appropriately into the artillery.[11] The departure of his head keeper must have been felt keenly by Charles Thellusson, whose game books show a marked decline in number of birds shot after 1916. New keepers were taken on, including wounded servicemen, who continued to have 'affrays' with poachers.[12] The head keeper's wife, Mrs Colledge, also assisted with some tasks relating to the shoot until 1919, being paid for 'nest money' and beaters' wages.[13] Nearby convalescent homes were added to the list of recipients of gifts of game, and Mrs Thellusson decreed that the household would eat only game in order to preserve meat in the shops for others.

---

11 Short service attestation for William Colledge, regimental No. 166406 (TNA, WO 363).
12 *Doncaster Gazette*, 13 Sept. 1916, records an assault on George Bufton, a former keeper who returned to Brodsworth after service in the Dardanelles.   13 Estate accounts, 1918 DA, DDBrod 11/6.

New tenant farmers during the war were still expected to be 'good preservers of game'. But there were persistent complaints by farmers of damage to crops by rabbits and crows, and keepers, including William Colledge, were granted early demobilization after the Armistice to return urgently as 'vermin catchers' – partly, it seems likely, in order to get the shooting back to pre-war standards.[14] While shooting provided employment, one vitriolic letter reveals how resentment of this pastime of the privileged could be sharpened by wartime circumstances. C.L. Robinson, the dairy manager for a neighbour, was outraged at being forbidden to pick blackberries along a certain boundary; his anger at the waste of food in a country under strict rationing turned into an attack on the structure of society:

> Is it conceivable that those millions who are just now being called heroes for risking their lives in defence of what they are told is their country and the land of freedom, will, after the war settle down again tamely in an atmosphere of autocratic domination which can decree, for instance that masses of delicious fruit are to rot to the ground (as they did last year) rather than risk the possibility of a few 'sacred' pheasants seeing a strange face? ... And what makes it worse is that in this year of national shortage we are ordered to allow nothing to be wasted. Many things point to the coming of a revolution at home following on the crushing of foreign oppression; it is devoutly to be hoped that it may arrive without the help of anything more violent than voting. But that will depend – as history shows.
>
> Signed, C L Robinson, MA, FRAS,
> Extension Lecturer for Oxford University.[15]

Mrs Colledge was not the only woman to take on men's work during the war. The *Live Stock Journal* had mentioned that 'the man in charge of the poultry was superseded by a woman'. This was a considerable responsibility given the scale of the Brodsworth poultry farm, whose extensive pens and new buildings held 1,500 birds in 1916. On the wider estate women and children had always helped seasonally in the fields, but their burden must have increased during the war. The log-book for the estate school at Marr records two girls returning after a prolonged absence, from April 1917 to January 1918, due to their mothers working in the fields; the girls had presumably taken on the care of younger children and running the homes.

The Brodsworth estate engaged some Women's Land Army girls in the dairy and gardens. Correspondence sheds light on the arrangements made between Mrs Margery Williams, the efficient local organizing secretary of the West Riding Women's War Agricultural Committee, and Mr McKee, who paid

14 Agent's correspondence for Nov. 1918 (DA, DDBrod 15/47).   15 DA, DDBrod 15/45,

eighteen shillings a week, slightly less than elsewhere on account of also giving board and lodging. While some girls gave excellent service, being granted leave to attend a recruiting rally and receive their long service badges, another, Miss Sires, was sacked for impertinence and persistently refusing to be in by 9.30 p.m. Unfortunately there is no record of her side of the story.

The Brodsworth estate archives reflect the increasing pressures on farming and food supply during the war. Grassland was ploughed up for crops and land taken for allotments for the nearby mining village, where permission was sought for tenants to keep pigs and poultry. In 1916 returns were requested on the types and dimensions of trees on the estate, for the war made huge demands for timber. Labour for agriculture was so stretched that a scheme was agreed with the War Office whereby soldiers with agricultural experience – 10,000 in 1917 – could be released to help at home, particularly with harvest. Jim Woodward was one estate worker who benefited; he applied to come home in 1917 and had this permission extended till the end of the war (fig. 5.7).[16]

Many children, like Jim Woodward's on the Brodsworth estate, would have had family members on active service. The log-books of the three village schools give insights into children's experiences and their involvement in activities to support the war effort. The schools enthusiastically took up gardening, selling potatoes in aid of the Red Cross and picking blackberries to be made into jam for the troops. The schoolchildren from Hampole were taken to Doncaster to see 'Egbert the Tank' on its fundraising tour and given sixpence each by Mr Thellusson to start their own war savings. Celebratory teas and peace mugs were presented to the children when the war ended, although the schools were soon to suffer closures and some deaths when the influenza epidemic reached the area.

One of the main activities in support of the war effort undertaken by members of Brodsworth's community of all ages was knitting and sewing. Providing garments for troops on active service, for those that were wounded and in hospital, and for refugees was one of the major voluntary activities undertaken on the home front throughout the country. With the rapid enlistment of so many men at the beginning of the war, uniforms and equipment of every kind were in very short supply. Queen Mary called on the women of the empire to knit and sew for the troops, and established the Queen Mary Needlework Guild to make, collect and distribute garments sent in to them. Ladies like Constance Thellusson took up the call, organizing the making and sending of garments. Mrs Thellusson herself provided wool for the children to use, and read them a thank-you letter from Captain Bowering of HMS *Violet*. To ensure these well-meaning efforts were directed where they were needed, Sir Edward Ward was appointed Director General of Voluntary Organisations in 1915, and each county's work was organized by their lords lieutenant, mayors and leading ladies,

Aug. 1917.   16 Agent's correspondence Nov. 1917–Dec. 1918 (DA, DDBrod 15/45–46).

5.8 Amy Tyreman, second left at the back and her siblings wearing their Queen Mary Needlework Guild badges (Private collection).

with eventually each group of workers being officially recognized. The Drapers' Chamber of Trade made flat patterns for garments like shirts, wool could be bought at reduced cost, and centres were set up for packing and distribution. This structured arrangement continued into the Second World War, when the Brodsworth Estate Workers Group was registered and once more knitted in great quantities.

A remarkable piece of evidence surviving at Brodsworth reflects this call for greater efficiency and the involvement of almost the entire estate. A notebook of 1915–16 filled with names and lists of garments records over 2,000 items such as socks, shirts and caps being made by 129 people, mostly women, and including all of the Hall's female staff. Mrs Catton, the wife of the head herdsman, was the most prolific, making 115 shirts.

The local press celebrated the efforts of the estate's 'little war workers', several of whom received Queen Mary Needlework Guild badges and certificates.[17] Even Father Christmas (in reality the vicar of Brodsworth) sent them thank-you letters and gifts of patriotic mugs. The children of the stationmaster at Pickburn, Mr Tyreman, were especially productive (fig. 5.8). A label with the name of the

17 *Doncaster Chronicle*, 13 Aug. 1916.

5.9a&b The badge and thank you letters received by Amy Tyreman for her knitting (Brodsworth Hall).

maker and her or his village was attached to each garment, resulting in many thank-you letters being received. A small bundle of fragile letters was kept by Amy Tyreman; these provide glimpses into the lives of men on active service and record their reactions to this contact with an unknown schoolgirl (figs 5.9a&b). Some letters are cheery, others brief; among the most touching is one from twenty-six-year-old James Norman, serving with a machine-gun company in the Mediterranean Expeditionary Force in December 1915, his first Christmas away from home: 'I think it awful good of you children to make such things for they are needed very bad when us chaps are in the trenches but thank God I have finished with the trenches and I wish that I had finished with the war.' He asked his wife in Bristol to send Amy a small gift. Norman survived the Dardanelles but was killed at Ypres in 1917.

After the Armistice had been signed the slow process began for men to be demobilized and returned home. A welcoming party was held in Brodsworth's village school in March 1919, with speeches by some of the senior staff who had served. Mr Larner, the head gardener, tactfully paid tribute not only to the men who had fought but also to 'those at home who had done all possible to keep things going … and borne themselves bravely in their anxiety', and who had sent 'beautiful presents' and 'warm comforts'.[18]

It was not long before subscriptions were raised to install a stained glass window in Brodsworth's church of St Michael and All Angels, inscribed with the names of ten men who had given their lives. The service of dedication in 1920 drew the community together but also reflected how it had changed.[19] It was unveiled by the young son of one of those commemorated, groom Walter Sanderson. Others had worked as a footman, gardener, gamekeeper, clerk, and

18 *Doncaster Chronicle*, 7 Mar. 1919.   19 Ibid., 4 June 1920.

some had been labourers on the estate and in the nearby pit that increasingly offered work to men from the estate. The 'Last Post' was played by Thomas O'Connor, a bugler from the colliery who had served with the Royal Medical Corps, and who had kept a remarkable diary of the evacuation from Gallipoli. Charles Thellusson's niece, Adeline, was among the family members attending, accompanied by a party of blind ex-servicemen from the St Dunstan's hostel in Ilkley, where she was then nursing. At the service the bishop of Sheffield remarked that the estate village of Marr was unusual in not needing a memorial, as every one of the twenty-five men who had fought in the war from its population of 170 returned safely. This has earned it a place among the fifty 'Thankful Villages' in the country.

Two further windows were unveiled, in thanksgiving for the safe return from the war of the two Grant-Dalton brothers, and in memory of the squire, Charles Thellusson, who had died in March 1919. His death, almost as much as the war, triggered change on the Brodsworth estate. While Captain Mellor's return brought a steadying hand to its management, he soon had to close down Charles' prize cattle, pig and poultry enterprises with the loss of several jobs. The household and garden staff – though not the gamekeepers – were reduced as Charles' brother Augustus Thellusson lived mainly in Kent. Circumstances at Brodsworth after the war were more straitened for all than they had been in August 1914.[20]

20 The author would like to acknowledge the Historic England Archive for permission to use all images included in this essay.

'Lay spring flowers on our boy's grave': Norman Leslie's short war

IAN d'ALTON

'If the European thing by chance settles, I shall get to Glaslough in August', wrote Captain Norman Jerome Beauchamp Leslie to his mother, Leonie, at Castle Leslie, Co. Monaghan, in late July 1914 (fig. 6.1).[1] He was never to see home again, though; he was killed by a sniper at Armentières, northern France, probably on 18 October.[2] A fellow-officer described a reconnaissance that went wrong: 'he was dead in 5 minutes and never spoke, shot through the body'.[3] Leslie was a professional soldier, and thus war was what he did. He had attended Eton College in 1899–1902, and left 'hating it'. He was commissioned as a 2nd lieutenant in September 1905, a lieutenant in October 1909, and a captain in May 1914.[4] A member of the elite Rifle Brigade, he was one of its 546 officers who were killed during the Great War.[5] He took his chances. But the war produced hazards of a magnitude that could not be foreseen. While it was a catastrophe for him, and a tragedy for his family and friends, it also had ramifications for the class of which the Leslies were members – the upper tiers of Protestant society in Ireland, the gentry and aristocracy, the erstwhile Ascendancy, now on an observable path towards decline and eclipse – politically, culturally, economically.

Monk Gibbon, self-styled 'inglorious soldier', wondered if this war, ultimately, had any purpose or objective other than prestige and subservience. Gibbon surmised that a war fought for such abstractions would be the most bloody and ruthless of all.[6] And bloody and ruthless it was; yet in a perverse way, it had some coincident meaning for Leslie's people; for, in the Ireland of 1914,

1 Norman Leslie to Leonie Leslie, n.d., but postmarked late July 1914 (NLI, Leslie Papers, MS 49, 495/2/66). Norman's military records can be accessed in TNA, WO 339/6313. I am indebted to Mr Felix Larkin, sometime Academic Director of the Parnell Summer School, where a version of this paper was originally presented in August 2014. 2 There is considerable confusion about his date of death, variously given as 15, 18, 19 Oct. (TNA, WO 339/6313.) For the battle at Armentières, see J.E. Edmonds, *Military operations France and Belgium 1914. History of the Great War based on official documents by direction of the historical section of the Committee of Imperial Defence. 1 Mons, the retreat to the Seine, the Marne and the Aisne August–October 1914* (London, 1926), pp 94–123, 231. 3 Fragment of typescript 'Letter from Lady Falmouth "My Boy Tommy [Boscawen] wrote the following on Nov 2nd"' (NLI, MS 49,495/2/132). 4 TNA, WO 339/6313. 5 Service sheet for a memorial service for the King's Royal Rifle Corps and the Rifle Brigade, 22 July 1919 (NLI, MS 49,495/2/65). 6 Monk Gibbon, *Inglorious soldier* (London, 1968), p. 256.

they had little left but the increasingly empty prestige of lineage and the remnants of a false subservience on which to rest. In that wholly negative sense, the war provided purpose for Norman Leslie and his ilk. Yet the war was a two-edged sword. At once it restored their *raison d'être*, while at the same time wreaking further destruction on these remnants of the Anglo-Irish gentry.

Of their families, one in four or five suffered fatal casualties.[7] They fought alongside many Irishmen from other traditions, religions and classes of course; and while every death diminished a family, the generality of deaths was not as great as among other groups, at about one in thirty families.[8] The Anglo-Irish contributed proportionately far more than most. A journey through *Burke's landed gentry of Ireland* and *Burke's peerage, baronetage & knightage* brings forth the sheer greatness of the Great War for the Anglo-Irish. From Abercorn to Wolseley, three-quarters of the families to whom Ireland was still significant had close military connections with the conflict.[9] This marked the class as fundamentally different from what Joe Lee has suggested was the 'relatively weak sense of identity with the war effort' that existed among the Irish generally, where only a little more than one-tenth of the men that could have served, did.[10] That this was a caste-led inclination and tradition is clearly demonstrated if one looks at the proportion of Protestants of all classes who joined up; in Leslie's county of Monaghan, the Protestant townspeople and farmers showed a reluctance to join the colours, thus in stark contrast to the gentry's preparedness to join in the war.[11]

Were the Anglo-Irish thus inordinately decapitated? Mark Bence-Jones thought so, apocryphally characterizing 1914 as 'not just the beginning of a war, but the end of a nation'.[12] Only a couple of months after its outbreak, Leslie's father was found writing to his wife with a catalogue of the casualties suffered among people they knew: 'Cecil Leslie's son wounded in the eye … Lady Erne is perfectly satisfied that Harry Crichton is alive. I hope he is.' As it turned out, Harry, heir to the earldom of Erne, did not come home; he was killed a fortnight after Norman Leslie, on 31 October 1914.[13]

---

7 See Nicholas Perry, 'The Irish landed class and the British Army, 1850–1950', *War in History*, 18:3 (2011), 328; David Fitzpatrick, 'The logic of collective sacrifice: Ireland and the British Army, 1914–1918', *Historical Journal*, 38 (1995), 1018.   8 Using the number of households from the 1911 census, and total fatalities at about 30,000; see John Horne, 'Our war, our history' in John Horne (ed.), *Our war: Ireland and the Great War* (Dublin, 2008), p. 6.   9 This corroborates the conclusions of Terence Dooley, *The decline of the big house in Ireland* (Dublin, 2001), p. 122; also Patrick Buckland, *Irish Unionism I: the Anglo Irish and the new Ireland, 1885–1922* (Dublin, 1972), p. 30; and Perry, 'The Irish landed class', 328.   10 J.J. Lee, *Ireland, 1912–1985: politics and society* (Cambridge, 1989), p. 23; David Fitzpatrick, 'Home front and everyday life' in Horne (ed.), *Our war*, p. 134.   11 Terence Dooley, *The decline of unionist politics in Monaghan, 1911–23* (Maynooth, 1988), pp 8–9.   12 Mark Bence-Jones, 'The changing picture of the Irish landed gentry' in *Burke's landed gentry of Ireland* (London, 1958), p. xxviii; Lennox Robinson, *Bryan Cooper* (London, 1931), both quoted in Dooley, *Decline of the big house*, pp 124–5.   13 Jack Leslie to Leonie, n.d., but probably

Yet the headship of most families remained undisturbed by receipt of the dreaded orange telegram. Only six or seven heads of families in *Burke' peerage*, or one-fiftieth of the total, lost their lives. While twenty-four families, or nearly eight per cent, lost eldest sons, this did not unduly disrupt the succession – all but three had either a son of their own, or brothers to succeed. It is arguable, indeed, that death duties wreaked more havoc on gentry families than death itself.[14] But the numbers do not express the logarithmic power of death within the small, interrelated, interbred community, which meant that a loss for one family was a loss for many – simply put, everyone knew everyone else, so that the scale was amplified and magnified through an intimate consanguine connectivity. Death was an intensely communal experience. It came to the Leslies, baronets, of Glaslough, Co. Monaghan, early on in the war.

Castle Leslie, in Co. Monaghan – known as 'Glaslough House' in the early twentieth century – was the home of Sir John Leslie, the 1st baronet, and his wife, Constance; his son Colonel John [Jack] Leslie, his wife Leonie; and his sons Norman, John ('Shane'), Seymour and Lionel.[15] The Leslies moved in influential circles, and were noted for a somewhat contrarian streak.[16] Leonie was an American Jerome, and was the sister of Jennie Churchill, wife of Lord Randolph Churchill. The Leslie siblings and Winston Churchill were thus first cousins.

'We live our little lives and die', Norman Leslie had written to a friend,[17] but he lived no little life in his twenty-seven years. Despite an indifferent induction into the military – he failed to get into the Royal Military Academy, Woolwich, and came 57th (out of 67) in the examinations for his cohort at the less prestigious Royal Military College, Sandhurst[18] – by the time of the outbreak of the war in August 1914, he had served in outposts of the empire, in Malta, Egypt and India. Malta was sunshine and polo; Egypt turned out somewhat differently. In August 1908 Sir John Maxwell (later military governor of Ireland during the 1916 Rising) wrote to Leonie to enquire whether Norman would like to go there as his ADC.[19] He duly went, and got into a right mess.

Rather fond of the ladies, Leslie was encouraged by his grandfather who, as early as 1903, wrote to him in Germany, where Leslie was supposed to be learning the language – 'No better way to improve in a foreign tongue than to

around the second week of Oct. 1914 (NLI, MS 49,495/2/41). **14** See Andy Grainger, 'Killed in war exemption' in *Christie's Bulletin for Professional Advisers*, 18:1 (Summer 2014), 12–13. **15** Sir John (1857–1944); (Sir) John (Shane) (1885–1971); Norman (1886–1914); Seymour (1889–1979); Lionel (1900–87). **16** Otto Rauchbauer, *Shane Leslie: sublime failure* (Dublin, 2009), pp 4–6, 16, 30. 'Winston's aunt' got Norman's effects quickly after his death, see War Office letter, 12 Nov. 1914 (TNA, WO 339/6313). **17** Quoted at his memorial service in Glaslough by the Church of Ireland Primate, Most Revd J.B. Crozier (NLI, MS 49,495/2/65); the address was given in full in the *Northern Standard*, 7 Nov. 1914. **18** TNA, WO 339/6313; NLI, MS 49, 495/2/68. **19** Sir John Maxwell to Leonie Leslie, 5 Aug. 1908 (NLI, MS 49,495/2/64); Col. E. Graham to Leslie, 20 Aug. 1908 (NLI, MS 49, 495/2/65); Norman Leslie to the duke of Connaught, n.d. (NLI, MS 49,495/2/64).

6.1 Norman and Leonie Leslie, September 1914, image courtesy of Castle Leslie Archives.

practice with a young lady'.[20] He made a habit of practising with quite a number
of young ladies. He wrote from New York to his mother early in the century,
about an American society family – 'Ye Gods, what a pair of sisters, nothing in
all England to meet the young one'.[21] In 1908 he had been embroiled with a
Frenchwoman, who addressed him as 'Mon Bebi cheri', and whose letters were
annotated by Leonie as from 'the French tart' after Norman's death.[22]

In Egypt, it was no 'French tart', but rather the Turkish Princess Shevikar,
the wife of Yousury Pasha, a Turkish diplomat (and subsequently Eygptian
Minister to the US in 1924) that caught Norman Leslie's roving eye.[23] An
indiscreet letter of his was intercepted.

> Crash came April 13th [1910] … They sent for me – desperate agitation on
> Y's part who paced up and down the room like tiger … saw him alone in
> my room – he threatened to shoot me where I was – offered him my
> revolver – on 2nd thoughts he said he wouldn't murder me, but would
> wring my neck in the street unless I was man enough to see it through.
> Awful thought that he meant me to marry the lady … This passed, when
> in another fit of passion he said he'd send me his seconds tomorrow – felt
> inclined to say what I would do with them, but refrained fearing he would
> break furniture over my head …. Gen[eral Sir John Maxwell] raged for
> some minutes, told me I'd have to depart 8 am next morning.[24]

If this had elements of high farce – or at least Edwardian melodrama – it could
also have had serious consequences for Leslie. Yousury subsequently challenged
him to a duel. This placed Norman in a quandary. To accept would have risked
the loss of his commission; not to, would have impugned his sense of honour and
meant losing respect among the Egyptians. The duke of Connaught, Leonie's
devoted admirer and Norman's patron, intervened.[25] A 'committee of honour'
consisting of R.B. Haldane, General Sir Ian Hamilton, Lord Cromer, Lord
Charles Beresford and Sir Ernest Cassel (Beresford and Cassel were Leslie
family friends) advised that the duel could take place so long as no report
appeared in the newspapers. Leslie was an international swordsman, but he took
the precaution of undergoing an intensive six weeks' tuition with a French
fencing-master.[26] The duel took place in Paris at Cassel's house on 15 May 1910.

20 'Daddypa' (Sir John Leslie) to Norman, 10 Aug. 1903 (NLI, MS 49,495/2/64). Norman
Leslie had had a German governess, Clara Woelbe (NLI, MS 49,495/2/38).   **21** Norman
Leslie to Leonie?, 17 Nov. n.d. (NLI, MS 49,495/2/66).   **22** A bundle of letters, Sept.–Dec.
1908 (NLI, MS 49,495/2/64).   **23** Elizabeth Kehoe, *Fortune's daughters: the extravagant lives
of the Jerome sisters: Jennie Churchill, Clara Frewen and Leonie Leslie* (London, 2004), p. 279.
24 Leslie, fragment of autobiography [1897–1913] (NLI, MS 49,495/2/133).   **25** For
Leonie's curious relationship with the duke of Connaught, see PRONI, 'Introduction, Leslie
papers' (Belfast, 2007), p. 26; also Kehoe, *Fortune's daughters*, pp 240–2.   **26** Kehoe, *Fortune's
daughters*, p. 280, states that his father trained him.

Leslie drew first blood, but Yousury insisted on continuing. This went on for a further forty minutes, eventually ending when Leslie received a hand wound.[27]

Maxwell's rage took some time to subside; he wrote an exasperated letter to Leonie, blaming her son for the entire *contretemps* and ordering that 'he will not attempt to write or communicate with the lady, he has done quite enough mischief'.[28] Nevertheless, the 'mischief' appears to have done no harm to Leslie's standing among his peers (he is reputedly the last British officer to have fought a duel) – 'How magnificent to have fought a long duel with a terrible Turk and to have come through the ordeal with only a scratch', wrote one admiring friend.[29]

This episode did not cramp Leslie's romantic style: in September of that year a press photograph showed him in the company of Lady Marjorie Manners, society beauty and 'Soul',[30] daughter of the duke of Rutland and later wife of the marquess of Anglesey.[31] He got into further trouble two years later. Shipped off to India, he arrived in Madras at the end of January 1912 as an ADC to the Governor, Sir Thomas Gibson-Carmichael. Another affair ensued, with a married British lady, apparently resulting in a pregnancy. In September 1912 Carmichael wrote to Leslie, advising 'If I were you, I'd keep out of Calcutta or places where people talk for a bit … I daresay you were a bit silly … it wouldn't do to ask you to come on my staff again for a time'.[32]

Apart from women, Leslie's other passions appear to have been horses – buying and selling polo ponies – and card gambling. This caused financial difficulties. Leonie, with whom he had 'an almost classically Freudian relationship',[33] bailed him out in Malta, and then had to do the same in Egypt;[34] and in January 1912 Leslie wrote to his mother to tell her that he was going to India 'to recuperate my shattered finances'. He was sufficiently self-aware to recognize that 'some people are idiots gambling and I am one of them'.[35] He was not very good at managing his affairs, financial or otherwise: he died without having made a will, which, for a career army officer going into a terrible war, was inexcusable.[36]

27 See report in *Morning Bulletin* [Rockhampton, Australia], 1 Aug. 1938, http://trove.nla. gov.au/ndp/del/article/55984895 (accessed 2 May 2014); Kehoe, *Fortune's daughters*, p. 280; also papers and letters relating to the duel in the Leslie Papers (NLI, MS 49,495/2/64). **28** Sir John Maxwell to Leonie Leslie, 22 Apr. 1910 (NLI, MS 49,495/2/66). **29** Paul Kennedy to Norman Leslie, 25 May 1910 (NLI, MS 49, 495/2/64). **30** The 'Souls' were a group of the glamorous, beautiful, rich and effortlessly charming British *beau monde* of the turn of the century. See Jane Abdy and Charlotte Gere, *The Souls* (London, 1984). **31** *Tatler*, 21 Sept. 1910. **32** Lord Carmichael to Leslie, 14 Sept. 1912 (NLI, MS 49,495/2/64). **33** Kehoe, *Fortune's daughters*, p. 240. Norman Leslie's relationship with his mother was intense (NLI, MS 49,495/2/65). **34** Kehoe, *Fortune's daughters*, p. 241; Sir John Maxwell to Leslie, 15 Oct.? (probably 1908 or 1909) (NLI, MS 49,495/2/64, 66). **35** Norman Leslie to Leonie, 29 Jan. 1912 (NLI, MS 49,495/2/65); also fragment of autobiography [Oct. 1905] (NLI, MS 49,495/2/133) concerning polo pony sales, racing and *chemin de fer*. **36** An undated letter from Norman Leslie to Leonie (late July 1914) assured her that all his affairs were in order; they weren't (NLI, MS 49,495/2/66).

Leslie's intestacy caused death duty problems, stemming from the fact that, following the resettlement of the Monaghan and Donegal estates in 1908 after his elder brother Shane's conversion to Roman Catholicism (and the then suggestion that he might become a priest), Norman Leslie, who was the younger brother, was destined to succeed.[37]

Leslie was a raffish rogue in many respects, a stereotypal elite British Army officer of high birth and higher connections. Yet, beneath the tiger shoots and tourneys, the flighty women and the flying machines,[38] there was another side to him. He was something of a Renaissance man, an accomplished musician, interested in opera, Roman mythology, classical history, Greek numismatics and literature. And it was that side which transformed him into the *beau ideal* of the almost perfect chivalrous knight: he carried into battle a sword given him by the duke of Connaught, a useless weapon in the new arsenal of tanks, gas and machine-guns, but an emblem of what he stood for.[39] These 'traditional establishment values'[40] were encapsulated in a letter Leslie wrote to Mrs Zoe Farquharson at the outbreak of war: 'let us forget individuals and let us act as one great British unit, mixed and fearless. Some will live and many will die, but count the loss not. It is better far to go out with honour than survive with shame.'[41]

His last letter to his mother is insouciant, almost unfeeling, reciting the numbers game of the professional soldier. He wrote that 'I can't see that our losses have been heavy at all.' And continued: 'What are 2000 killed and 8000 wounded out of a force of 80 or 90,000 British who repelled 200 or 300 thousand Germans. It's wonderfully small ... only 2½% killed. One would imagine it would be much more like 10%.'[42]

It is unlikely that Leslie would have agreed with his brother's excoriation of war as 'simply waste, waste of limb and life, waste of time and talent, waste of heroism and prudence, waste of all things useful and beautiful. And the same iron rain – it raineth upon the fit and the unfit alike.'[43] For Norman, the 'iron rain' was just one more way of killing Germans.[44] But Leslie was more reflective

37 See various letters concerning Norman Leslie's death duties, 1929–34 (TNA, WO 339/6313); also NLI, MS 49, 495/2/68; also income tax returns and insurance policies of the Sir John Leslie Estates Co. (NLI, MS 49,495/1/94A–94C); Kehoe, *Fortune's daughters*, pp 294–5.   **38** Press cuttings of a boxing tournament organized by Leslie in April 1910, and of a tiger shoot in India (NLI, MS 49,495/2/65). Norman had thought of becoming a pilot; see Sir John Maxwell to Leslie, 15 Oct. 1908(?) (NLI, MS 45,495/2 64).   **39** http://www.castleleslie.com/castle-hotel-normans-room.html# (accessed 1 May 2014); NLI, MS 49,495/2/66. The sword was lost in France in 1914, but returned to Leslie's father in 1934. There is considerable correspondence in Leslie's War Office papers concerning the loss of the sword (TNA, WO 339/6313).   **40** Rauchbauer, *Sublime failure*, p. 183.   **41** Shane Leslie, *Long shadows* (London, 1966), p. 163 (note); also Leonie to ? in the US, 13 June 1917, concerning the letter, which was reproduced in the *Daily Mail* in Nov. 1915 (NLI, MS 49,495/2/39).   **42** Norman Leslie to Leonie, n.d. (Oct. 1914) with annotation 'his last to his mother?' (NLI, MS 49,495/2/42).   **43** Shane Leslie to John Leslie, 17 Dec. 1914 (NLI, MS 49,495/2/42).   **44** See Norman Leslie to Leonie, 7 Sep. 1914 (NLI, MS 49,495/2/42).

than might appear. Assuming victory, he thought forward to the peace, focusing on the effect on Europe, how to neuter Germany, and on the empire, especially the African colonies.[45] In these imperial interests he was following in well-trodden steps. His father had served in his own faraway wars in Egypt and South Africa, and although nearly sixty in 1914, played his part in training men in Donegal for the slaughter in France.[46]

To this class, and to that generation, military service in time of war was axiomatic, requiring an almost unthinking sense of duty and unity. As the brothers Ross-Lewin, offshoots of the Clare gentry, wrote in bad, but sincere, verse in 1917, 'No longer divisions of class or of creed / By danger united in Britain's sore need.'[47] Norman Leslie fought in Britain's need; and he could write more lyrically than the Ross-Lewins. Although not in the literary class of his brother Shane, a piece published in the *Westminster Gazette* eleven days after his death, 'A typical night in the British trenches', was an atmospheric re-construction of the front:[48]

> The light creeps up, and all the lovely wooded slopes stretching down to the river and canal in our rear begin to show themselves … high up an English aeroplane sails over us, the red lights glinting on some metal, a moment's glow, then silver – a flash – and it resumes its normal colouring, humming strongly over us – it is impossible to describe its beauty and grace, passing through the different layers of light …

And then contrapuntal to the description of a peaceful bucolic scene: 'the 4-inch and 8-inch howitzers are a very different thing. When their earth-shaking shells begin to drop, everybody hides. There is something peculiarly terrifying about their noise and the disturbance they cause to earth and air.'[49]

Leslie harboured hopes that he could have chronicled the war for others – his last letter to his father was in the cigarette case given to him by his mother in 1909: 'There's so much to write and so little time you'll have to wait for most of it at the end of the war in my diary', which, he felt, 'should be good'.[50] The diary – found on the battlefield – indeed showed promise in its arresting vignettes and spare, economical descriptions, often varying between the ghastly and the ridiculous:

> 18 September Biddulph CO shot in the foot by one of our own men. Rickman dead, shrapnel in the stomach – Foljambe dead, hit in a worse place – many wounded – Salmon run over by a cart …

45 Norman Leslie to Leonie, 3 Oct. 1914 (NLI, MS 49,495/2/65).   46 Letters from Sir John Leslie to Leonie (NLI, MS 49,495/2/41).   47 The brothers Ross-Lewin, *In Britain's need* (Dublin and London, 1917), p. 13.   48 *Westminster Gazette*, 29 Oct. 1914; also (NLI, MS 49,495/2/65).   49 A similar description is in Leslie to Edward Hudson, 28 Sept. 1914 (NLI, MS 49,495/2/65).   50 Unposted letter from Norman Leslie to John Leslie, n.d. (Oct. 1914)

22 September B Co.'y lost 7 men, 5 of whom were in my part of the
trench. I hauled them out and did what I could to tie them up – broken leg,
thigh, lung wound, arm and body shattered, foot shot off, etc. By 9 a.m.
I was covered with blood and slightly tired ...
2 October [resting behind the lines] had honey for breakfast and the most
gorgeous lunch of apple tart and goose cooked by our soldier servants –
after lunch we 5 officers solemnly slept for the rest of the evening ... we
only think and talk of food ...[51]

The entries were a far cry from the excitement that he had exhibited earlier – as
he wrote sarcastically to his mother, 'what fun it will be in November lying with
our Mackintosh in a frozen turnip field!'[52] By mid-October, fun had been
replaced by a biting reality:

I was never colder in my life – had been up to my waist in the stream for
4 hours spent a miserable rainy night till dawn (17th Oct) I was woke at
4.00 a.m. and got orders. The battalion marched away ... in the direction
of Armentières ... all the inhabitants here are in a wild state of excitement,
welcomed us with open arms and showered all with hot coffee and food.

That was his last diary entry. The next day, at Armentières, he was shot dead.[53]
Leslie had had an entirely pragmatic view of what the war would entail, and the
risks posed. Leonie had visited him at Cork before his eventual embarkation for
France from Southampton on 7 September 1914;[54] in his barracks he wrote a
wistful testamentary letter ('To be opened in the event of my death by my
Mother') with an assurance of assets greater than liabilities, and little legacies for
his ladies.[55]
    If Leslie's life was conventionally iconic, so, too, was his death. After solemn
memorial services in London and Monaghan and the pious utterances of the
clergy[56] (the Church of Ireland Primate at Glaslough spoke of a 'pure-souled,
clean-living man with high ideals of life and duty'), ghostliness took over – it was
said that Leslie was seen as an apparition at Glaslough a week before he was
killed.[57] The spirits were everywhere, and yet nowhere. Some two months after
his death, his elder brother Shane, in France, came upon his hastily buried body.
He wrote to their mother that 'He lies about a mile behind the trenches occupied

(NLI, MS 49,495/2/132); Leslie to Leonie, 3 Oct. 1914 (NLI, MS 49,495/2/65).
51 Norman Leslie diary, various dates (NLI, MS 49,495/2/132).   **52** Norman Leslie to
Leonie, 28 Sept. 1914 (NLI, MS 49,495/2/65).   **53** *Northern Whig*, 24 Oct. 1914.
54 Norman Leslie diary, p. 1 (NLI, MS 49,495/2/132).   **55** (NLI, MS 49,495/2/65).
56 *Morning Post, The Times, Daily Telegraph*, 27 Oct. 1914; see also death notices and reports
of memorial services in various papers (NLI, MS 49,495/2/66).   **57** http://www.castleleslie.
com/castle-hotel-normans-room.html# (accessed 1 May 2014).

by his regiment and within sound of the guns of both armies whose shells pass daily above his head ... the sky was ripped with the flashes of the guns, while a gigantic German searchlight threw the surrounding countryside into sepulchral relief'. Norman's grave, he said, 'seemed to rock with the thunder of the gunfire'. When men from the Rifle Brigade opened it, Leslie's clothes were unsoiled and clean; his hands were white and pink at the edges, and rested on the wound that killed him. To fit him into a new pine coffin they had to remove his footwear. Shane did not cry until he saw 'that lonely pair of boots' sitting on the wretched earth. His brother seemed to have borne 'no trace of suffering or contortion ... [and] as one who had reached his appointed end with credit and dignity.' 'Poor dear Norman – he is well away – for his spirit was not there and I had no feeling of his presence.'[58]

It seemed that Leslie had purposes in mind other than just being a part of the dying of the Irish gentry's light. He, like his brother, saw a future for himself in politics – in April 1914 he had talked of quitting the army when he was thirty-five[59] – but it was to English politics he looked, not to the brand of Irish nationalism that had Shane standing for the Irish Parliamentary Party in the Londonderry City seat in the two general elections of 1910.[60] This may have been bound up in his perception of being more a Jerome than a Leslie – 'my chief asset [is] to be able to say that I am Leonie Jerome's *son*', he had written in 1912[61] – but perhaps his Anglo-Irish gentry ancestry ('coming of a race of gentlemen') persisted in emerging, like damp in a wall, in his unashamed preference for aristocratic government. As between Conservatives and Liberals, there was little to choose, a question of 'greater patriotism with lesser brains, versus moderate patriotism with greater brains'.[62] There spoke a true 'Soul'.

In a commentary on his death, *The Lady* magazine (appropriately enough) described Leslie as having 'Irish humour and a natural gaiety combined with American opportunism, independence and sagacity'; a later historian wrote of his 'enormous capacity for happiness'.[63] And yet, there is one final puzzle about Norman Leslie. It may have been prompted by the trauma of the recent Yousury Pasha affair, but on 26 June 1910 he wrote an extraordinary self-assessment in a fragment of private autobiography. A visit to the pilgimage site of St Patrick's Purgatory, Lough Derg, Donegal (owned by the Leslies) provoked a searing critique of his own life. He described 'the smell of the heather and all the Creators gifts which he had given me to enjoy and which I slumbering in gloom had forgotten'.

58 Shane Leslie to Leonie, 22 Dec. 1914 (NLI, MS 49,495/2/42).   **59** Norman Leslie to Leonie, 14 Apr. 1914 (NLI, MS 49,495/2/65).   **60** Brian Walker (ed.), *Parliamentary election results in Ireland, 1801–1922* (Dublin, 1978), p. 296; Rauchbauer, *Sublime failure*, pp 34–5. **61** Norman Leslie to Leonie, n.d. (1 June 1912) (NLI, MS 49,495/2/65).   **62** Norman Leslie to Leonie, 20 July 1911 (NLI, MS 49,495/2/65).   **63** *The Lady*, 5 Nov. 1914; Kehoe, *Fortune's daughters*, p. 240.

They met me in little groups along the road – they, the country folk and
men of my race, men of the same spirit and tongue as myself, and whom I,
even I, had despised for their narrow lives and desires. The sight of their
honest rugged faces … went through me with a thrill, a thrill of delight
and of peace, a thrill of sorrow at my own state compared to them … did
the glitter of the salons, the clink of the restaurant glasses, the fair faces,
the dazzling dresses, did they shine before me and gleam as brightly as
before? No, they felt unutterably sham and faded before these people.[64]

'God grant you may come out of it all right', wrote Leonie to her son on
8 October 1914.[65] It was not to be. Ten days later he was dead. At the end,
though, those left, like Leonie, had to cling to some promise of light. Shane
Leslie found what he called 'solace and oblivion in the rhythm of words'.[66] Jack
Leslie, away in Donegal, wrote to Leonie on Armistice Day: 'I wish I was with
you to embrace you … I feel excited almost to insomnia. The news is the most
wonderful since the world began.'[67] In great measure, though, the Leslies' world
had ended with the loss of Norman. Shane's advice to his mother in November
1914 had been 'Stay at Glaslough where Norman's memory is vivid in the minds
of all whom you meet … stay there where the whole atmosphere yearns for him
and where his name will outlive ours'.[68] But once the guns had fallen silent and
stillness had crept over the cemeteries, those from home could not stay away. At
the memorial service in London four years previously, his mother had 'looked
overwhelmed with grief' – 'she carried a beautiful bunch of violets, and stopping
before the lectern, she tenderly laid down her floral tribute'.[69] A few days after
the Armistice, Jack Leslie suggested more flowers, in another world and for
another time: 'I should like to go to Armentières in the Spring, not in cold dreary
winter, and lay spring flowers on our boy's grave, both of us together. His spirit
knows what is going on, and that his life was not lost in vain.'[70]

64 Fragment of autobiography (NLI, MS 49,495/2/133); see Shane Leslie, *Saint Patrick's
purgatory: a record from history in literature* (London, 1932).   65 Leonie to Norman Leslie, 8
Oct. 1914 (NLI, MS 49,495/2/65).   66 Shane Leslie to Leonie, 3 Nov. 1914, quoted in
Rauchbauer, *Sublime failure*, p. 247.   67 Sir John Leslie to 'Puss Cat' (Leonie), 11 Nov. 1918
(NLI, MS 49,495/2/41).   68 Shane Leslie to Leonie, 3 Nov. 1914, quoted in Rauchbauer,
Sublime failure, p. 247.   69 *The Lady*, 5 Nov. 1914; *Northern Standard*, 7 Nov. 1914.   70 Sir
John Leslie to Leonie, n.d. (*c*.11 Nov. 1918) (NLI, MS 49,495/2/41).

Augusta Bellingham and the Mount Stuart Hospital: temporary therapeutic transformations

RONAN FOLEY

While much has been written about the sheer level of death and injury that took place during the Great War with the image of the mutilated 'soldier-body' a common trope, less has been said about the geographies and histories of care for those wounded combatants away from the front.[1] In addition, while many of the inhabitants of the country houses lost their lives in the war, less is known of the specific roles of the houses and their occupants, in caring for those same wounded bodies. Many country houses became literally parts of the war network, through their transformation into auxiliary hospitals or convalescent homes, of which Highclere House (fictionalized as Downton Abbey) was a classic example.[2] Country house owners also gave service through the running of such medical centres and equally became active elements within a wider wartime therapeutic assemblage. The coalescence of histories of health, medicine and welfare in the context of the Great War is particularly fertile ground for describing and understanding the complex networked nature of wartime care. Within current geographical writing, the idea of a relational mapping of specific components of the war connected across time and space has become a valuable methodology.[3] Finally, the term therapeutic landscapes, and the ways that geography was enrolled in the creation of places and spaces of healing and recovery, is one which has some purchase in wartime writing, for example in the role of Craiglockhart Hospital in the treatment of wounded officers.[4] In developing the concept of the therapeutic landscape in history, this essay describes one such Auxiliary Hospital, Mount Stuart, on the Isle of Bute (fig. 7.1), and one such owner, Augusta Bellingham, marchioness of Bute, to show how the country house had a specific role as a node in the relational networks of wartime care; within a therapeutic landscape such places became sites of transformation, in both terms of self and terms of place, during and after the war.

1 Mark Harrison, *The medical war: British military medicine in the First World War* (Oxford, 2010); Emily Mayhew, *Wounded: the long journey home from the Great War* (London, 2014); Leo Van Bergen, *Before my helpless sight* (Farnham, 2009). 2 J.M. Robinson, *Requisitioned: the British country house in the Second World War* (London, 2014); Countess of Carnarvon, *Lady Alminia and the real Downton Abbey: the lost legacy of Highclere Abbey* (London, 2011). 3 Doreen Massey, *For space* (London, 2005); Jon Murdoch, *Post-structuralist geography* (London, 2006). 4 W.M. Gesler, 'Therapeutic landscapes: medical issues in light of the new cultural geography', *Social Science and Medicine*, 34 (2002), 735–46; Ronan Foley, 'The Roman-Irish Bath: medical/health history as therapeutic assemblage', *Social Science and*

7.1 Mount Stuart today (source: author).

Augusta Bellingham was born in 1880 and brought up in the town named after her family, Castlebellingham, in Co. Louth. She was introduced to the 4th marquis of Bute and they married at Castlebellingham on 6 July 1905; the wedding, unusually for the time, was captured on film.[5] Augusta then moved as the new marchioness of Bute to the family seat at Mount Stuart on the island of Bute, situated in the Clyde estuary in the west of Scotland. Like many patriotic subjects, on the outbreak of war the Butes offered their home as a temporary hospital space to treat wounded officers. Set up in August 1914, it initially took soldiers, but the intent was always for the house to become a naval hospital and it assumed this role from January 1915 until the end of the war.[6] During the war, 2,120 soldiers and sailors were treated at the hospital and it was generally full, with a mean daily patient count of 48.6 in 1915 that increased to 67.4 in 1916 and 84.1 in 1917 as war at sea intensified. Augusta was centrally involved in all aspects of the running of the hospital, as were many of the house's domestic staff, who were retrained for wartime medical service (fig. 7.2).[7] At the end of the war

Medicine, 106 (2014), 10–19; Pat Barker, *Regeneration* (London, 1996).   5 Referred to as the world's first 'wedding video', the film showed the wedding party at home, at the church and boating in nearby Annagassan; http://ssa.nls.uk/film/6774.   6 Augusta, marchioness of Bute, 'Description of Mount Stuart, Bute, as a hospital with full report of the life and work there during the Great War, 1914–19' (Scottish National Library, MS H8.96.722).   7 SNL, MS H8.96.722.

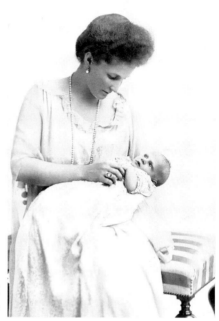

7.2 Augusta, marchioness of Bute (Imperial War Museum: WWC D8–3–320).

she and some senior medics and nurses were thanked by the state for their service, and the episode still forms an important part of the house's historic legacy.[8] In this history, the marchioness of Bute would not have been unusual, and in many ways her story illustrates both typical and unique features of the contributions the country house made to the war effort and the toll it took. Yet Mount Stuart was also relatively unique in its naval function, its island-location and the specific role that geography played in its therapeutic function through the war years.

It is not the intent here to provide a detailed account of the wider histories of wartime care; more eminent writers have covered this fully.[9] Debates around frontline medical services and the slowly shifting capacities of the military machine to improve treatment of physical and mental wounds are well established.[10] Geography appears in such discussions, in relation to the different classes of treatment spaces on or near the front, the locations of mobile 'behind-frontline' services and the different transport networks required to move wounded soldiers across that system.[11] In the early years of the war and during

8 SNL, MS H8.96.722. 9 Harrison, *The medical war*; Mayhew, *Wounded*; Roger Cooter, Mark Harrison and Steve Sturdy (eds), *War, medicine, and modernity* (Stroud, 1998). 10 Peter Barham, *Forgotten lunatics of the Great War* (New Haven, 2004); Edgar Jones and Simon Wessely, *Shell shock to PTSD: military psychiatry from 1900 to the Gulf War* (Hove, 2005). 11 Ronan Foley, 'From front to home and back again: relational geographies of

particular prolonged battles, the need for networks of auxiliary support to augment the overstretched existing military medical network at a distance from the front, including 'at home', have been less fully discussed.[12] The intent here is to focus on the specific sub-networks of treatment and care associated with Mount Stuart in order to provide a broad context as to where the country house fitted in. Conceptually, it is possible to place it in its position within what might be referred to as a topology or network of care. In addition, the specific interior and exterior spaces of the house functioned as examples of therapeutic landscapes, where recovery and restoration in soothing locations contrasted sharply with the traumatizing surrounds of front-line combat.[13]

Geographers increasingly discuss the idea of relational space. While most traditional understandings of space are focused on locations and descriptions of a topography or landscape, relational geography focuses on how space is connected up and how different actors move around and along networks.[14] In this way, rather like the London Underground map, the topologies of place matter more than precise locations, and can be better understood as a series of nodal points connected along networks. The locational networks of wartime medicine moved from node to node, for example from dressing-station to casualty clearing stations (CCS), to base hospital, and along connective networks (road, rail, canal, ship) that moved wounded bodies up and down that line.[15] Away from the front, key nodes included Etaples, the central location on the French coast for the arrival and onward dispersion of wounded troops, and Netley near Southampton, the main home-based receiving and distribution point from where many soldiers were moved on.[16] Their final destinations, back in the British Isles, were existing hospitals and other paramedical institutions, but also a whole series of previously non-medical spaces that had assumed new functions as working auxiliary hospitals and convalescent homes.[17] Within the topology of wartime care, the country house was enrolled as a common node, somewhere towards the end of that network. We think of hospitals as fixed places, but wartime introduced a type of spatial contingency that produced a constantly mobile network. CCS, for example, moved several times through the

medical treatment in World War I' in Ian Miller and David Durnin (eds), *Medicine, health and Irish experiences of war, 1914–45* (forthcoming, 2016). **12** Harrison, *The medical war*, p. 14; Mayhew, *Wounded*, pp 2–5. **13** Foley, 'From front to home and back again'. **14** Murdoch, *Post-structuralist geography*, pp 19–23. **15** *War record of the St John Ambulance Brigade and the British Red Cross Society in Leinster, Munster and Connaught, 1914–1918* (Dublin, 1919); *Reports by the Joint War Committee and the Joint War Finance Committee of the British Red Cross Society and the Order of St John of Jerusalem in England on voluntary aid rendered to the sick and wounded at home and abroad and to British prisoners of war* (London, 1921). **16** Netley hospital is fully described in Philip Hoare's evocative book, *Spike Island: the memory of a military hospital* (London, 2001). **17** There was a broad typology of auxiliary hospitals, from existing military and naval hospitals to requisitioned hospitals but down to paramedical, public and private buildings as well. Annmarie Adams, 'Borrowed buildings: Canada's temporary hospitals during World War One', *Canadian Bulletin of Medical History*, 16:1 (1999), 25–48.

war as they tracked the front line, while there was a similar mobility in the bodies moving backwards and forwards through the network. Indeed such fluid networks were marked by a peculiar mobility wherein the hospital literally followed the patient.

This mobility applied equally to the country house as a material setting, as it received wounded troops, treated and cared for them, yet often sent recovered patients back to war.[18] Equally, that mobility applied to the inhabitants of the country houses. The men folk were central figures on the nodes and connecting lines of this network, as both military and medical men. Many followed the paths to war and/or medical service and never returned and their contribution is covered elsewhere in this book. As exemplified in this essay, the women of the country house also emerged as important actors on the scene, initially in the absence of the men but quite quickly after, with a function/identity of their own. While many women served on or near the front as trained nurses or Voluntary Aid Detachments (VADs), their 'home' work was less well known but equally substantial.[19] In the case of Mount Stuart, all of these mobile elements were visible and the auxiliary hospital acted as an exemplary representative of such topologies of care, although the specific form and nature of the site had its own unique characteristics.

Archival material and sources on auxiliary hospitals are relatively limited. Many images and documents exist in relation to the wider network, especially at the front and in the other medical nodes across France.[20] In addition, good records exist from some of the more formal domestic hospital spaces.[21] But in the case of the auxiliary hospitals, most were administered and run by a joint committee of the Red Cross and St John's Ambulance organizations. Information on these sites is available from a number of comprehensive publications produced by the joint committee along with archival material on military visits, pension management and other activities recorded at these more informal settings.[22]

Mount Stuart was unusual in a number of ways. Unlike many auxiliary hospitals, it was primarily a naval hospital and worked relatively independently in terms of its own record keeping. Fortunately, a full publication was produced on the house's wartime history, available from both the Mount Stuart archive itself and also via the Scottish National Library.[23] Though no specific authorship is identified, it does seem as if it was written by Augusta Bellingham and contains valuable accounts of the multiple transformations to the place, the people who worked in it, the naval military establishment and the wounded combatants who passed through its rooms and grounds.

18 Mayhew, *Wounded*, pp 225–7.   19 Thekla Bowser, *The story of British VAD work in the Great War* (London, 2003), pp 20–7; Joint War Committees Reports, 1921.   20 'The long long trail: the British Army in the Great War', www.1914-1918.net/wounded.htm (accessed 28 Aug. 2014).   21 Hoare, *Spike Island*, pp 371–3; Barham, *Forgotten lunatics*, pp 371–6.   22 *War record of the St John Ambulance and British Red Cross*, 1919; *Report by the Joint War Committee*, 1921.   23 SNL, MS H8.96.722.

In looking at Mount Stuart's place on the wider wartime therapeutic network, geography played a role in both its choice as a working hospital and in the specific spatial sub-networks by which wounded combatants got there. Its choice as a naval hospital location was in part to do with its location on the more remote western coast, free from submarine attack and bombardment threat on the more risky east coast, and finally its protected location within the Firth of Clyde. More relevant to the idea of a therapeutic network, it was suggested as an ideal site in part because of its position on a linked train-ferry access route, while the 'compensatory' therapeutic qualities of the house and its surrounding grounds were also considered significant.

> The Isle of Bute was particularly well situated for a naval hospital in the North. On the West Coast of Scotland it was to a large extent free from the alarms of war. At the same time it is but a short train journey from the clearing hospital in Edinburgh, and the difficulty of transporting patients to an island was more than compensated for by the ideal surroundings of the hospital once the cases had been installed here.[24]

Almost immediately upon the outbreak of the war, Mount Stuart was offered to the navy as an auxiliary hospital but was initially declined. In the meantime, the new 'Mount Stuart Hospital', as it was called, took in soldiers for convalescent purposes from the 4th Scottish General Hospital (Stobhill) in Glasgow in 1914.[25] It is likely that the evidence of its ability to operate effectively convinced the naval authorities to think again, and the house was granted naval hospital status in 1915. The map of the identified locations in Scotland of joint Red Cross/St John's Ambulance hospitals does not list Mount Stuart, in part due to its direct naval role, but also due to more direct local running of the hospital, with a more limited role for the joint agencies.[26]

In identifying Mount Stuart's specific function within the therapeutic network, and more specifically the mobile processes that connected the front to the house and back again, there were some unique features. While most of the rest of the network followed the route through Etaples and Netley, the 'front' for the navy covered quite a different geographical space (fig. 7.3). Many of the wounded sailors who ended up at Mount Stuart received their wounds in naval service and combat, primarily in the North Sea and associated coastal channels, though with some links to the wider Atlantic sea-front. Although the battle of Jutland was not specifically mentioned, skirmishes in autumn 1917 at the 'Cattegat' were noted as sending a substantial number of long-term casualties to Mount Stuart.[27] The typical routing for sailors coming to Bute involved initial

24 Ibid.   25 Stobhill was one of the major nodes on the therapeutic network in Scotland and even had its own customized railway siding (as many of the bigger hospitals did) to connect it to the main rail network.   26 Joint War Committees Reports, 1921, pp 716–17.   27 Wounded

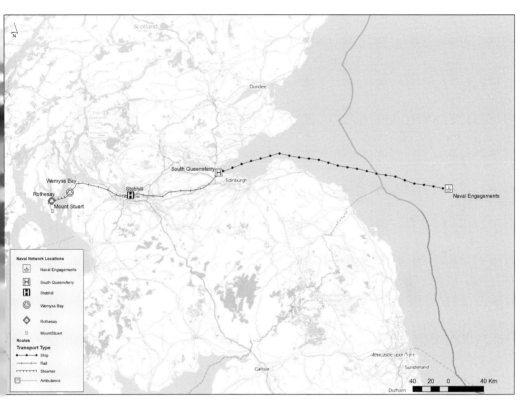

7.3 Location map of wartime networks linked to Mount Stuart
(Open Street Map, Creative Commons).

arrival at South Queensferry (the main receiving node for Scotland), rail transfer to Stobhill and then further along to Wemyss Bay. There a ferry transferred the combatants to Rothesay, from whence local ambulance buses brought them the last few miles to the house.

In line with the interest in relational geographies, Mount Stuart's spatial network involved a wide range of transfer processes and travel modes, and connected the front to the hospital via ships, railways, steamers and ambulance, all operating through a range of different reception, assessment and transfer points. In practical terms, technologies such as the telegram were important in delivering notifications of 'incoming' patients, in order that appropriate preparations could be made. Typically, wounded sailors arrived in batches of fifteen to forty, requiring many vehicles to transport them to Mount Stuart. For example, they were collected at Rothesay by, among others, Abel Seaman Hill, the former private chauffeur at Mount Stuart. Initially this involved a modified

sailors were usually recorded with their ship name as their 'home place' on arrival at Mount Stuart (SNL, MS H8.96.722).

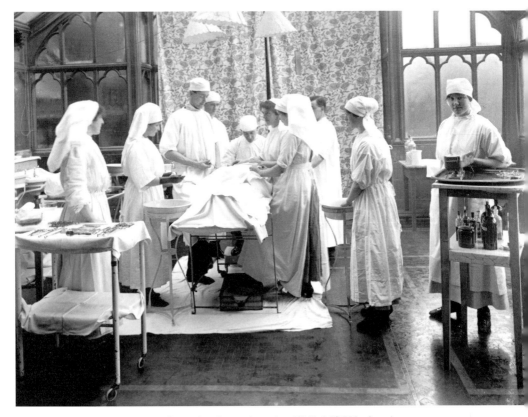

7.4 Operating theatre in action (SNL MS H6.96.722).

version of one of the house's Gobron-Brillé cars, though the navy later provided
a Renault and a second ambulance as well.[28]

As a therapeutic setting, the new Mount Stuart Hospital was, like other
country houses, ideal for its new function, with lots of room, light and space for
treatment, recuperation and recovery.[29] Functionally, the hospital operated under
the rules of the navy and as such was regularly inspected before, during and even
after its operational years. While the medical and rehabilitative work on the
ground was organized with the Red Cross and used VADs for nursing support,
the marchioness was very actively involved in the whole process. The
professionalization and training required for running the house as a hospital
extended in different directions. There was a main medical superintendent and
visiting surgeons who provided the core medical expertise. In addition,
professional nurses served throughout the war in a range of capacities as working
lives and identities developed in tune with that of the auxiliary hospital's needs.

28 Ibid.   29 Foley, 'From front to home and back again'.

7.5 Mount Stuart Royal Naval
Hospital, ward, 1914–19
(Wellcome Library, London).

Untrained staff, primarily VADs, but also the marchioness herself, her sister and
several of the domestic staff received training in-house; there were at least four
trained and additional probationary nurses on call at all times. The medical staff
included a mix of the qualified and unqualified, incorporating the marchioness,
naval and medical personnel as well as members of the house staff. In one image
we see direct evidence of the role of the marchioness as right-hand woman to the
surgeon (fig. 7.4).[30] In total, 834 operations, of 90 different types, were carried
out under anaesthetic at the hospital throughout the war.[31] The most common
were actually routine, such as hernias, haemorrhoids, varicose veins and
tonsillectomies, but there were also fourteen amputations, a number of tumour
removals and many forms of orthopaedic operations of different types.

More specifically, the new function as a working hospital meant many of the
larger reception and drawing-rooms were given over as wards. Much of the
house was still used by the family, so there was a clear demarcation between
medical and domestic spaces, examples of what Marchioness Bute herself
referred to as a 'compartimental' scheme.[32] The dining-room became the

30 SNL, MS H8.96.722.   31 Ibid.   32 Ibid.

medical ward with twenty-two beds, the drawing-room the surgical ward (fig. 7.5), also with twenty-two beds, and the marble hall was partitioned off to become an airy general ward with fifty beds. Small ward rooms for officers (two to four beds in each) were located upstairs, as other 'compartmentalisations' reflected naval traditions. The Purple Library became the x-ray room, while the upstairs conservatory became the operating theatre. Different spaces outside were used as workshops, gardens for growing vegetables and rehabilitation rooms. In addition, the wider grounds with their extensive woods, walkways and coastal views functioned as part of a wider therapeutic landscape.

From a patient perspective, the hospital must have seemed like a safe haven after the months at sea and at battle. There are some detailed records, based on a careful recording at both admission and discharge stage. A summary table (fig. 7.6) shows the broad classification of diagnosis and discharge for the years, 1916–18.[33] Within these broad classes there were multiple sub-categories that identify distinctions between war wounds and injuries/illnesses contracted while on active service. Around twenty cases of neurasthenia (the wartime code for shell-shock) are listed and such cases were typically either cured or moved on elsewhere. There were four listed types of discharge from the hospital, which marked the differing therapeutic outcomes: A 'Discharged Cured to Duty', B 'Discharged to Shore Leave', C 'Discharged for Survey for Invaliding', and D 'Discharged to RN Hospital for further treatment'.[34] Types A and B were generally sent directly or indirectly back into service, and this recirculation back into the networks of war was a common narrative for all branches of the armed services. The other two classes were essentially those who were less likely to go back to war. Throughout the conflict, very few deaths were recorded at Mount Stuart.[35] In truth, many of the worst casualties either perished at sea or were treated at South Queensferry; it was generally the less acute cases that arrived for treatment at Mount Stuart.

As a representative location, Mount Stuart exemplified many of the trans-formations that took place in the country house at war. Those transformations took multiple forms, applicable in different ways to the place itself, the people in it and, through the 'external' patients who moved through its rooms, to relationships with an 'outside' world. In particular, the production of an ephemeral medical space within a domestic setting was something that occurred not just in the country houses of the British Isles, but across Europe too. At Mount Stuart, as elsewhere, the process involved a conversion that was carried out relatively quickly and easily. Beds and screens were items that could be moved around, and required relatively limited structural alteration, a feature common to many auxiliary hospitals and the relatively unsophisticated medical requirements of the age.

---

33 Ibid.   34 Ibid.   35 *The War Record* shows images of the funeral of a Stoker Samson, HMS *Tiger*, in May 1915, p. 66.

Discharged cases	1916–18
Infective	118
Constitutional	8
Diseases – nervous	95
Diseases – blood	34
Diseases – circulatory	122
Diseases – respiratory	119
Diseases – digestive	442
Diseases – genito-urinary	69
Diseases – bones/joints	75
Injuries	527
Special departments (ORL)	230
Sub-total	**1,839**

7.6 Summary of medical activity at Mount Stuart, 1916–18
(SNL MS H6.96.722).

Many of the larger public and reception rooms, as noted above, acquired new identities and functions during the war. Where specific transformations did take place, they used the particular advantages of some of the domestic rooms. This applied specifically to the rationale for the choice of the glass-roofed conservatory, on the house front, as an operating theatre (fig. 7.4).

> The Conservatory was in every respect an excellent Operating Theatre. The light was perfect. The floor of stone tiles might have been made for the purpose. Hot and cold water were laid on, and a small cooking stove for boiling water was installed. The Theatre was heated by this and … there was no difficulty in keeping the temperature to the required degree.[36]

Not all of the house was given over: some domestic space remained, partitioned off from the military area so that the 'big house' assumed a split identity, both physically and in human terms for the course of the war. In addition, there was a clear and well maintained partitioning of officers and soldiers, reproducing the upstairs/downstairs hierarchy of the country house, with wards for officers upstairs and those for other ranks on the ground floor.

These transformative processes of conversion and medicalization applied equally to the people in and around the house. The specific demands of the navy and of being an auxiliary hospital involved a degree of human transformations as well. Medicalization occurred with a mix of formal medical bodies, surgeons, physicians, GPs, trained and probationary nurses and VAD volunteers coming

36 SNL, MS H8.96.722.

in to the house on a regular basis. In gender terms, alongside the marchioness, there were also a range of new roles for women in the house. The volunteer staff tended to come from within the house pool, but also from nearby Rothesay. Domestic staff assumed new medical roles during the war as orderlies, cooks and laundresses, as did the men who worked at the house; examples included carpenters, gardeners and drivers, who combined medico-military roles with their original or ongoing domestic roles. Indeed much of the objects used in massage and rehabilitation were made by the house's carpenter, Andrew Lamont.[37]

Finally, we must also consider the patients, whose transformations took on a number of corporeal dimensions. Bodily changes were part and parcel of the wounded sailor's life – amputations, injuries, disabilities, burns, and the specific impacts of explosions on bones and joints that changed the victim's physical appearance. Rehabilitation was a core feature of the house/hospital activities – evident in the massage and physical therapy rooms – to prepare the body either for a return to service or for non-active work. There were also to a lesser extent some occupational health and retraining activities. Examples included fresh-air therapies, taking full advantage of the therapeutic potential of the grounds and water around the house. One wonders at the value of taking the sailors out in small sailing boats on the Firth of Clyde – given their recent traumatic experiences in much bigger boats – but there were many indoors entertainments to keep the sailors amused, from both within the patient community but also from outside troupes and local entertainers.[38] Yet there is no doubt as to the likely sense of luck many sailors felt in ending up in the kind of fine and restorative locations that they would not have had access to in peacetime.[39] It has also been argued that this opening up of the country house, out of necessity and duty, accelerated the breakdown of social divides in the post-war period.[40]

Notification of the closure of the hospital arrived in November 1918, and after the slow re-housing of the wounded it finally closed in January 1919. In appreciation of the role of the country house in the war – quite apart from the huge emotional loss of its many sons and some daughters – there was a heartfelt thank you from the nation for the provision of auxiliary hospital services. Several of the nurses at Mount Stuart were given honours. Augusta received a citation, thank you letter and DBE, while Staff Nurse Alice Marion England and Theatre Sister Isabella Frame Lang were awarded the Royal Red Cross, 2nd Class. A wider legacy perhaps was the opening up of big house spaces to new uses and identities. These houses were chosen for their suitability as auxiliary medical

37 Ibid. 38 Ibid. 39 This reflects narrative from places like Brighton Pavilion, where Indian patients send photos home pointing out they were currently living in 'the King's Palace'. Samuel Hysen and Alan Lister, 'British India on trial: Brighton military hospitals and the politics of empire in World War One', *Journal of Historical Geography*, 38 (2012), 18–34. 40 Simon Greaves, *The country house at war: fighting the Great War at home and in the trenches* (London, 2014), pp 4–5.

spaces, and many reverted after the war with very little markers or evidence of that function beyond the photos and documentary evidence. Yet that opening up was still fairly tightly controlled, at least at Mount Stuart. This was a military/naval space, as exemplified by a set of standing orders that moderated and controlled behaviours.[41] Access to outside visitors was also controlled, as was permission to leave and arrive.

One could argue, however, for a greater permeability of the Big House space during the war and envisage the 'mucking in together' (although always hierarchical) as a form of democratization in action and even the foundations for new ways of thinking about societies of care. The older models of paternalism and informal provision were severely tested in the war, as was a sense of duty in return from the state for the sacrifices made by its citizens and an intensification of the pre-war social insurance acts led the way in time to the National Health Service. That paternalism also extended to the social activities on the site. Parties tended to be focused on Bute family events, though the allowance of Stoker Philip Lang's wedding (to Theatre Sister Lang mentioned above) in August 1915 provides a nice counterpoint as a marital, as opposed to martial, starting-point.

In terms of transformations and mobile medical knowledge, research from Highclere Castle suggested that the learning gained by surgeons at the house was transferred back to improved orthopaedic practice in the main London hospitals.[42] These shifting mobile processes of medical learning moving from medical to non-medical spaces and back to medical space again can also be associated with the rehabilitation work at Mount Stuart. On a wider scale, the typical auxiliary hospital history exemplified by Mount Stuart was repeated across all combatant countries; multiple narratives from different geographical locations would help to illuminate the wider roles played by the country house during and after the war period and especially clarify common experiences and outcomes for comparative histories.[43]

This essay argues the case for recognizing how auxiliary hospitals acted as key nodes within a complex networked geography of wartime care, while the country house had an important and undervalued place within that network. Each house had its own individual history but was also, in Veronica Strang's words, both typical and unique.[44] Inside the wartime country house we get a glimpse, through the lens of medical contingency, of the transformation of people and place that arguably triggered longer-term transformative impacts and modernizations of society that resonate to the present day.

41 SNL, MS H8.96.722.   42 Caernarvon, *Lady Alminia and the real Downton Abbey*, p. 290.
43 Jay Winter, *Sites of memory, sites of mourning: the Great War in European cultural history* (Oxford, 2005), pp 29–36.   44 Veronica Strang, *The meaning of water* (Oxford, 2004), p. 9.

The Bellingham family of Castlebellingham, Co. Louth, 1914–24

DONAL HALL

On Wednesday, 10 June 1914, Lieutenant Roger Noel Bellingham, aide-de-camp (ADC) to the lord lieutenant of Ireland, Lord Aberdeen, inspected a parade of Irish National Volunteers (INV) in Castlebellingham, Co. Louth. In the course of an address, Bellingham asserted that the Volunteer movement as a whole supported the leader of the Irish Parliamentary Party (IPP), John Redmond, and that 'the immediate and manifest duty of the Volunteers was to secure the triumph of the Home Rule movement, and to defend [an Irish parliament] which had been so shamefully lost and nobly won.'[1]

A week later, in the House of Lords, in response to questions from Viscount Middleton, the marquis of Crewe reported that Bellingham had retracted his comments and 'admitted he was under the influence of being at home, forgot the obligation of reticence that rested upon him as aide-de-camp to the lord lieutenant, and regretted any offence.'[2]

Soon afterwards, Joseph Devlin, IPP MP for West Belfast, addressing Prime Minister Herbert Asquith, listed six occasions when the marquis of Londonderry, ADC to the king, had appeared at Ulster Volunteer Force rallies in opposition to Home Rule, and asked whether the marquis had been required to justify his actions and if not, why not? The prime minister dismissed Devlin's question, explaining that 'there are more than seventy Aides-de-Camp to the King, and that the office, unlike that of an acting Aide-de-Camp to the Lord Lieutenant of Ireland, does not normally carry with it any active duties or responsibilities ... I have not thought it worthwhile to take any notice of the matter'.[3]

The disparity between the political repercussions to the actions of the marquis of Londonderry and those of Lieutenant Roger Bellingham caused momentary uproar in the nationalist press: 'Let us have the same sauce for the most noble marquis as for the lord lieutenant's ADC. These Ulster notables have played with treason. They should be taught that the law expects from them the same obedience that it exacts from the most humble citizen.'[4] Lieutenant Bellingham's potential as a nationalist martyr was short lived, however, when political attention shifted as the month of July 1914 progressed and Ireland

1 *Dundalk Democrat*, 13 June 1914.   2 *Irish Independent*, 17 June 1914.   3 HC Deb, 29 June 1914, vol. 64, cc28–30.   4 *Dundalk Democrat*, 30 June 1914.

8.1 Bellingham Castle in 1900 (private collection).

seemed daily to slip inexorably closer to civil war. Bellingham did not comment publicly on the subject again; however, a certain amount of insouciance can be reasonably inferred when he shortly afterwards sent a letter of public support to the organizers of an INV rally held on his father's lands in Castlebellingham on 12 July 1914 (fig. 8.1).[5]

The squabble highlights an idiosyncratic vein in the political and cultural tenets of the Bellingham family at that time. According to the Royal Irish Constabulary (RIC), the Irish National Volunteers in Co. Louth drew its recruits, from '… the farmer, farm labourer and working classes'.[6] The respectable middle classes, including Roman Catholic clergy, members of urban and rural councils, and justices of the peace also played prominent roles in the organizing committees and by August 1914 the INV in Louth had reached a membership of just under 5,000. The local gentry, of either religious persuasion, had shown little interest in the Volunteers, the one notable exception was the Bellingham family. Sir Henry Bellingham, Roger's father and lord lieutenant of Co. Louth, actively supported Irish cultural organizations, including the Gaelic League. Sir Henry hosted on his land the annual Féis, or cultural gathering, organized by the Louth Gaelic League, and it was a short step from that to permitting drill practice by the Volunteers on his demesne in Castlebellingham. The Grove Field in Castlebellingham, a football field that was owned by him, and used by the Gaelic Athletic Association, was the venue on 12 July 1914 for a march-past and parade of some 2,000 members of the INV. In this major event, three great organizations that were the muscular and energetic realities of Irish

5 *Freemans Journal*, 13 July 1914. 6 County Inspector's Confidential Monthly Report (CICMR), Louth, May 1914.

nationalists' perception of their own uniqueness within the union of Great
Britain and Ireland, the Gaelic League, the Irish National Volunteers and the
Gaelic Athletic Association, co-operated in a highly organized propaganda event
which was filmed for posterity, with the full encouragement of Sir Henry
Bellingham, to proclaim their readiness to train, arm and fight in support of John
Redmond and Home Rule.

There was little in the Bellingham family history to suggest that Sir Henry
Bellingham would be amenable to the Home Rule movement, never mind
actively encourage the growth of an armed militia to fight for it. The Bellingham
family were descended from Henry Bellingham who acquired lands in Co. Louth
in the mid-seventeenth century, as part of the Cromwellian settlements. Henry's
son, Col. Thomas Bellingham, took the Williamite side in the war of the 1690s,
and built Bellingham Castle around 1700. His descendant, Sir William
Bellingham (*c*.1756–1826), was a member of parliament, secretary to Prime
Minister William Pitt, a commissioner in the navy, and was created a baronet in
1796. The title then passed to William's nephew, Sir Alan Bellingham (1776–
1827), and in turn to the latter's son, Sir Alan Edward Bellingham (1800–89), the
3rd baronet. During the 3rd baronet's time, the Bellinghams, like many other
landlords in Co. Louth, were on the receiving end of agrarian violence, the worst
occasion being in 1832 when a determined attempt was made to burn Bellingham
Castle, while Lady Bellingham and children were in residence. On this occasion
Sir Alan Bellingham was threatened with death, 'if you do not alter yourself for
the better'.[7] Sir Alan was one of the largest landowners in Co. Louth whose
holdings totalled 4,100 acres with an annual valuation of £4,300.[8] In 1889, the
3rd baronet's son, Alan Henry Bellingham, commonly called Henry (1846–
1921), became the 4th baronet.[9]

Henry Bellingham was politically astute, having served for one five-year-term
as MP for Co. Louth from 1880, asserting then and afterwards that he was a
'Conservative Home Ruler'.[10] His life and actions were, however, dominated by
religious piety, and from the time he was received into the Roman Catholic
Church in 1873 he worked assiduously and publicly for the advancement of the
Church. He was privy chamberlain to three Popes, Pius IX, Leo XIII and Pius
X, and was a frequent contributor to religious tracts. When he inherited the
Bellingham estates, he opened up his demesne to the annual village Corpus
Christi procession, and had the lintel on a number of his tenants' houses
decorated with religious icons. On the death in 1891 of Sir Henry's first wife,
Constance, daughter of the 2nd earl of Gainsborough, he erected a roadside
crucifix in her memory, which still stands. Sir Henry remarried in 1895 to Bertha
Clifton, Baroness Grey du Ruthyn.

---

7 Deposition of John Reece, butler to Lady Bellingham, concerning attempt to set fire to
Bellingham Castle on Sunday 23 December 1832 (Bellew Archive, Barmeath Castle, N/3/9
also N/3/10).   8 John Bateman, *The great landowners of Great Britain and Ireland* (1883, repr.

8.2 (*left*) Sir Henry Bellingham, 4th baronet (County Louth Archaeological and Historical Society).　8.3 Roger Bellingham (Heber Russell).

Sir Henry had four children by Constance. They were Edward and Roger, Mary, who became a Roman Catholic nun, and Augusta whose marriage ceremony to the 4th marquis of Bute in 1905 was an ostentatious social event, the moving images of which were captured on film now held by the National Library of Scotland.[11] Edward, the oldest son, was born in 1879 and served with the British Army in the Royal Scots (Lothian Regiment) in the Boer War, 1899–1902. Life in peacetime was difficult for Edward, and on his marriage to Charlotte Gough (née Payne) he resigned his commission in 1904 and spent some years in the United States of America, before taking up a position as secretary to the British embassy in Guatemala.

Roger, born in 1884, was gazetted second lieutenant in the British Army in 1903 (fig. 8.3). He inherited his father's Roman Catholic piety, contributing to Catholic Trust Society pamphlets and also working as a helper during pilgrimages to the Marian shrine in Lourdes, France. As ADC to the lord lieutenant of Ireland he was also a popular habitué of the Dublin Castle social scene, contemporaneous 'Court Reports' recording the presence of Roger and his wife Alice at numerous social and official functions, sometimes together, sometimes separately, but always recording Alice's ensemble in great detail. More so than his brother who was abroad, Roger was an up-and-coming man, and could have confidently expected that he would play an influential role in any future Home Rule administration.

1971), p. 36.　9 Owen McGee, Julia Sammler and Mary Free, 'Collection List 167', Bellingham Papers, National Library of Ireland, 2000.　10 See, for instance, *Dundalk Democrat*, 22 May 1880 and *Irish Independent*, 4 May 1912.　11 http://movingimage.nls.uk/film/6774.

War between Britain and Germany was formally declared on 4 August 1914. The next day, one hundred Volunteers accompanied by the Armagh Pipers Band paraded at Castlebellingham train station to see off two of their number who had been called up for service in the British Army. As the train pulled out, the Volunteers cheered and sang 'Come Back to Erin'.[12]

At the outbreak of the war, the 28th Brigade of the Royal Field Artillery occupied Dundalk military barracks. Roger Bellingham immediately reported for duty in Dundalk and prepared for embarkation to France. Reflecting his own deeply held religious feelings, Roger arranged for special Masses in St Patrick's church in Dundalk for all Roman Catholic soldiers serving in the barracks:

> No sight could be more edifying than that of these men attending two special early Masses in St Patrick's just before their departure, when every man, with Captain Bellingham at their head, approached the altar and received Holy Communion.[13]

The brigade marched out of Dundalk Barracks on the night of 15 August 1914, escorted to the train station by friends and a company of buglers from the Irish National Volunteers. The actions of the buglers were to trigger bitter recriminations and a disastrous split in the organization in Louth. Roger Bellingham in the meantime was amused to note that the train that carried him and his men, many of them Roman Catholic nationalists, was cheered loudly as it passed through loyalist Lurgan, Co. Armagh, which was festooned with anti-Home Rule flags and bunting.[14] The brigade embarked from Belfast, and landed in Le Havre in France on 19 August. It went into action only a few days later, on 24 August, at the battle of Mons and again on 26 August at the battle of Le Cateau. Bellingham transferred to 8 Brigade Royal Field Artillery, which operated in and around the Ypres sector. A report in the brigade's war diary of 1 March 1915 noted: 'Lieutenant Bellingham spotted bomb gun on right front of a fusilier and shelled it. Also searched wood in front of T-trench for another bomb gun which was stopped firing. Bomb gun opened again so Lieut. Bellingham went forward to the trench and located gun but did not shoot.'[15] Sadly, only a few days later on 4 March, Roger Bellingham was found dead in bed, having just come off duty. It is thought that he suffered from heart failure, brought about by the stress related to his duties. He was buried on the following day, 5 March, in Dickiebusch churchyard.

The death of Roger Bellingham triggered a remarkable outpouring of sympathy for the family with obituaries emphasizing both his religiosity and

12 *Dundalk Democrat*, 8 Aug. 1914.   13 *Dundalk Democrat*, 13 Mar. 1915. On this date Roger was still a lieutenant. He was appointed posthumously to the higher rank of captain with effect from 30 Oct. 1914 (*London Gazette*, no. 29171, 25 May 1915, p. 5012).   14 Letter from Roger Bellingham to Alice Bellingham, 20 Aug. 1914 (private collection).   15 'War Diary 8 Brigade

8.4 Edward Bellingham, 5th baronet
(National Portrait Gallery).

nationalism. A Mass was held in his honour in St Patrick's church in Dundalk, and a memorial plaque was installed near the high altar. Unfortunately, that plaque was removed about twenty years ago during renovations and is now lost, and this was also the fate of a portrait of Roger which was presented to the Louth County Council by Sir Henry.

Edward Bellingham returned from Guatemala immediately on the outbreak of war and took a commission in 8th Battalion Royal Dublin Fusiliers (RDF) (fig. 8.4). Within a few months he was promoted to the rank of captain and by the time his battalion landed in France on 20 December 1915, he had reached the rank of major, effectively second-in-command of the battalion. On 1 January 1916, the battalion began its first tour of the front-line trenches, and by the time they returned to billets on 14 January, they had lost five men killed and nineteen wounded. On 3 February, it was noted that Major Edward Bellingham had assumed command of the 8th Battalion, RDF, which at that stage comprised of 26 officers and 774 men.[16] From the time that Bellingham took command of 8th RDF, the names of all casualties, both officers and men, were recorded in the war diary, a relatively unusual practice, as usually only casualties amongst the officer corps were named, while the men were bracketed with the acronym OR (Other Ranks).

On 27 and 29 April 1916, the 8th RDF was subjected to prolonged attacks from the German Army, and suffered in the region of 500 casualties, killed wounded, gassed and missing. The roll of casualties, which noted each man's serial number, name, rank, date and casualty type, took up nine closely typed foolscap pages of the war diary. These diaries were never intended for publication, so it is by coincidence that the detailed casualty list can now be viewed not only in the context of the prolonged horror of 27 and 29 April at Ypres, but also in the context of the coincidental events then occurring in Ireland. During that same week, the Easter Rebellion had broken out in Ireland, and had even touched Edward's home when RIC Constable Charles McGee was shot and killed by Irish Volunteers outside the gates of Bellingham Castle. The bitterness that Edward felt towards the rebels whose proclamation of the Irish Republic made particular reference to the support of 'our gallant allies in Europe', that is, the Germans, was expressed in a letter to his father:

> We were in action on the 27th and 29th April. My battalion bore the brunt of the right attack, and behaved archly ... Poor George Magee and Thomas Lambe, of Castle Bellingham; Wm Hoey, of Darver, P. Macken of Ardee; and J. Murphy of Drogheda are among the killed. Please express to their people my profound sympathy in their losses. We had heavy casualties, but 50 per cent will return eventually. Our men are furious with the Sinn Féiners, and asked to be allowed to go and finish them up. We were defending the Empire with serious losses the very day these people were trying to help the Germans that we were fighting. It is all too sad.[17]

Edward Bellingham continued to serve with distinction during the war. He was awarded the Distinguished Service Order for his actions at the battle of Guinchy on 8–9 September 1916, when he took command of two battalions and 'at a time when troops were elated with success and without officers, was able to control the situation and organise the defences'.[18] He received the medal personally from King George V in a private audience in Buckingham Palace on 10 October 1916.

As lord lieutenant, Sir Henry Bellingham played a major role in recruiting for the British forces. Centrally, Sir Henry was president of all county recruiting committees; locally he was a member of the recruiting committees for Co. Louth, and also for Castlebellingham.[19] In 1915, recruiting campaigns began in earnest, with frequent advertising in the local newspapers, and public meetings held in various parts of Louth in efforts to drum up enthusiasm. Supporters of John Redmond were notably in attendance, at meetings addressed by 'celebrity' soldiers, such as Lieutenant Tom Kettle MP. Edward Bellingham addressed a meeting only a few weeks after the death of his brother Roger, where it was publicly recorded that Sir Henry was 'prostrate' with grief. This meeting was notable when a man named Thomas Walsh was arrested for making fairly mild

17 *Dundalk Democrat*, 20 May 1916.   **18** F. Ramsey, Brigadier General Commanding 48th Infantry Brigade, *Report on operations of 48th Infantry Brigade on 8th and 10th September, 1916 in attack on Guinchy*, 15 Sept. 1916 (TNA, War Diary 7 Battalion Royal Irish Rifles). **19** Department of Recruiting for Ireland, *County Louth Area 6, committees, voluntary helpers, recruiting officers and agents*, 1916 (author's collection).

anti-recruiting statements in the presence of Edward, who didn't seem to take the matter too seriously. However, it was enough to upset the local RIC and Walsh, who was the first man to be tried in Co. Louth under the Defence of the Realm Act, was sent to prison for three months with hard labour.[20]

An impressive infrastructure of voluntary support for the war effort was set up after the outbreak of hostilities in 1914. The Dundalk War Relief Committee, with the long-term objective of seeing to the needs of returned soldiers and their families after the war, was established in 1914. In the same year a branch of the National War Relief Fund 'for the relief of women and children who are faced with privation as a consequence of the war' was set up under the stewardship of Sir Henry Bellingham.[21] A branch of the Red Cross under Lady Bellingham was established in November 1914 to organize first aid and nursing classes, to establish hospital supply depots, and to provide nursing care at home and abroad by trained voluntary aid detachments of Red Cross volunteers. The Red Cross was dependent on voluntary subscriptions to carry out their work and under the energetic stewardship of Lady Bellingham by the end of July 1915 had collected £412.[22] Later in the same year, in one day alone, £100 was collected to go to base hospitals at the war front.[23] A Red Cross sale of farmers' produce donated free of charge in May 1916 raised £800.[24] In 1917, thanks to Lady Bellingham's energetic canvassing and organizational flair, a Red Cross hospital for the war wounded was established in Dundalk that was largely paid for by public subscription. By the end of the war the Louth Red Cross had made 75,000 items such as dressings and bandages for distribution to the forces, and had also funded the purchase of a Red Cross ambulance for use in France.[25] The various funds operated by Lady Bellingham raised £12,000 for the Red Cross by the end of the war.[26]

By 1918, Edward had reached the rank of brigadier-general, and he had been awarded the Companion of the Order of St Michael and St George in the New Year's Honours list. On 21 March, a much-anticipated German spring offensive was launched, designed to crush the Allies before the army of the United States had an opportunity to fully deploy. On 28 March, Edward was on the front line inspecting defences and directing troops when he was somehow cut off from his command, taken prisoner, and spent the last six months of the war in a prisoner-of-war camp.[27] On release, he returned to his old regiment, the Royal Scots, and served with the army of occupation in Germany. He also found time to take up the cause of ex-soldiers and on Edward's instigation, a branch of the Demobilised Sailors and Soldiers Federation was established at a public meeting

20 *Dundalk Democrat*, 27 Mar. 1915.   **21** Ibid., 15 Aug. 1914.   **22** Ibid., 7 Aug. 1915.
23 Ibid., 30 Oct. 1915.   **24** Ibid., 3 June 1916.   **25** Joseph Gavin and Harold O'Sullivan, *Dundalk: a military history* (Dundalk, 1987), p. 55.   **26** *Dundalk Herald*, 2 Aug. 1919.
27 War Diary 118 Infantry Brigade (TNA, WO 95/2589/2).

8.5 Castlebellingham war memorial 2014 (photography by author).

in Castlebellingham on 11 January 1920. On that occasion, Edward promised to do all he could to address the needs of ex-soldiers in relation to anticipated land re-distribution. Edward remained as a serving officer in the British Army until he retired with the rank of brevet-lieutenant colonel on 14 August 1922.[28]

With the ending of the war, Red Cross activities in Louth were wound down. At a private function in 1919, Lady Bellingham was presented with an album containing an illuminated address with the signatures of 400 subscribers, and a case of treasury notes. Lady Bellingham refused the offer of a personal gift, and pledged the money instead for the families and dependants of sailors and soldiers in Co. Louth.[29]

On 8 March 1919, a letter from Sir Henry Bellingham was published in the *Dundalk Democrat* proposing the erection in Castlebellingham of a memorial to those from that area who fell in the Great War, and invited anyone who wished to submit a name for inclusion to do so. It is apparent that Sir Henry proceeded

28 *London Gazette*, 32738, (15 Aug. 1922), p. 6020.   29 *Dundalk Herald*, 2 Aug. 1919.

with energy with his task as by the end of the year, he had published three updated lists of names and had secured a design for the memorial. The Castlebellingham memorial cross was dedicated on 5 February 1920, in an impressive ceremony officiated by Cardinal Logue, Roman Catholic Primate of All Ireland (fig. 8.5). The unveiling of the memorial was preceded by a solemn requiem Mass in Kilsaran church, about a mile from Castlebellingham. Two hundred ex-servicemen under the command of Edward Bellingham marched in military formation from Kilsaran to the memorial, where a very large crowd met them.[30]

The unveiling of the memorial in Castlebellingham is a key to understanding the ability of the Bellingham family to survive. This ceremony occurred just as the War of Independence was moving into a more violent phase, and while Co. Louth was comparatively quiet, the local IRA was sufficiently active to make it seem likely that both the memorial and the family would come under threat. Sir Henry Bellingham was after all, still the lord lieutenant of the county, he had two sons who served in the British Army, and he had been highly active in promoting recruitment to the British forces, from which many hundreds of men from Louth had not returned, or had returned wounded. However, even the IRA admitted to the 'deserved' popularity of Sir Henry Bellingham,[31] and whether intentionally or not, with the presence of Cardinal Logue at the dedication of the memorial, and the overtly Roman Catholic nature of the ceremony, Sir Henry had cloaked the memorial, and his family, with the protection of the Roman Catholic Church. Even more importantly, the fifty-five names on the memorial were submitted by local families, and with that, it took on an intensely local significance, being dedicated to 'those of the three parishes of Kilsaran, Dromiskin and Togher who died for Ireland in the Great European War of 1914–1918'. The dedication did not claim that the men died for the King, or to make the world safe for democracy, or for the freedom of small nations, but 'for Ireland', a stark and defiant challenge to those who would doubt their motives.

Sir Henry Bellingham died on 9 June 1921, while the War of Independence still had a month to run. His son Edward inherited the baronetcy and in July was appointed lord lieutenant of Louth, the last person to hold that position (while he was still serving with his battalion in Germany). Further distinction was bestowed upon him when in December 1922 he was nominated to the Free State Senate by the president of the Executive Council, William Cosgrave. However, the nomination did not translate into a seat, but he was made a peace commissioner for Louth. Having once been closely identified with the British administration, Edward Bellingham transferred his allegiance with little difficulty to the newly established Irish Free State. Notable supporters of the Free State were however being targeted, and in early 1923, during the Civil War,

30 *Dundalk Democrat*, 7 Feb. 1920.   **31** Statement of James MacGuill (Bureau of Military History, WS 0353), p. 17.

anti-Treaty forces commenced a concerted campaign against houses and property owned by persons with close connections to the Free State administration and whom they regarded as being inimical to the republican cause. A couple of hundred yards away from Bellingham Castle, Milestown House occupied by Major Barrow was destroyed on 29 January; Ballygassan House owned by J.J. Russell, sub-sheriff of the county, also close to Bellingham Castle, was burned on 2 February. Less than three miles away, Clermont House at Blackrock, owned by Col. Charles Davis Guinness, high sheriff of Co. Louth in 1918, was also destroyed on 2 February; Knockabbey Castle, owned by the O'Reilly family, one of the principal Catholic families in Co. Louth, was destroyed on 2 March. With the Bellingham family's obvious ties with the ousted British administration, with Edward's appointment to various positions in the new Free State administration, and the fact that he was still a serving officer in the British Army, Bellingham Castle should have been an obvious target for republicans. Yet for some reason Bellingham Castle was never attacked and it must be assumed that the traditional popularity of the family somehow contributed to its survival.

Edward was elected a senator in 1925 and was victorious in three subsequent Senatorial elections, serving until the Senate was abolished in 1936. In 1927, he provoked a near riot when, under the auspices of the British Legion, he called an electioneering meeting of ex-soldiers in the Town Hall, Dundalk, probably with the intention of sounding out his chances of a Dáil seat. But his speech was drowned out by hundreds of ex-servicemen expressing their support for both republican and resurgent Redmondite candidates.[32]

Edward served again in the British forces during the Second World War, this time in the Royal Air Force, and later in occupied Germany in 1945–6. He died in a Dublin nursing home in 1956, and being without a male heir, the title was passed to his brother Roger's son, also called Roger Bellingham. Edward was buried, along with his father and mother, in a simple grave in Kilsaran churchyard, the stone merely recalling his name, and his date of birth and death. Bellingham Castle was subsequently sold and for the most part since then has operated as a hotel.

The Bellingham family has not died out in the area and continues to thrive. The war memorial unveiled in 1920 also survived, although with the passing of time, it became neglected. Approaching the centenary of the Great War, the local community had the cross cleaned, landscaped and an interpretative plaque erected. At an impressive and touching interdenominational rededication ceremony in 2014, Roger Bellingham's grandson, Heber Russell, laid a wreath at the base of the newly restored memorial which his great-grandfather built, and on which his grandfather is commemorated (fig. 8.6).

32 *Dundalk Democrat*, 17 Sept. 1927.

8.6 Heber Russell, laying a wreath at the rededication of the Castlebellingham war memorial, September 2014 (photograph by Luke Torris).

By all that is now accepted, the Bellingham family of Castlebellingham, Co. Louth, could have been victims of the overthrow of the political and social ascendancy that occurred between 1912 and 1922. They were at the centre of the administrative and legal system in Louth, where they visibly and volubly supported the British war effort, campaigning for recruitment and providing for the well-being of soldiers and their families. Unusually for their class, they had publicly taken a nationalist stance in the Home Rule campaign of 1912–14, but by supporting Redmond they had ultimately backed the wrong side in the internecine war within nationalism, and compounded this stance by publicly excoriating the 1916 Rising. Other prominent families in Louth, with less to be apprehensive about in the new order, had their houses burned and property destroyed, although it has to be recorded that few, if any, of those families fled the country, applying for and accepting compensation from both the Irish Free State and the British government. The Bellingham family somehow managed to find a way through the political minefield of early twentieth-century Irish politics, seemingly without compromising their own principles, without alienating those who disagreed with them, and more than that, by retaining local respect and popularity. It does not seem paradoxical therefore that, on the modest family gravestone in Kilsaran, the incongruity of the Bellingham perspective is by chance manifested. The identity of the stone-mason who made the memorial reads 'J Pearse Brunswick Street, Dublin'. That the English father of the first president of the Irish Republic as proclaimed in Dublin at Easter 1916 carved the Bellingham family memorial in stone seems somewhat ironic.

Lanhydrock: a Cornish parish torn apart

PAUL HOLDEN

On 6 August 1910, Mary Agar-Robartes (1853–1921), Viscountess Clifden, launched HMS *Lion*, a 31,000-ton battle-cruiser, at Devonport dockyard (fig. 9.1).[1] The story travelled all over the world. The Singapore newspaper, the *Straits Times*, reported that 'the weather was anything but ideal … heavy rain falling all afternoon, but this did not prevent 80,000 persons from assembling to witness the great vessel take to the water.'[2]

The viscountess was a caring and benevolent lady who took a lasting interest in the fortunes of the ship and its crew. After the launch she invited those who built the *Lion* to a garden party at her Cornish home, Lanhydrock, where she was presented with an ornately carved box containing the hammer and chisel used during the ceremony. Subsequently, she corresponded with a former member of her house staff whose son served on the ship during the Great War. In one of these letters, dated November 1915, the viscountess wrote at long length, first as a proud patron of the ship, concerned about the hardships on board and the perils the crew faced on a daily basis; but she also wrote as a thoughtful friend showing concern for the son's personal welfare, as well as a devoted mother, sharing the worry of having her own sons serving on the front line. On the fourth and last page of the letter, as if an afterthought, she referred to her own private loss – the death of her eldest son, the Hon. Thomas Agar-Robartes (1880–1915), MP: 'we do not know how to bear our grief'.[3]

The loss of the heir to the Lanhydrock estates and title of Viscount Clifden reversed the fortunes of the family during the twentieth century; it is fair to say they never recovered. Moreover, the ramifications extended well beyond the gentry family to the estate workers and parishioners, all of whom did their bit for the war effort. This essay will explore the effect war had on a single parish in rural Cornwall.

Lanhydrock is a small parish situated on the edge of Bodmin Moor. Of its 2,400 acres, roughly half is now owned by the National Trust. At its centre is a magnificent Jacobean house (fig. 9.2). The parish borders are defined by the

This chapter is the result of a decade of research into to the war dead of Lanhydrock parish. During that time I have been grateful for the help of Helen Charlesworth, Mike England, Ray Hingston, Kathryn and Eleanor Holden, Peter Mortimer and Nick Thornicroft.
1 www.youtube.com/watch?v=ct_sHYooHt8 (accessed 24 Nov. 2015).   2 *The Straits Times*, 7 Sept. 1910. It was originally intended that a member of the royal family would launch the battle cruiser; however, the court was still in mourning after the death of King Edward VII. 3 Private collection held by descendants of Marion Brown.

9.1 Mary Robartes, Viscountess Clifden (1853–1921). Wife of the 6th Viscount Clifden and mother to ten children, four of whom served on the front lines during the First World War. Mary is pictured here in her coronation robes of 1902. © National Trust/Lanhydrock.

9.2 Lanhydrock House, Cornwall. Completed by 1651, the house was rebuilt after a fire on 4 April 1881. © Paul Holden.

salmon-rich river Fowey, the beautiful Glynn valley, the remote Helman Tor and large tracts of agricultural lands owned by the duchy of Cornwall. Much of the parish was attached to Bodmin priory until the dissolution of the monasteries, when it passed into private hands. The stone-built church dedicated to St Hydroc is a tangible reminder of the medieval monastic community that lived and worked there.

In 1621, Richard Robartes, a middle-class merchant from Truro with huge social aspirations first made his home at Lanhydrock. Robartes was a money-lender, and he amassed a huge landed estate scattered across the county. In 1624, he purchased a baronial title for £12,000. His son John was created 1st earl of Radnor in recognition for, among other things, his active support in restoring the monarchy in 1660. After a disastrous spell as lord lieutenant of Ireland he served more successfully as lord privy seal and lord president of the council. However, despite the earl having nineteen children by two wives, the subsequent three earls did not produce heirs, and the Radnor title died out in 1758.

Lanhydrock house and estate, with its huge mineral wealth, passed into the nearest bloodline, the Cheshire-based Hunt family. In 1804, Anna Maria Hunt married Charles Bagenal Agar, youngest son of Viscount Clifden of Gowran

9.3 The war memorial positioned above the south door in St Hydroc's parish church, Lanhydrock. © Paul Holden.

Castle in Co. Kilkenny, and in 1822 the Agars restored the Robartes name by deed and warrant. Lanhydrock then passed through three generations of the Agar-Robartes family until 1953, when, due to a failure in the male line, Gerald Agar-Robartes, 7th Viscount Clifden, gave the property to the National Trust. Today Lanhydrock house and estate is one of the Trust's flagship properties.

In the fifty years prior to the Great War the parish had undergone some considerable change. A new turnpike road had connected Bodmin with the neighbouring town of Liskeard, which diverted traffic away from the heart of the parish and, in consequence, made redundant its busiest hamlet, which hosted a public house, several private homes, a blacksmith's shop and poor houses. This hamlet was cleared soon after the railway arrived in 1859. Mining had flourished in the parish from the 1860s, and the influx of people created a demand for new facilities, including a school, orphanage and vicarage. Artisans and tradesmen came to work at Lanhydrock in 1881 after the mansion suffered a huge fire. The zenith of the Agar-Robartes family was between the years 1885 and 1915; but this period saw a decline in the parish population, a consequence, in part, of the collapse of agriculture and mining. Despite this, the 1911 census returns still shows agricultural labouring as the predominant occupation.

9.4 The Honourable Thomas Charles Reginald Agar-Robartes, MP (1880–1915). As son and heir Tommy was set to inherit the Viscount Clifden title and vast, mineral rich, lands in Cornwall. © National Trust/Lanhydrock.

This is how the small, sleepy, parish of Lanhydrock stood on the eve of the Great War. Over the next four years men from this rural backwater experienced slaughter on an unprecedented scale, inconceivable fear and hardship, and depravity beyond imagination. Those who died have their names cold-chiselled onto the war memorial situated in the south aisle of the church (fig. 9.3).

The first name on the memorial, taking alphabetical not social precedence, is the Hon. Thomas Agar-Robartes, MP – affectionately known as Tommy by the Lanhydrock staff (fig. 9.4). Tommy was son and heir to the 22,234 acre Cornish estate with a rental income in 1872 of £30,730 per annum.[4] He was a charismatic Edwardian playboy, elected Liberal member for South-East Cornwall in 1906 but disqualified within months for electoral 'treating' or fraud.[5] He returned as member for St Austell in 1908 and, in the lead up to war, championed the potential of volunteer forces to protect the country against invasion. Indeed, Tommy and his valet and coachman, William Cole, were volunteers in the Devon Yeomanry.

Tommy insisted that his life was of no more importance than that of any other Englishman, so by example he enlisted into the Royal Buckingham Yeomanry

4 *The return of owners of land 1873: Cornwall* (Woking, n.d.), p. 25. **5** Paul Holden, 'A very English gentleman: the Honourable Thomas Charles Reginald Agar-Robartes (1880–1915)', *Journal of Liberal History*, 66 (Spring 2010), 8–18.

(Hussars), where he was active on Norfolk coastal defence duty. From January 1915 he served as a captain with the 1st Battalion, Coldstream Guards, with whom he transferred to the front. On 7 April 1915, he returned to England to perform best-man duties for Neil Primrose, son of the former Liberal prime minister Earl Rosebery, at St Margaret's, Westminster.[6]

The following month Tommy wrote a letter to his constituents headed '1st Coldstream Guards May 17, 1915 in a dirty ditch somewhere in France', in which he voiced a familiar wartime cry:

> Every man can help! Every effort is required, for although our ultimate victory is certain, I would venture to remind the delegates that it is a long, long way to Berlin. So one and all must help.[7]

Tommy was summoned by parliament in September 1915 to vote in the House of Commons on the Conscription Bill. On his return his battalion had advanced on Loos. What happened next is recorded in the regimental war diary:

> At about 6 a.m. on September 26 1915, two sergeants, Hopkins and Printer … went out in front of our trenches at the chalk pit … to bring in a wounded man. When they were about to return Hopkins was shot down by a German sniper. Sgt Printer continued on with the wounded man and brought him into the lines. Captain Robartes who had been watching the whole episode, at once went out with Sgt Printer and brought back Sgt Hopkins who was severely wounded. The whole ground in front of the chalk pit was covered in enemy machine guns, Captain Robartes was severely wounded shortly afterwards.[8]

Two days later Tommy was unsuccessfully recommended for a Victoria Cross for conspicuous gallantry in the field, but it was decided he would be considered for a high military decoration if he were to survive his injuries. Two days later, Tommy, aged thirty-five, died in the 18th Casualty Clearing Station. He was mentioned in despatches on 30 November.

On his death the local newspaper, *The Cornish Guardian*, reported: 'His Death was Grand, The Cause was Just'.[9] At the local Liberal Club meeting on 8 October 1915, a deep gratitude was tendered by the constituency members and

6 *The Aberdeen Journal*, 8 Apr. 1915, reported 'Mr Agar-Robartes … is regarded as the Beau Brummell of the House of Commons. He also has the distinction of being the only bachelor now of a trio of inseparables of which Mr Primrose and Mr Lionel de Rothschild were the other two'. For more on Primrose see Martin Gibson, *Captain Neil Primrose MP, 1882–1917* (Wisbech, 2015).   7 Uncatalogued letter in the Lanhydrock collection, reproduced in full in Holden, 'A very English gentleman', 16.   8 Thanks to the Regimental Headquarters, Coldstream Guards, for this information. The 'Intelligence Summary' (TNA, WO95/1219) recorded on 28 Sept. 1915 also lists 'Cpt T.C. Agar-Robartes MP (wounded)' among 229 casualties.   9 *Cornish Guardian*, 8 Oct. 1915.

his local Liberal agent commented on the fact that on his last encounter with Tommy he had conveyed the impression that he never expected to see England again.[10] Sergeant Hopkins survived the war and sent a letter of gratitude to Viscount Clifden.[11] Tommy has several memorial plaques, with the most poignant positioned above the speaker's chair in the House of Commons alongside one to fellow parliamentarian and best friend Neil Primrose, who died in Palestine leading a charge on Gezer on 15 November 1917.

Tommy's privileged life is well recorded in the family archives, photograph albums and contemporary newspaper coverage, but details of the others listed on the war memorial are not so well known.

William Beare, son of a local miller, and Thomas Fewell of Chelmsford in Essex were best friends.[12] They first met while serving in the duke of Cornwall's Light Infantry stationed at Gravesend Barracks in 1911. Two years later Private Beare married Emily Rusk, daughter of an Irish farm labourer living in the parish. Thomas Fewell was his best man that day, a duty that William reciprocated in 1915 at the wedding of Thomas and Emily's sister, Sarah Rusk. Private Beare had joined the army in 1910 and served on the home front. In March 1918, he was sent with comrades to France to reinforce the front line after severe losses. In April he transferred to the 1st Battalion of the Somerset Light Infantry, was promoted to sergeant and ordered to lead his men towards the French/Belgium boarder. On 15 April, during the battle of Hazebrouck, Beare led his men through barbed-wire defences into relentless German machine-gun fire in an attempt to gain control of Pacult Woods. They failed, and were driven back. He was listed as one of 215 who died during the assault; his name now appears on the Loos memorial, the Lanhydrock memorial and the memorial in Chelmsford. By the end of hostilities four further members of his immediate family had been killed in military action, one of them, his brother Harvey, having been killed only seven days earlier.

Thomas Fewell, the son of a Chelmsford tanner, was stationed in Ireland at the outbreak of the war but was soon transferred to France. He was among the first British infantrymen to engage the enemy at the battle of Mons. Perhaps injured, Fewell was returned to Falmouth, where he was deployed in training new recruits. It was here he married Sarah Rusk of Lanhydrock. In July 1916, he joined the British and Commonwealth forces on the Somme, where, under the flag of the Duke of Cornwall's Light Infantry, he advanced to relieve the Royal Warwickshire Regiment and engaged with a prolonged and destructive enemy artillery barrage, described by a contemporary as 'a truly terrible sight

10 *Western Morning News*, 11 Oct. 1915. **11** Uncatalogued letter in the Lanhydrock collection. **12** These stories have been uncovered from accessing census records, battalion histories, medal history cards, foreign service record documents in Australia and Canada, the Commonwealth War Graves Commission, war diaries, newspaper archives, personal correspondence and other published, unpublished, online and private resources.

and a nerve-wracking experience for those who had to endure that awful holocaust'. On this day Acting Corporal Thomas Fewell, aged twenty-five, was 'killed in action'. He has no known grave and his name can be found on the Thiepval memorial to the 72,000 missing of the Somme. On 25 August the *Essex County Chronicle* reported his death and added 'Mrs Fewell has four other sons … serving with the Colours'.

One of the witnesses to Thomas Fewell's marriage was William Roberts, father of William who had worked on the Lanhydrock estate between 1904 and 1912. William jr signed his enlistment papers in Sydney, Australia, and in June 1915 transferred with the Australian Engineers to Gallipoli as a sapper. In July 1916, promoted to 2nd corporal, he led a successful attack on Pozieres during the Somme offensive. During August the Australians, despite heavy German gun-fire, were repairing captured trenches, during which time Roberts received, according to his casualty record, a gunshot wound to the head. He was buried in a small military cemetery that was violated by further fighting in 1918.

Another local man who lost his life on the Somme was Clarence Hawken. Clarence lived on the Lanhydrock estate and was an assistant gardener to his father, James, who was also a local Methodist preacher. Like William Roberts, Hawken sought his fortunes overseas, and his attestation papers show that in June 1915 in Ontario he joined the Canadian Overseas Expeditionary Force. Private Hawken arrived at the Somme in the summer of 1915 and by 9 October was reported 'missing' near Courcelette.

Another reported missing at the Somme was Private Alfred Walkley. His association with the parish is unclear, but he was living in Bodmin (just a mile from Lanhydrock parish) in 1916 when he enlisted in the 23rd Battalion of the London Regiment. In August 1916, an assault was made on an area known as High Woods, where four companies of the London Regiment advanced through a strong mist towards the enemy lines. Some ninety minutes into the advance, reports indicate that the soldiers had advanced beyond their target. Confusion reigned when the Germans launched a counter-attack that resulted in 22 officers and 565 men killed, wounded or reported missing from the London Regiment alone. Walkley was among them. But High Wood was taken over two hours later.

Another member of the parish, Private William Vanderwolf, survived the Somme. The 1911 census shows a dozen members of the Vanderwolf family employed in the local community as blacksmith, dressmaker, assistant school-teacher, labourers, parlour-maids and farm-hands. William Vanderwolf enlisted with the 10th Battalion of the Royal Warwickshire Regiment in 1916 as soon as he turned eighteen. After the Somme he served at Ypres, in a force tasked with recapturing a strategic position known as the Messines Ridge. Within a fortnight of his arrival he was dead. He has no known grave.

Joseph Coad was brought up at Trebyan on the western edge of the parish. His father, also Joseph, was a butcher and farmer and a loyal member of the

Lanhydrock church bellringers. In 1911, the young Joseph Coad was married with a son, William, and living in nearby Lostwithiel while working as a butcher's apprentice. After enlisting in the Devonshire Regiment, Private Coad transferred to France with the 9th Battalion in 1916, most likely serving on the Somme before participating in an offensive on the heavily fortified Hindenburg Line in France. In August 1916, he was moved north to Flanders to fight on the flooded battlefields of Passchendaele. On 9 October, the Devonshires were called into action on the front line at short notice. The conditions were horrendous: it was impossible to dig new trenches, and enemy gun positions soon found an accurate range; 270 officers and men of the 9th Battalion were killed. Coad was hit by a sniper's bullet. His commanding officer told his widow that 'He did not suffer, death was instantaneous'.[13] His body was never recovered.

Not all from the parish served in Europe. At the outbreak of war Sergeant Charles Johns was in the Territorial 4th Duke of Cornwall's Light Infantry based in Truro. Johns was listed on the 1911 census as a car driver, so possibly he served the gentry family as a chauffeur. His military service is equally sketchy; however, he is commemorated on the Basra memorial in Iraq, one of over 40,000 men who died in the campaign against the Turks. He has no known grave. In 1911, Frank Blake from St Winnow on the edge of the parish was a 'domestic groom', living above the stables at Lanhydrock. After turning eighteen he sailed for Gallipoli with the Royal 1st Devon Yeomanry. The main fighting was over by the time of his arrival and so the regiment transferred first to Egypt, and then to Jerusalem along with the 16th Devonshire Regiment. Severely weakened by weeks of extensive fighting, shortages of food and ineffective horses, the Devonshires braved very difficult terrain and strong Turkish opposition, much of which involved close-quarter fighting. The Devonshires were obliged to retreat from the encounter in which Frank Blake was killed. Like others on the memorial, his body was never found.

One member of staff who was buried in a marked grave was Sidney Smith, a groom at Lanhydrock, who is buried at St Martin's church, Liskeard, some six miles from Lanhydrock. Smith, who lived above the Lanhydrock stable-block, most likely served either on the Western Front or in the Middle East until injury forced him home. Once fit he was attached to the labour corps, which afforded non-combatant roles to men still in uniform. As part of an agricultural company, he worked hard to maximize home-grown food supplies. Private Smith died in Wandsworth four days after the Armistice was declared, possibly of the influenza virus that was sweeping the country.

Mary, Viscountess Clifden, a devout high Anglican, was a benevolent landlord and charitable pillar of the community, observing the conflict from afar and living with her own personal loss. As the war progressed her sense of sacrifice grew, as her other sons were pulled deeper into the conflict. Soon after the loss

13 Personal papers of the Coad family.

9.5 Officers of the No. 4th Coy. Guards Machine Gun Battalion, March 1917. The Honourable Arthur Victor Agar-Robartes, MC (1887–1974), later 8th Viscount Clifden, is seated 2nd from left © National Trust/Lanhydrock.

9.6 The Honourable Alexander Agar-Robartes, MC (1895–1930). Alexander served with distinction in India after the war before committing suicide in 1930 © National Trust/Lanhydrock.

of Tommy she wrote to a friend, 'I still have four sons in France', even though her eldest was by now dead and buried.[14]

Tommy's brother, Victor, later 8th Viscount Clifden (1887–1974), served with the Devon Yeomanry before transferring first to the 2nd Battalion, Grenadier Guards, in July 1915 and then to the 1st Guards Brigade Machine Gun Regiment (fig. 9.5).[15] He was wounded three times and was later awarded the Military Cross. Cecil Agar-Robartes (1892–1939) left Cambridge University in 1915 and after a brief period with the Rifle Brigade he volunteered to join the newly formed Tank Corps, where he saw action with the 11th (K) Battalion in Europe during the so-called '100 days war' that led to the final victory. The youngest of the Agar-Robartes children was Alexander (1895–1930), who was twenty when he joined the 3rd Battalion, Grenadier Guards (fig. 9.6). He served at Loos simultaneously with his elder brother Tommy and within days of his brother's death received severe facial injuries. He returned to see action on the Somme and at Ypres and was awarded a Military Cross for conspicuous gallantry and leadership under shellfire. However, Alexander was a very sensitive character: traumatized by war he wrote moving poetry and struggled with his homosexuality after the Armistice.[16] In 1930 he jumped to his death from a Belgrave Square window.

The Agar-Robartes girls also served the war effort on the home front. In January 1916 Tommy's twin Everilda set up a Bodmin branch of the Kensington Pioneer Depot and later became director of the War Hospital Supply Depot. Her mother served as president, her sister Violet was a joint-treasurer and Emily Bone, wife of the Lanhydrock vicar, was secretary. Much of the money was raised from fêtes held at Lanhydrock; by the end of the conflict the depot had supplied 300,000 swabs, 20,000 bandages, 3,500 splints, 3,000 slings and 3,000 hospital bags as well as socks, bedsocks, handkerchiefs, flannels, shirts, pillows, pneumonia jackets, pyjamas, mufflers, mittens, slippers, bed jackets, pillowslips, helmets, crutches and vests.

When Viscountess Clifden launched HMS *Lion* in 1910 she could never have envisaged what the next few years had in store. It is fair to say that neither the family nor the parish were ever the same again. After hostilities had ceased she addressed the local Women's Institute and spoke of:

> the tremendous task of rebuilding all that has been so shaken by the terrible experiences of the past years. In the heart of all there is a desire that the new England should be worthy of the sacrifices made by her, and we look around for a sure foundation on which to build. The courage which helped us through the years of war is needed still.[17]

14 Private collection held by descendants of Marion Brown. **15** His application to join the Devon Yeomanry is dated 25 Dec. 1911. **16** Alexander published a poem in memory of Tommy entitled 'To a Brother' in the *Eton College Chronicle*, 11 Nov. 1915. **17** Quoted from Mike England, *A Victorian family at Lanhydrock: gone the happy dream* (Bodmin, 1999), p. 92.

Despite her outward reassurance, rebuilding her own family and the wider parish proved impossible. Tommy's death was a huge blow to the family. He was the most charismatic and confident of the children as well as a popular Liberal politician; indeed the future of the estate rested on him. Of his eight adult siblings, only two married and only one had a child. This heir, Rachel, went to live in Africa and wanted little to do with Lanhydrock, so in 1953 Viscount Clifden gave Lanhydrock House and 600 acres of estate land to the National Trust. By 1974, with the death of Victor, 8th viscount, the Agar-Robartes family line became extinct.

The parish too was in decline. With the loss of men during the war, numbers in the parish dwindled, a situation made worse by the collapse of agriculture and mining. None of the families named on the war memorial remain in the parish today. Lanhydrock's story is far from unusual; indeed most parishes contributed and suffered in this way – the many war memorials up and down the country are a reminder of that sacrifice.

'Let each man do his best': the Percy family and their staff in the Great War

CHRISTOPHER HUNWICK

This essay describes the experience of developing and delivering an exhibition (with the same title as this essay) at Alnwick Castle to mark the centenary of the First World War.[1] Work on the project began in 2012 at the duke of Northumberland's instigation. Staff of the collections and archives department worked very closely with the castle visitor experience team. At first there were two main sources that invited examination: the Roll of Honour for the Northumberland Estates, which hangs in the estate office, and letters to the 7th duke of Northumberland from his children.

The Roll of Honour lists the names of all those staff members and Percy family members who served in the war (the names of those who were killed are highlighted in gold) (fig. 10.1). A great deal of information is recorded: name and estate department; date of enlistment; which military service and regiment; field of service; date of demobilization and rank at that date. There is also a note column recording extra information such as 'wounded', 'gassed', 'frostbitten', 'PoW', and the award of special medals. An analysis of the roll led to initial surprise among the exhibition team at how few men, comparatively, had been killed in the war: eight names in gold from a total of eighty-one names. The pre-research inclination had been to assume a much higher proportion of fatalities than one in ten. The great variety of different services and regiments, serving across the globe, not just in France and Belgium, was also striking. It was quickly apparent, however, that there were omissions from the roll. For example, members of the household staff were entirely absent. This appears to be as a result of the administrative structure, whereby the estates office departments were under the aegis of the commissioner or head agent (who commissioned the roll in 1924), while the household staff reported to the constable of the castle. As research progressed, further names, absent perhaps through oversight, also became apparent.

The second main source, family letters of the period written to the 7th duke, was found to be a rich vein of material. One of the most frequent correspondents was Lord William Percy, one of the duke's younger sons, whose story turned out

---

1 The quotation at the chapter opening is taken from Harry Hotspur's speech to his men before the battle of Shrewsbury in Shakespeare's *Henry IV, Part I*, yet it sounds as if it could have been taken directly from one of Kitchener's recruitment posters. The essay is based on a talk given to the Yorkshire Country House Partnership seminar in Feb. 2015.

10.1 The Northumberland Estates Roll of Honour (Archives of the duke of
Northumberland at Alnwick Castle).

to be most interesting (fig. 10.2). He was born in 1882 and educated at Eton and
Christ Church, Oxford, before being called to the Bar by the Inner Temple in
1906. A man of firm morals and high standards, Lord William left the Bar in
disgust after disagreeing on principle with a judge in a murder case. He never
returned to the law except for a brief spell during military service in the Great
War. He concentrated instead on his ornithological interests, notably in species
of duck. At one time he possessed perhaps the best collection in the world of
duck skins, which he subsequently passed to natural history museums (1,200
skins, for example, went to the American Museum of Natural History in 1932).

10.2 Portrait photograph of Lord William Percy in legal attire
(Archives of the duke of Northumberland at Alnwick Castle).

In the spring of 1914, Lord William set off on an expedition to north-east Siberia in search of the spectacled eider duck, then thought to be extinct.[2] He had heard a story from a whaler who had been wrecked in Siberia and had survived by eating this rare bird! Lord William joined the *Bear*, a forty-year-old Dundee whaler that had been converted into a cutter, and which was familiar with Arctic waters. The *Bear* sailed from Seattle through the Gulf of Alaska and the Bering Sea via Unalaska and Nome to the Siberian coast. On this voyage Lord William's survival skills were severely tried. The most testing period, however, was when Lord William, a travelling companion and an Eskimo were stranded together on an island in a tent and came near to starvation. He wrote in his diary: 'I always thought one could live on anything for a week or ten days, but none of us can eat ducks without anything else any more. They simply won't go down.' He was later to write home from the trenches: 'I can't say this last week has been the height of comfort. It has rained and blown a gale for six whole days and the place is a sea of mud. However it is not nearly so bad as Siberia!' Luckily the stranded threesome were rescued by natives and Lord William was reunited with the crew of the *Bear*. It was aboard this ship that he heard about the outbreak of the war:

2 The following details are extracted from Lord William's arctic journal in the Archives of the duke of Northumberland at Alnwick Castle (henceforth Alnwick Castle), DNP: MS 807.

Got news about war. I heard of war first on August 3 by the merest
accident. We were 200 miles north of Bering Straits, and out of range of
the small Marconi set on the ship, but picked up what they call a 'freak'
message out of the air (not sent to the ship at all). It said that 'Lipton says
he won't race ... Cup England ... engaged war.' Also 'Belgian King ...
supreme appeal ... England ... Belgian neutrality.' Putting the two
together I asked the Captain to put me ashore at once and he did so at
Kotzebue, where there is a white man or two and a big native village, on
August 4.

He then had a thoroughly frustrating wait for eighteen days at Nome until the
next ship could take him. He finally arrived back at Liverpool on 24 September
and rushed to rejoin his regiment, the Grenadier Guards. In early November,
Lord William was sent out to France, where he served for five months at the
front and often in the trenches. His letters to his father during this period are an
excellent eyewitness account of life at the front. For example, writing from the
trenches on 20 November 1914, his ornithological interest is undaunted by shell
fire: 'One of the things that astonish me is the apparent indifference to the noise
displayed by the small birds. Great flocks of larks etc. just fly up when a battery
starts shooting and settle again within fifty yards!'[3] Later that month he
commented that his sister had sent him more supplies than he could carry, but
'There is only one thing I do want and that is a small tin of Vaseline once every
ten days. All our feet are more or less frostbitten and I find a copious dose of
grease is the best thing to keep them in commission.'[4]

On 11 March 1915, Lord William was shot at the battle of Neuve Chapelle
and sent back to England. He had been hit by a machine-gun bullet at 200 yards
range. His brother, Alan Ian, was able to see him shortly afterwards and sent the
following report in a letter to the duke:

He was wounded about 7 a.m. this morning, with a bullet through the
upper part of the left thigh ... As far as I could see it had gone through the
leg sideways starting on the inside where there was a small hole and
making a larger one on the outside. Of course he was weak as he had lost a
good deal of blood, but quite cheerful and full of conversation ... He lay
out under heavy shell fire for nearly two hours when the stretcher bearers
got him away most gallantly.[5]

The archives of the Grenadier Guards and The National Archives at Kew
shed further light on his war service.[6] In May 1915 the Medical Board reported
that the thigh wound had healed, but that the leg muscles were weak and that

---

3 Alnwick Castle, DP: D7/I/245.   4 Ibid.   5 Alnwick Castle, DP: D7/I/256.   6 TNA,
WO 339/8854.

Lord William could only walk short distances. A sedentary occupation was recommended. He therefore joined the Judge Advocate General's (JAG) Department in London, a fitting position given his legal training. Treatment on his leg by electricity and massage continued through May and June, until he was declared fit for duty at home or abroad with the JAG Department in mid-August.

Lord William transferred to the Mediterranean Expeditionary Force to cover for a sick deputy JAG, serving in Gallipoli for four months. He wrote to his father on the 22 September: 'We live within easy sight of Achi Baba and the sounds of war, and get bombed a good deal by aeroplanes, on four different occasions within the last few days. Damage practically nil. We had a great shoot at 2 aeroplanes that came and bombarded us this morning. The bombs make more noise than they do damage unless they get just the right place.' And he added that 'We are living in tents and at present that's all right, though the sand and dust go into and through everything and fill one's mouth with grit. What it will be like later on I don't know.'[7]

From January 1916 to May 1918, Lord William served in Egypt as a deputy JAG with the Egyptian Expeditionary Force. His letters give a sense of what this entailed: 'I sit on the bank of the canal and work in my office from 8.30 a.m. till 1 p.m., go for an hour's ride from 2.30–3.30 and then on with intervals for tea and drinks till 11 p.m. That is the daily routine'.[8] Asked about his work, he replied:

> I can only give you the words of Field Service Regulations at p. 48, Deputy JAG … advises a Commander 'on matters of military, martial and international law'. This country is under Martial Law, we try civilians for every sort and kind of offence in considerable numbers: questions about arrests of neutrals and others in every part of the Aegean … are always coming up. Every single trial by Court Martial or Military Court that is held in Egypt, Salonica, Mudios, Lemnos etc. comes through my hands.[9]

In May 1918, Lord William was promoted to assistant adjutant general, Jerusalem District, with the Occupied Enemy Territory Administration under General Allenby. Palestine had been a province of the Ottoman empire and the vast majority of its inhabitants were Arabs. Proclamations from the British military administration were issued in Hebrew, English and Arabic, and Lord William was involved in fearsome debate with Muftis, Patriarchs and Zionist leaders. An amusing anecdote from this time is related by Ronald Storrs, one of the governors during Lord William's time in Jerusalem:

> I was relieved to find that it was not only with me, or on literary topics, that Percy knew no compromise. He was an ornithologist of wide reputation

7 Alnwick Castle, DP: D7/1/262.   8 Alnwick Castle, DP: D7/I/270.   9 Alnwick Castle, DP: D7/I/274.

and I therefore asked him to show the Commander-in-Chief, on his first visit to my new Governorate, the Natural History Museum which the Germans had formed in the basement. On the way down I heard the Field-Marshal describe in detail a bird he had seen on the way up to Jerusalem, and ask its name. 'There *is* no such bird,' said Percy. At the first case they reached, I heard again: 'Why here's the very bird', but 'No one could have guessed that from *your* description', said Percy.[10]

Lord William resigned his commission in March 1920 and returned to his ornithological pursuits, travelling the world in the process.

His eldest brother's letters were also heavily drawn on for the exhibition at Alnwick in 2014. Alan Ian, Earl Percy, later 8th duke of Northumberland, was already a veteran by the outbreak of the war, having joined the Grenadier Guards in 1901 and fought with them in the South African campaign, followed by a spell in the camel corps of the Egyptian Army on the wild frontier at Kordofan. He served with distinction in the Great War as part of the Intelligence Department, co-writing the war communique concerning operations on the Western Front, known as 'Eye Witness', from 1914 to 1916. Earl Percy's letters to his father are filled with heated debate about the military tactics he saw being employed. The duke and his son disagreed strongly on several points. For example, in 1913 Earl Percy put his support behind Lord Roberts' campaign for universal compulsory military service, with which the duke could not agree. Many of Earl Percy's phrases in his letters have a prophetic quality, foreshadowing with startling accuracy the events that split Europe during the war. For example, in a letter of September 1915, he states that 'the whole social life of England is going to be entirely altered by this war'.[11] He was also outspoken on the disastrous Dardanelles campaign: 'All this business of the Dardanelles is very foolish. There is no harm in bombarding the ports but to land troops is suicidal. There is only one theatre of war for us – Belgium.'[12]

At this stage in the preparation of the exhibition, a concern was emerging that it would be very Percy-family-centric, given how rich was the material in the letters. The team turned to searching for sources for those on the Roll of Honour, and crucially those missing from it, especially household staff. Records of servants, however, are not particularly rich at Alnwick. As ever, the most reliable sources are financial records. The accounting ledgers for the period 1913–20 were scoured for lists of wages paid to household staff, and a list of servants was compiled.[13] It cannot be comprehensive, as certain types of employee tend to be grouped together for payment, such as carpet-beaters and boilermen, so individual names are not recorded. There are also periods when

10 Ronald Storrs, *Orientations* (London, 1937), pp 353–6 (I am grateful to Algernon Percy for this reference).   11 Alnwick Castle, DP: D7/I/262.   12 Letter written two months before the troops landed there; Alnwick Castle, DP: D7/I/256.   13 Alnwick Castle, uncatalogued material.

10.3 Sir Francis Walker, Bt, commissioner to the duke of Northumberland
(Archives of the duke of Northumberland at Alnwick Castle).

household staff were not in residence at Alnwick, when the ducal family resided at one of the other seats. Nonetheless, a fairly detailed listing has been compiled and it is quite clear that there was a gradual falling vacant of household positions during the war, which tended not to be refilled afterwards.

Employment ledgers were also consulted,[14] although these were difficult to interpret: one had been amended over decades with various coloured inks representing names and information for different years, with strikings through and tiny illegible scrawls between lines, while the other was in census format, giving only snapshots of staffing with intervals of several years between. The latter volume, however, does contain comments about wartime allowances to those serving, and at its front is a list of 'Office Boys' employed on a sort of apprentice scheme, which had begun in 1906. This list of boys records the date each boy entered the scheme, the date he left, and gives details of his subsequent employment (many having gone on to positions within the estate office). The entry for William Wood simply reads that he began in the office on 2 September 1914, and then in pencil is a note: 'killed in Great War'. This is the only mention

14 Alnwick Castle, A8/3–4.

of William Wood to be found in estate records, giving a further example of employees of the estate missing from the Roll of Honour.

The difficult job of running the estates with a depleted staff and extra wartime demands fell to Sir Francis Walker, as commissioner or head agent to the duke, a man with a dry wit easily discernible in his copy letter-books (fig.10.3). For instance, in August 1914, writing to the district valuer for Newcastle upon Tyne, concerning two pieces of land in Tynemouth:

> Dear Sir,
> I beg to acknowledge the receipt of your two letters of the 10th inst., which I hope to attend to at the end of the War, if the land in question then forms part of the British Empire.[15]

The copy letter-books are also an excellent source for military service information, particularly after the end of the war when Sir Francis was imploring the War Office to release his key office staff, saying the payment of death duties for the 7th duke would be impossible unless his staff were returned. The letter-books record, too, what the duke instructed with regard to care for the families of his staff absent on military service: that the families left were to be housed rent free; that a suitable weekly allowance should be made, to enable them to live in all respects as hitherto; that any further allowance should be made in case of sickness or other special occasion arising requiring help; furthermore, wherever possible, jobs were to be kept open for men who had served to resume their former position after the war.

Another record series, the business minutes, documenting the business activities of the estates from the mid-nineteenth century to the present, contains a vital source: a list of all staff on military service and their dependants who were to receive free accommodation. There are several more names appearing on this list than appear on the Roll of Honour, including members of household staff.

External sources were then used to cross-check military service and to try to flesh out some individual stories. Ancestry.com was utilized to search medal index cards, census records and service records. Often the census records highlighted siblings who might otherwise have been overlooked. The Northumberland County Record Office holds a complete run of the *Alnwick and County Gazette*; this local newspaper was a key source, containing reports of woundings and deaths, often with photographs. In many cases, the *Gazette* photograph was the only image we could trace of members of staff. Other photographic sources were very scarce, comprising irregular estates office staff photographs every decade or two, and one football team photograph (figs 10.4 & 10.5). The *Gazette* also featured correspondence home from the troops; several letters from or concerning estates staff were discovered. For example, one was

15 Alnwick Castle, uncatalogued material.

W.H. Hendry, G.E. Wilson, A. Douglas, R. Steven, J.A. Anderson, J.H. Ferguson, J.W. Elliott,
R. Kyle, F. Temperley, R.S. Wright, Sir F.E. Walker Bt, G.R. Darling, T.F. Hedley, W.F. Meech,
S. Vernon, G.N. Lowes

10.4 1925 Estates office staff photograph (Archives of the duke of Northumberland at Alnwick Castle).

10.5 Park Farm football team photograph (Archives of the duke of Northumberland at
Alnwick Castle).

published from a chaplain, describing the burial of John William Ternent, a former farm labourer on the estate who was killed in action on 25 January 1916. The letter mentioned that John's brother had been present at the funeral. John is on the Roll of Honour, but his brother, David, is not. David was traced in the employment ledgers as a woodsman, and his military service record was discovered, proving that he ought to have been included on the Roll.

Once research was completed, various individual stories were chosen to be highlighted in the exhibition. A certain story might have a strong element of pathos, such as Robert Dalgarno Chrystal, the woods foreman, who died in a train accident just three days before the Armistice; or a story was chosen to illustrate the different experiences of the war encountered by estate staff. For example, John Stewart Carr, an office boy, joined the RAF in 1918 and found himself in the Black Sea on board a converted packet ship acting as an aircraft carrier. Another staff member served on the home front: Frederick Eli Silk was a veteran of twenty-three years in the Royal Navy, had seen active service in the Zulu War, and served on the royal yacht. He had retired and become a lodge-keeper for the duke of Northumberland (since the eighteenth century, many of the duke's lodge-keepers had been retired military personnel). Silk was summoned out of retirement, aged fifty-three, as a naval reservist and served for the duration of the war at Portsmouth Barracks, charged with keeping 14,000 men entertained with twelve billiard tables and a gymnasium converted for showing films. After the war he returned to Alnwick as a lodge-keeper and worked until his ninety-fifth birthday, when, in his own words: 'His Grace was pleased to allow me to retire'![16] (fig. 10.6)

An appeal was also launched in the local newspapers and online asking for descendants of those on the Roll of Honour to come forward with information. Quite a significant response was received, with much extra information gathered and even offers of loans of material for the exhibition. One very poignant example was the loan of the personal effects of Joseph Forster as returned from the German prisoner-of-war camp where he died, in the original envelope labelled 'Nachlassliste [personal effects] XXXV'. Forster was the youngest son of one of the duke's gardeners. By 1898 he was a plumber's labourer on the estate. He enlisted with the 7th Battalion of the Northumberland Fusiliers in 1915 and was taken prisoner in March 1918. He died of illness in captivity six months later, on 15 September. The items returned to his family included photographs of his wife and three daughters, a sewing kit, a prayer card and a letter from his daughters. Forster was one of the men puzzlingly missing from the Roll.

A suitable location for the exhibition within the castle site was decided on. The visitor exit route from the castle's state rooms utilized the servants' staircase and below-stairs corridor, which during the twentieth century had been appropriated for office space, with grey carpet tiles and modern lighting.

16 Memoirs of Frederick Eli Silk; Alnwick Castle, DNM: H/3/9.

10.6 Frederick Eli Silk on his ninety-sixth birthday (Archives
of the duke of Northumberland at Alnwick Castle).

Utilizing a floor plan from *c*.1900 and an inventory of 1908, the original
Edwardian era look and feel of this part of the castle has been restored. The
butler's room has been set dressed with period furniture, gramophone and
books, and the exhibition has been placed within this setting. This room is
indeed where news might have been received about household staff absent at
war.

The butler's bedroom has been decorated in the same fashion, but not set-
dressed. This room has been set aside as a memorial room containing an audio-
visual installation and a new Roll of Honour in the form of vinyl lettering applied
to the wall. This new Roll includes all the extra names discovered during
research, taking the total number of names to 112, with 13 deaths highlighted in
gold, compared with 81 and 8 respectively on the original version.

The audio installation features the names from the new Roll being read out,
along with their occupations and ranks, where known; wherever possible, the
person reading the entry is the successor in office today or a descendant of the
named person. There was a strong level of participation in the exhibition by staff
across the estate and by the descendants who contacted us. The result is a very
moving tribute to all those who served on the occasion of the centenary. The
results of the research undertaken on each of the men are also now available in a
searchable database on the Alnwick Castle website, which is intended as a
permanent feature.

Lady Londonderry and the Great War:
women, work and the Western Front

BRETT IRWIN

Edith Chaplin was born in 1878, the eldest daughter of Henry Chaplin, a landowner and Conservative Party MP, and Lady Florence Levenson-Gower. Edith's mother died when she was just four years old. She and her brother and sister were largely raised by their uncle and aunt, the duke and duchess of Sutherland. On 28 November 1899, she married Charles Stewart, the then Viscount Castlereagh. In February 1915, on his father's death, Charles became 7th marquess of Londonderry and heir to a vast fortune. Edith played a leading role in Irish and British social and political life from her estate at Mount Stewart in Co. Down and the renowned Londonderry House in London's Park Lane. She was vice-president of the Ulster Women's Unionist Association from 1919 until her death in 1959. She inspired awe and affection in equal measure and many found her energy and enthusiasm hard to resist; but she was so much more than a *grande dame*. She was devoted to helping other women in the search for equality, and sometimes, against very personal criticism, she strove to win the vote for women, and challenge views commonly held at that time regarding women and their role in society. Although she was more suffragist than suffragette, she showed great conviction in her endeavours for women to be given the opportunity to prove themselves in supporting the war effort and thereby play a full role in society. Her papers form part of a wider collection, the Londonderry Papers, held in the Public Record Office of Northern Ireland (PRONI). This essay, while looking at the effect of the Great War on a prominent Anglo-Irish family, will also examine the effects a member of that family had on the war itself.

A fascinating aspect of Lady Londonderry's war was her club, the Ark, formed in 1915. The Ark was established to provide relaxation and escape for friends involved in war work. It soon took on the role of a *salon* and became a select social club that maintained the Stewart family's influence at the heart of the British establishment during the war years. Lady Londonderry also inspired great loyalty and confidence in her many military friends who served on the Western Front. The letters from her sister, Florence Chaplin, serving as nurse with the International Red Cross in Serbia, provide some fascinating insights into the situation in the field hospitals on the Eastern Front. These provided information on the conditions and effects of the war that few outside the military command could possibly know. Such were her connections and influence that much of the correspondence bypassed military censors and she knew what conditions on the Western Front were actually like, contrary to the widely held 'great adventure' that was prevalent particularly in the early stages of the war.

The Women's Volunteer Reserve formed by Evelina Haverfield began to provide a role for women in the early stages of the war. It was one of the first women's voluntary organizations, but members had to pay for their own uniform, which at £2 excluded many would-be volunteers. Lady Londonderry became involved and relished her role as colonel-in-chief of the Women's Volunteer Reserve but was aware of the limitations of the organization. She realized the potential for a more inclusive women's movement to be involved with the war effort and in July 1915 she founded the Women's Legion (fig. 11.1). She used all of her connections and influence to recruit women to this movement. Lady Londonderry, writing after the war in her book *Retrospect* (1938), pondered what had been done: 'It became obvious that there was room for some organization of women on a large scale, not only for emergency work as and when required, but for all those other duties where women could take the place of men called to the colours.'[1] This was a non-political, cross-class organization structured along military lines. Lady Londonderry wanted working women to replace working men, thus freeing men to fight at the front and giving women an essential role to play in the war effort despite initial ridicule from prominent members of the establishment.

Lady Londonderry set up a military cooking section that became the nucleus of the future Women's Auxiliary Army Corps of the British Army. This section produced as many as 40,000 trained cooks, many of whom worked at army camps and military hospitals during the war. Other Women's Legion members became motor and ambulance drivers, despatch riders and technicians, from whom the Motor Transport Section was later formed. The Women's Legion drivers played a vital role in driving ambulances sometimes during air raids and meeting trains at all hours to bring home wounded soldiers. After the war a large number of drivers were sent to France to help with demobilization. In one of her letters Lady Londonderry recounts a humorous exchange between a Women's Legion driver and an American general at the end of the war. The general was waiting impatiently for his car: 'Hurry up, Hurry up', he said, 'you are two minutes late.' 'Well, jump in,' said the Women's Legion driver, 'You are three years late.'[2] The Women's Legion agriculture unit also played a vital role: ploughing, tractor-driving, thatching, threshing and fruit-picking needed to be done and the population had to be fed. Lady Londonderry was at the heart of ensuring women stepped in to do this essential land work.

1 Marchioness of Londonderry, *Retrospect* (Manchester, 1938); see also Diane Urquhart, *The ladies of Londonderry: women and political patronage* (London, 2007).   2 PRONI, Londonderry Papers, D3099/3/25/1/1.

11.1 Lady Londonderry in Women's Legion Uniform.

Lady Londonderry also supported the establishment of aid stations in France with the help of the YMCA and Princess Victoria. She gave over two of the family's grand homes, Londonderry House in London and Wynyard House in Durham, for use as military hospitals. She made a personal visit to France in November 1914 to support the work of the YMCA (fig. 11.2). The field support services set up by it offered troops a welcome respite from the trenches and somewhere they could relax, drink tea and write letters home. These became known as 'welfare huts' and would prove to be of vital service.

The success of the Women's Legion was a definite factor in influencing the government to organize female labour along official lines during the latter part of the war. Lady Londonderry's contribution to the war effort was recognized when she was made a Dame Commander of the Order of the British Empire on the 25 August 1917. The following January her DBE was upgraded from a civilian honour to a military one in acknowledgment of the military contribution of the Women's Legion to the war. The influence and commitment of Lady Londonderry and the Women's Legion made a significant contribution to the lives of thousands of women in Ireland and Britain and arguably paved the way

11.2 Lady Londonderry's YMCA Identification Card.

for the Representation of the People Act of 1918, whereby 8.4 million women gained the right to vote. It cannot be denied that the act, with its age and property limitations, still favoured middle-class women; but it shook and changed the orderly routine of the British parliamentary system. It was a decisive step on the long road to full women's suffrage. The old arguments of women being unfit to vote because of inferiority to men were discredited in a post-war world. It had been a hard-fought campaign, but women proved that they could serve the war effort by commitment, talent and heavy toil.

Lady Londonderry's Ark club was based in Londonderry House (fig. 11.3). Originally, the male and female members of the club were involved in war work, and the purpose of the club was to provide relaxation. The Ark was a place of safety and companionship, although puns on *archaic* were made in jest. Lady Londonderry later reflected on the formation of the Ark:

> We decided that once a week, at any rate, we would relax from serious events and to be thoroughly frivolous. Any friends, who were on leave from the front used to turn up. Some of our friends were Cabinet Ministers or Secretaries of State … We decided to call ourselves the Ark, feeling that Londonderry House was sufficiently antiquated to merit the title.[3]

The Ark had a rather strange entrance code whereby members had to adopt an animal name (real or mythological) to gain admission. Lady Londonderry's Ark name was Circe, the enchantress who seduced Odysseus and turned his crew into

3 PRONI, D3099/3/12/5.

Yᵉ Archaic Ark Association.

Yᵉ arrival of yᵉ Ancient Ark on Mount Ararat situated on yᵉ Island of Æǣa.

(Note the Sorceress receiving the inmates as they disembark and transforming them into animals).

11.3 Ye Archaic Ark Association.

swine. All members were referred to by their Ark name, which bore some alliterative relationship to their own name: thus, Winston Churchill was Winston the Warlock, Admiral Lord Beatty was David the Dolphin and Lady Londonderry's daughter Maire became Maire the Mare. Other members

11.4 David the Dolphin.   **11.5** Linky the Lemur.

included Princess Helena Victoria (Victoria the Vivendiere); General John Cowan (Merry John the Mandrill); Unionist leader Edward Carson (Edward the Eagle); Lord Balfour (Arthur the Albatross); Lady Londonderry's husband, Charles (Charlie the Cheetah) and Lord Hugh Cecil (Linky the Lemur) (figs 11.4 & 11.5).

The Ark seems to have lasted until well into the 1930s and came to include many distinguished figures in politics, society and the arts during the inter-war years. While undoubtedly fabulously eccentric, the Ark also served a political purpose. Edith secured the family's place at the centre of politics such was the illustrious members' list. Lady Carson famously remarked that the Ark was 'not as silly as it sounds and outsiders are very jealous and inquisitive'.[4] The name also suggests a sanctuary from the storms of war and an Arcadian Revellers Committee consisting of nine members decided on the election or rejection of members. The Ark's composition was never exclusively political. Membership grew to include literary and artistic figures, among them Edmund Gosse, Sean O'Casey, Philip Sassoon, John and Hazel Lavery, and Peter Ward Price, editor of the *Daily Mail*.

Among the papers relating to the Ark held in PRONI is a poem entitled 'Arkeology', which although riddled with puns, captures something of the spirit of the Ark. One verse goes as follows:

4 PRONI, D1507/C/2.

> You will find there a Queen, a jockey, a Dean,
> With perfect affinities sorted;
> A sculptor, an actress,
> A world – benefactress
> By crowned Heads and clergymen courted.[5]

Another revealing component of Lady Londonderry's Papers at PRONI from this period is the often candid correspondence she received from influential figures serving in the British military. Such was the range and depth of her friendships that she was privy to information that appears on occasion to have bypassed strict military censorship. A great friend of Lady Londonderry's was General William Pulteney, commander of the British Army's 3rd Corps. These letters describe in detail the German retreat from the Marne river. The first battle of the Marne, fought between 5 and 9 September 1914, was a strategic victory for the allied forces and halted one of the major objectives of the Schlieffen Plan, the capture of Paris. Pulteney, in a letter to Lady Londonderry, voices his displeasure in taking over a chateau formerly occupied by the Germans and the lack of suitable refreshments: 'Took good care to take the sheets off the bed the last two nights as Germans had slept there the previous nights, the brutes had drunk all the champagne here the previous nights'.[6]

Lady Londonderry's husband Charles was General Pulteney's aide-de-camp, a posting he frequently complained about due to the initial lack of military action (fig. 11.6). Although Pulteney's earlier letters to Lady Londonderry have a somewhat candid and jolly tone and are meant to reassure her that her husband was in no danger, the mood darkens as the war continues and harsher realities regarding the preparedness of the British Army in dealing with trench warfare became clear:

> We are in little danger here except for the odd shell on the top of the hill … You must start conscription at home, get the depots built to hold the recruits, physical training is what the nation wants, and do it on proper lines … Jack was killed yesterday morning looking over the parapet in broad daylight, it really is too sad, such splendid soldiers, knowing our strategy was faulty.[7]

Charles, writing to Lady Londonderry in the early stages of the war, vented his annoyance and frustration at his staff job and the situation that had developed on the Western Front:

> I realised that I am doing no good here. There is a certain amount of honour and glory in being 'at the front' and not left behind in England;

5 PRONI, D3099/3/12/2.   6 PRONI, D3099/3/9/1/1.   7 Ibid.

but for useful work I should be doing more of it anywhere but here ... However I made my own choice, worked tooth and nail to get this job, worried and bothered you to get it for me and now when I have got it I am not pleased ... We have got Armentieres I understand. One ought never be pessimistic I know; but I really don't feel very hopeful about it all. The Germans seem to do exactly what they want; they take Antwerp, Ostend, Lille etc etc and we never seem to be able to stop them, and all we have to set against that are little short advances at the capture of a village.[8]

Florence Chaplin, Lady Londonderry's sister, volunteered as a nurse for the International Red Cross in Serbia in February 1915. She wrote candid letters to her sister describing the conditions of the field hospitals and the problems she had to face:

The only way the infection spreads is through lice, and then it has to be one that has bitten a typhus patient, so, provided you are careful not to get the creatures on you, there is no reason for catching it ... It is when you get a whole crowd of dirty patients that it is so difficult to keep them clean and prevent the bugs getting on to other people. There is a Greek doctor in charge, who, mercifully, speaks French, but two other Servian doctors appear at moments, and I have to struggle with them in German. I have a German orderly, and bitterly regret not having worked more industriously with Fraulein. Incidentally, there is a Russian Masseuse who only speaks atrocious German, and I have to struggle to translate the doctor's orders for him, so you can imagine the confusion. What with Centigrade and Fahrenheit temperatures and their measures for medicines, the few brains I have are getting thoroughly addled.[9]

These letters from Serbia provide insights into the lesser documented war on the Eastern Front. This arena also saw slaughter on an industrial scale, with large, set-piece battles over expansive landscapes. It did not have the stalemate of the Western Front and yet it has to take second place to English-speaking military historians who have been preoccupied with events in France and Belgium.

In another letter from September 1915, Lady Londonderry recounts the first time she experienced a Zeppelin attack on London:

We had a great excitement here on Wednesday night. Six or seven bombs were heard. I saw the Zeppelin beautifully, about two miles up, and the shells of the anti-aircraft guns were distinctly visible, but they were bursting a long way beneath her. The guns made a good deal of noise and added to the excitement, as most people thought they were bombs dropping. The guns we heard were those in Hyde Park, St James's Park

8 PRONI, D3099/3/1/312.   9 PRONI, D3099/3/2/7/1.

and Green Park. The patients were very excited, and were hopping about in their pyjamas on the balcony. At the same time, the results of those huge bombs are not at all reassuring. They are about 240 lbs and go clean through everything. From what I saw myself, I am convinced if one struck this house it would go through it as if it were paper. One hit Liverpool Street Station, and went clean through the whole thing into the underground, smashed the water pipes and flooded the tunnel; ten people were killed here.[10]

Although there can be no mistaking the sheer terror the Zeppelins brought to London, Lady Londonderry's description gives it a certain surreal quality: the image of these enormous aircraft silhouetted against the night sky while London burns, and the patients in their pyjamas on the balcony of Londonderry House (in use as an officers' hospital at that time).

Another close friend of Lady Londonderry's was Captain William Cavendish-Bentinck of the Cavalry Corps. In one letter to her he describes poison gas being used on the Western Front for the first time. At 5 p.m. on 22 April 1915 the Germans released chlorine gas over a four-mile front of the line held by divisions of the French Army during the second battle of Ypres. The French troops caught up in the cloud of gas had thousands of casualties, many of whom died within minutes. Chlorine gas, denser than air, forced soldiers out of the trenches and into heavy fire. This letter records the near mutiny of the French units in what would prove to be a dark day in the history of the war:

> The scene the first night of this affair in Poperinghe was awful, as all the French Territorials and Zoaves who bolted from the gasses let off by the Germans, on their way to Poperinghe met their transport coming up and told them that all was lost and that the Germans had got hold of Ypres, We put a cordon of Infantry across the road with fixed bayonets, it was only with this persuasion that order was restored and the French troops persuaded to go back to their trenches.[11]

In other very poignant letters, Cavendish-Bentinck offers us some remarkable insights into the great feeling of pride and optimism expressed by the Cavalry Corps in August 1914 when they have 'just sighted the French coast and the troops are cheering'.[12] But later, in November, and in stark contrast, he informs Lady Londonderry of the grim realities and human cost of this new type of war on the Western Front in which cavalry would have a much reduced role: 'Of fifteen thousand that came out in August 1914, only five thousand now remain.'[13]

10 PRONI, D3099/3/2/25.   11 PRONI, D3099/3/8/1/2; see also R.J. Steel and J.L. Williams, *Gas!: battle for Ypres 1915* (Ontario, 1985).   12 PRONI, D3099/3/8/1/1. 13 PRONI, D3099/3/8/1/2.

11.6 Charles, Lord Londonderry, in the uniform of a staff officer
of the Royal Horse Guards.

Lady Londonderry had an impact on the war, just as it had on her. The
organization of female labour along military lines was a shock to some members
of the establishment, but by the end of the war an estimated eighty per cent of
the labour in Britain was performed by women.[14] The Women's Legion became

14 Londonderry, *Retrospect*, p. 110.

the most influential of women's wartime associations as it influenced the army to incorporate official women's military sections. By 1917 the armies of Australia, Canada and New Zealand had also formed women's military units. The Ark club kept the Stewart family at the heart of the political and social scene during the war, and heightened Lady Londonderry's prestige and aura, with her ability to bring people together and make things happen. The wartime correspondence offers us detailed and personal insights into the grim realities of a conflict for which there was no precedent. Lady Londonderry was a feminist, albeit with a strong sense of familial bonds and a sense of duty, but a feminist nonetheless. The Londonderry Papers in PRONI are a major resource for the study of local and international history.[15]

15 All material used with permission of the deputy keeper of Records, Public Record Office of Northern Ireland.

The Hely-Hutchinson brothers of Seafield and the Great War: two sons, one inheritance

In November 2011, Fingal County Council Archives received a donation of the papers of the Hely-Hutchinson family, originally of Swords. A branch of the earls of Donoughmore of Knocklofty and later Palmerstown, they owned two Big Houses (with estates) in the Swords and Donabate areas of North County Dublin, namely Seafield and Lissenhall.

John Hely-Hutchinson, DL, JP and county sheriff for Dublin, had two sons, Coote Robert (b.1870) and Richard George (b.1871), known as Dick, as well as three daughters (fig. 12.1). Both boys were sent to boarding schools in England, which operated as preparatory schools for the British Military Academy. Both sons served with distinction with the Royal (London) Fusiliers before and during the Great War, reaching the rank of lieutenant-colonel, and both were decorated. Dick spent most of the war at the front and, fortunately, was an avid letter writer. As an officer he was able to write uncensored letters from the various fronts home to his wife, father, mother, brother and sisters, many of which survive as part of the collection. These give a detailed first-hand account of life at the front.

Their lives after the war were quite different. Coote returned to run the estate, was appointed a sheriff of Co. Dublin like his father, was elected as a member of Dublin County Council, and became heavily involved in the promotion of agriculture, particularly through the Royal Dublin Society, and the provision of mental health services. Dick, however, was cut off financially, just before the war, by his father, for marrying the 'wrong' girl, Alice Cunningham, from a well-to-do Church of England family in Belfast, and he remained in the army after the war, until retirement.[1] Almost every significant event in their lives is recorded in the documents that form part of the Hely-Hutchinson collection, including a vast collection of photographs, many taken by family members. This chapter draws on these original records.

Coote and Dick Hely-Hutchinson were born into a privileged Anglo-Irish family that had a long and distinguished military history. Their grandfather, the Hon. Coote Hely-Hutchinson of Palmerstown, Lucan, had gained the rank of captain in the Royal Navy, and it was he who brought the family to Swords, having inherited Lissenhall House and demesne through marriage. Coote's

1 See below, p. 149.

12.1 C.R. & D.G. Hely-Hutchinson © Hely-Hutchinson Collection, Fingal County Archives.

brother, the Hon. Henry Hely-Hutchinson of Weston Hall, Northamptonshire, was an army colonel. Their great-grand-uncle was Lt-General Richard Hely-Hutchinson, 1st earl of Donoughmore of Knocklofty, Co. Tipperary. While their father, John, as Coote's eldest son, returned from Oxford to take over the family estate, their uncle Francis followed in his father's footsteps and joined the navy. Through marriage they were related to numerous officers in both the army and navy.

Coote and Dick's father was an enthusiastic huntsman, who fished and rode, and he was an advocate of teaching boys to shoot from an early age. Among his papers is a selection of correspondence with a number of hunting-gun manufacturers and shooting magazines in England, in which he discusses the finer points of various aspects of the sport.[2] Possibly for financial reasons, only Coote was sent to the traditional Hely-Hutchinson alma mater, Harrow (fig. 12.2). Dick was sent to a newly opened school in Clifton, Bristol.[3] Both schools were regarded as 'feeders' for a life in the army or navy. Dick excelled at sports while in Clifton, and represented the school at boxing.

2 This correspondence is in the Hely-Hutchinson Collection, Fingal Archives (FCCA). The collection's original letters, postcards, documents, photographs and objects formed the basis of the exhibition entitled 'The Hely-Hutchinsons of Swords and the Great War' at Fingal Local Studies and Archives, Swords, in 2016. 3 There is a connection between the family

12.2 Coote (front left) at Harrow © Hely-Hutchinson Collection, Fingal County Archives.

The Hely-Hutchinson collection contains many of the original certificates awarded to the two young men during their training as soldiers. There are certificates in musketry for both from the School of Musketry in Hythe. Dick later qualified as a gymnasium and fencing instructor, while Coote became an instructor in musketry. They both ended up in cavalry regiments within the Royal (City of London) Fusiliers. There is no explanation, nor any obvious family reason, for their choice of the same regiment, but as members of the lower rungs of the Anglo-Irish landed gentry the more exclusive regiments were beyond their financial means. Coote reached the regiment by training as part of a militia.[4] Dick received his training as an ordinary cadet, not as a gentleman, as can be seen from the adjustments to his original examinations results sheet.[5] As soon as Coote had reached a sufficiently high rank, as the eldest son he was able to retire on half-pay to Dublin, and is pictured in Phoenix Park in August 1897 in full fusilier uniform after his regiment had received new colours from the duchess of York.[6]

Dick spent the next forty years in the army until he retired on full pay. He served as a cavalry officer in various parts of India, and in Malta. The photo

and Clifton. Their grandfather, Captain Coote, was born and died there.   **4** FCCA/HH/ 10/01.   **5** FCCA/HH/10/03.   **6** FCCA/ HH/PA/1/5.

12.3 Alice Cunningham
© Hely-Hutchinson
Collection, Fingal
County Archives.

albums in the collection dating from this period suggest that the greatest challenge he faced was probably boredom. There were certainly a lot of gymkhana and polo matches in India, and a lot of hunting, and there is one photograph of him accompanying a maharajah.[7] Writing to his mother on 3 October 1905 from Jalaphar, Darjeeling, he says: 'This place is cram full now, with people up for the poojah holidays, & a most dull & uninteresting lot they are. The next 12 days is full of diversion in the way of dancing, racing, etc.'[8] None of this was preparation for the type of war that Dick would encounter in France and Flanders.

The disapproval of the family regarding Dick's engagement to Alice Cunningham, and Dick's attempt to avoid a confrontation, can be sensed in this letter to his mother, written from Aldershot on 5 July, possibly in 1898: 'I hope you did not think me a beast running away & not waiting till you came home but I did so want to see my lady love. Give my best love to everybody at home. Write and tell me the news, you may tell anybody you like I am engaged now.'[9] Defying his father's wishes was to have major consequences for Dick.[10] Following his marriage, Alice, an accomplished sportswoman and horse-rider, accompanied Dick to his postings in Darjeeling and Secunderabad, and she contributed to the many photograph albums of that time (fig. 12.3).

At the outbreak of war in 1914, Dick, Alice and their new daughter, Pamela, were living in Kinsale, where he was attending an officer training camp in Fermoy. Before he was sent to France, Dick needed to settle his immediate

7 Ibid.   8 FCCA/HH/1/6/1.   9 FCCA/HH/1/10/00.   10 See below.

family, but rather than move them into Seafield with the in-laws, where there was plenty of room, Dick rented a house in Foxrock. Writing to his mother before sailing from Kinsale, he closed with: 'Well, best of love to you all & look after Pam & Alice; & keep your spirits up. I hope Kaiser Bill will take it in the neck before this war is finished.'[11] The 1st Battalion sailed from Kinsale direct to France. Dick spent the next four years in France and Flanders; he was wounded three times, cited in despatches and later histories of the Royal London Fusiliers, and earned a DSO (fig. 12.4). He would write home lengthy and detailed descriptions of a completely different type of war to that which had gone before, with descriptions of trenches, and snipers, and no-man's land, which though familiar to us now must have been shocking for his family to read back in Dublin.

For his elder brother, Coote, it would be a completely different war. Based in various training centres in England, he would spend the war teaching new recruits how to shoot, and how to use the new machinery of war, such as the Maxim machine-gun. Married to Julia Vere Browne Clayton of Carlow, he was able to go home regularly. He would become a father to twins in 1914, and three more children would follow.

The tone and content of Dick's letters depend very much on to whom he was writing. His early 1914 letters to his mother are full of assurances that he is fit and well, with descriptions of the French farms and countryside:

> We came in here at 3 a.m. yesterday morning. We are in a farm house & very comfortable, they have most beautiful farm buildings here, enormous barns & stables, & acres & acres of corn, most of which is not stacked yet. There are no fences, great big bare plateaus, with very deep valleys & thick woods, ideal places for artillery fighting, as they get very long ranges & good concealment, both sides use aeroplanes for fire detection.[12]

His letters to his sister Cissy are more revealing about life in the trenches, but maintain a matter-of-fact tone:

> We had a little fighting in the last place we were, but only a small affair, but we lost quite a lot of killed & wounded considering the numbers out. No officer was hit, but the C.O. in charge had two men killed on one side & two on the other; so he breathed a sigh of relief. The difficulty was getting the wounded into the trenches again, as we could not send out till dark, as the German trenches were only 700 yds away & we both sniped each other all day. We got them all in at night including the dead. There seems to be a pause here at present & we hear no news at present.[13]

11 FCCA/HH/1/10/01.   12 FCCA/HH/1/6/4.   13 FCCA/HH/1/6/5.

12.4 Richard George Hely-Hutchinson in uniform © Hely-Hutchinson Collection, Fingal County Archives.

He adopted a similar stance in his letters to Alice which begin to reveal more of the grim life in the trenches:

> We had a sad business last night. We had had no loss all day, till about ½ hour before dusk, when a Welch Fusilier was trying to get back to his trenches, with some tea, when he was hit by a sniper. The Artillery observing officer saw him & went out to try & get him in [but] he was hit, & then two of our men went to try to get him in & they were hit too all badly, & the cause of all the trouble was only very lightly hit, & could have remained out quite well where he was till it was dark.[14]

He shows that he is aware that the lists of dead, wounded and missing appear every day in the newspapers back home, and tells her that she 'must remember that a large number of those are not really seriously wounded & will all get alright'.[15] However, he also goes on to explain that 'these new sharp nosed bullets make worse wounds than the old ones, as when they meet a bone they turn over, which of course is very bad for the bone'.[16]

Writing to his father in December 1914 he joked: 'Many congratulations on your 78th Birthday, I had no idea you were that old … We spend so many days wading in mud up to our waists & then so many days getting dry again. You would not believe the state of the trenches its worse than any mud you can imagine. We came out the night before last, & the men are not dry yet.'[17] But his letters from January 1915 betray a growing exhaustion: 'we are becoming more like rats every day; it is very hard to say what is going on. The Germans attacked

14 FCCA/ HH/1/6/7. 15 Ibid. 16 Ibid. 17 FCCA/HH/1/6/10.

12.5 Richard George Hely-Hutchinson at Seafield, January 1915 © Hely-Hutchinson Collection, Fingal County Archives.

at La Bassée & lost heavily, they attacked again this morning & again lost very heavily somewhere near the same place. They can't go on doing this for ever.'[18] His father was spared none of the gory details in March, perhaps as Dick himself became more immune to the horrors he witnessed around him:

> The trenches were in an awful state, one trench we had to abandon & dig a new one, we filled in the old one with 26 dead bodies in it, some of them all swollen up & so churned into the mud & slush that we could not pull them out even with a rope. In another they had to take the bodies out in bits & bury them, as the arms etc. came away if you pulled them. I should think we buried at least 120 bodies, all under heavy fire at night.[19]

When Dick received news in the same month of his own mother's death, he wrote to Cissy: 'It is a great thing when you die to die without pain, & I can never make out why one man out here has a lingering death & the next man is shot dead'.[20]

In June 1915, Alice received a telegram from Dick: 'Slight wound in the head from shell graze. Will probably come over tomorrow or next day.'[21] He thought

18 FCCA/HH/1/6/11.   19 FCCA/HH/1/6/13.   20 FCCA/HH/1/6/14.   21 FCCA/HH/10/03.

he would be getting some sick leave, but the War Office thought better, and wrote to Alice saying he would remain on duty (fig. 12.5). In 1916, Dick was wounded more seriously, twice. He was shot in the foot in March and gave a vivid description of the event in a letter to Cissy from a hospital in London on 29 March: 'about this time some Boches suddenly appeared in the road & all the men wanted to leave, however I rounded them up & started them to return the fire, & at that moment I got a bullet in the foot.'[22] Dick returned to the front and in August sprained his ankle when he was thrown from a horse; he appeared in *The Tatler* in October 1916 on the steps of HM the King of Portugal's Hospital, Brighton, on crutches. The following month, his father celebrated his eightieth birthday. Happy though the occasion may have been, John Hely-Hutchinson took the opportunity to get his doctor to confirm that he was in full control of his faculties, and then wrote Dick out of his inheritance. Notes survive among his papers that outline the reasons for this decision: 'My will which I have just now read gives the whole of my property, real and personal absolutely to Coote.' John had made a previous will in August, but says he did not understand then that it would mean £5,000 for Dick. 'To give any such appointment', he writes, 'would be the act of a fool. It gives the Belfast woman [Alice] at Dick's death the power of putting £5,000 in her own pocket ... absolutely destroying Coote's estate.' 'What I wish to do is make Dick independent of his wife. Whether Dick will get possession of his daughter I do not know but am quite certain the Belfast woman would sell her soul much less her daughter for £5,000.' On another page he notes: 'For the past 30 years my chief desire has been to leave Coote an unencumbered estate.'[23] His desire to leave Coote an 'unencumbered estate' would not have been unusual around this time, with so many recent changes to Irish land ownership legislation as a result of the sale and break up of so many the large estates.

The family correspondence of 1917 shows that his father had neither discussed nor informed Dick of these new arrangements. On 1 February, Dick wrote that he noticed no payments had been made into his account since the previous July. By 18 February he had obviously received a reply from his father, and complains of his treatment 'over the allowance question'. He continues:

> When the war started, you at once cut down my allowance by £50, without ever letting me know, or giving me any intimation that you had done so; and now after having paid me an allowance for 25 years, you simply stop sending it, without any word of explanation or warning; a thing you could perfectly easily have done when I was staying in your house last Dec., just about the time it was done ... Here I am, a Lt. Col. with 26 years' service, doing my best in this great war, & you treat me with as little consideration as you would a clerk.

22 FCCA/HH/1/6/15.   23 FCCA/HH/71/3.

12.6   Coote Robert Hely-
Hutchinson in uniform
© Hely-Hutchinson Collection,
Fingal County Archives.

The second of the two letters is marked 'Dick's last letter'.[24] Dick returned to
France in November 1917 as Administrative Commandant of the British armies
in France until November 1918.

John Hely-Hutchinson died in 1919, and with the war over Lt-Col. Coote
Hely-Hutchinson retired from the army and returned to Swords to take over the
family estate (fig. 12.6). In that year he was awarded an OBE for his war service,
despite never, as far as we know, having set foot on continental Europe. How his
thrice-wounded younger brother, a holder of a DSO, felt about that we shall
never know. A year later Coote was appointed high sheriff of Co. Dublin, the post
once held by his father, and he was elected for the Swords area as a member of
the county council. He and Julia had five children. He spent his time farming,
and despite having been away at school from the age of nine, became a highly
regarded agricultural expert. He was appointed to the Dublin County Council
Committee of Agricultural and Technical Instruction and became very involved
with the Royal Dublin Society and its agricultural shows. He held strong views
on the wisdom or otherwise of breaking up large estates, and particularly stud
farms, and distributing them to those who he felt had little idea what to do with
them. As a member of the committee he seconded a motion proposed by Mr W.
Flanagan: 'That we view with grave doubts the advisability of the compulsory

24 FCCA/HH/1/6/19.

acquiring of Land used as Stud Farms for distribution among landless men, as Horse Breeding is one of the beneficial industries to the Country.'[25] Coote was also appointed to the first Dublin County Council libraries and scholarships committee, along with Hannah Sheehy Skeffington, whose husband, Francis Sheehy Skeffington, was shot by the British military during Easter Week 1916.

Coote's other main interest seems to have been in the development of mental health services. As a council representative on the board of Grangegorman Hospital, he was very involved in the improvements at St Ita's Mental Hospital in Portrane, around the corner from his Donabate residence. One of his recommendations to save money and improve efficiencies in the kitchens was to employ a former army mess sergeant, to which the board eventually agreed.[26] He died in 1930, and among the many letters of condolences his wife received was one from the president of the Irish Free State, Liam Cosgrave: 'His country will miss the splendid public services and activities which he contributed to her welfare for so many years.'

For Dick, life after the war was very different. In the first place, he couldn't afford to retire on half-pay, and had to remain in the army until 1926, when he was gazetted as retired on 15 July. He, Alice and Pamela had moved from post to post in Britain, including some rather meaningless postings in Scotland, until he could retire and settle down. On 13 August 1922, he wrote to his sister Cissy from the Western Club, Glasgow: 'I have been given the Hamilton Infantry Records for two years from now, which is good in a way, as I shall not have to go on half pay a while, of course the place is beastly ... the only fly in the ointment is whether Alice can stand the climate up here as I am told it is cold there in the Spring.'[27] He and Coote also corresponded, and their letters give an idea of how different one brother's life was from the other's. One from Dick, written while staying in the Oatsheaf Hotel in the town of Fleet, Hampshire, reported:

> We at once started house hunting ... we have to but, I was dead against it, but we have bought one, quite a little house, I daresay it will do us very well ... it is in a very good state of repair ... 40 miles from London by road. I have taken my name off the Naval & Military, as I can't afford £15 a year & a car as well ... Have you any word as to land purchase & when the estate is passing through ... This is not a bad sort of a pub, they take us in for 3 and a half guineas a week each. We stay here till the 4th of June & then go into another species of boarding house called Chernoke House, Fleet Rd. Fleet, & remain there till we get into the new mansion.[28]

---

25 Minutes of Dublin County Council agriculture and technical instruction committee, 11 Aug. 1925. 26 Joseph Reynolds, *Grangegorman: psychiatric care in Dublin since 1815* (Cambridge, 1992), pp 240–1. 27 FCCA/HH/1/6/20. 28 FCCA/HH/1/6/21.

There is, however, no hint of resentment in this letter. In later years Dick revisited some of the places in France where he had fought, and often received Christmas cards and invitations to regimental events from fellow fusiliers. Like his father he survived into his eighties, outliving Alice. His daughter Pamela never married. Coote's children, and one grandson, Michael, were the last Hely-Hutchinsons to live on the Broadmeadow estuary, and it was to be their descendants, Caroline Harlow and Fiona Selway, who donated the Hely-Hutchinson collection to Fingal Archives.

King Elmes: a Wexford Protestant doctor dies in Messines

IDA MILNE

In the 1970s a south Wexford country house lies silenced. The weight of its contents add layers of meaning to its past and its present. The dingy brown hall, once filled with generation after generation of childhood play and adult greetings, was hung with stuffed boa constrictors, a tortoise shell fashioned into a shield. Was it Zulu? They were the only African tribe we knew, apart from pygmies. Everyone knew they used poisoned darts, not spears and shields made of shell. A swordfish bill. In the drawing room, ancient layers of books long forgotten to be returned to the Penny Library, the dust obscuring their names. In the glass bookcase, miniature balsa-wood rickshaws, stuffed blowfish, abalone shells and the magical porcupine-quill box. Tourist catchpennies of another time and places. On a table, the display boxes of butterflies and blown-out eggshells beloved of collectors at the end of the nineteenth century. Another smaller display box, this one containing a scorpion, its stinging tail detached by age.

In the attic, a portrait of an ancient uncle, an army medical doctor in full dress uniform. The same uniform, neatly folded in a long untravelled trunk, last used to bring it back from the Crimean war. His medical instruments, including some rather sharp surgical knives.

In a drawer, the few belongings of a Royal Army Medical Corps officer who was killed by a shell as the Great War tottered towards its end. His Red Cross armband, his medical degree papers, the awarding signatures themselves a minor history of the medical profession in Ireland. The letter to his parents, the customary 'he died bravely as he had lived' testament from someone who knew and fought with him. The self-conscious army personalization of war, recognizing the need for grieving families to understand those last awful moments, to see the context and believe the occluded truths offered in comfort.

In the basement, seldom used by the remaining occupants, more of the professional clues left by the previous inhabitants. A skeleton, perhaps a prank from a medical school, its fingers clasping the bars of the wine-cellar door. Did it actually exist? Was it more fostered by the imagination, primed to add to the clues from the previous inhabitants? Hundreds of pharmaceutical bottles, their glass stoppers occasionally chipped, their contents long dried or used up.

This was the home of the Elmes family from Robinstown, Palace East, in south Wexford in the 1970s, as recreated from memories of the teenage years of myself, Ida Milne. My grandmother, Ruth Elmes Milne, and her six siblings were raised in Robinstown. It was a house with indications of the impracticality of the owners: a large three-storey, over-basement home with no inside lavatory, it had a dining table that could seat twenty-four, and every surface was covered in a dense and eclectic layer of books – *The Times history of the war* and La Fontaine's *Fables* mixed with penny-dreadfuls, *The Strand* magazine and Black's veterinary dictionary. As a teenager, Granny once chopped the legs off a four-poster bed, as no one had thought to organize firewood. The Elmes were demi-gentry, but not ordinary farming stock either, being eccentrically bookish. A Church of Ireland Wexford family, they had been constant on this same farmland close to Old Ross since before it was traversed by the rebels of 1798. As the house contents indicated, they were travellers, with sons moving around the world for work, for duty, and for adventure as seamen and medical doctors, over several generations. Their story is also one of an overwhelming loss, a sadness emanating from the death of that young RAMC officer that has transferred now across four generations.

When I used to visit the house before it was sold in the 1970s and the land acquired by the Land Commission, the last remaining inhabitants were Aunt Fran, my grandmother's sister, a shy, bookish woman crippled with arthritis, and her brother, blind and cranky Uncle Willie, who spent his days in front of the dining-room fireplace, fuelled by enormous logs that barely took the chill off the air. Willie's attention was permanently glued to a wireless on the mantelpiece, trying to alleviate the tedium of his life by listening to the BBC. Family lore had it that he had been a brilliant surgeon, and that his mentors in the Royal College of Surgeons had offered him a lectureship when his career was ended by failing eyesight. He told us of being trained in the operating theatre by Oliver St John Gogarty, who would try to prevent novices from fainting by relating saucy stories.

Granny, Fran and Willie had other brothers: the oldest, Tommy, farmed, while Sam and Euseby, like their brother Willie, sailed the world as young doctors on liners between the world wars; Sam and Euseby both married and settled with their families in England. Euseby was in the Pacific when his ship was taken over by the Royal Navy during the Second World War, and he told many lively stories about his subsequent service in the navy. Willie, sitting almost sightless in his chair by the fire, would pull down the album of his pictures from the Yangtse and other places in Asia.

Magical as their adventurous pasts seemed to us, in a world newly accessible by air travel, it was the story of their other brother, King, that most gripped us. He was hit by a shell in Flanders in the last few weeks of the Great War. Granny told us that he had been 'with Lawrence in Arabia', and that he had been moved to the Western Front when 'things went quiet' in the Middle East, and that he died in September 1918. We knew little factual detail of his service, other than that, but the little we knew filled us with excitement. We children camped in his army service tent, played with the solar topee he had acquired when he arrived in Egypt, and marvelled at a picture of him cooking his breakfast on the rocks in the desert.

Reflecting back, we as a family observed that his sisters and brothers never spoke of his actual death, or the way that they felt about it. And yet the trauma caused by the death of this much loved, and by all accounts gentle and charming, brother, was somehow more than evident in their silences. Sam's daughter, Judy Bull, told me that her father hadn't spoken of the loss of his brother: 'It was Mummy who told us how devastated they all were when they were told of his death, just when they were expecting him home soon.' His death hung over Robinstown like a shroud, a beautiful soul lost not only to his siblings but also to the rest of the family, the subsequent generations and their spouses who he never got a chance to meet. Judy Bull's husband, Brian, described visiting the grave in Flanders in 2003:

> When I first visited Kandahar Farm cemetery with two friends to lay a wreath which Judy had made for King's grave, I'm not ashamed to admit I completely broke down for a while in sorrow for a man I never knew, having already been that very day to several other war cemeteries and though deeply moved by them all, it was at this time and place, and the personal nature of this visit that really brought it home what an awful price thousands of families have paid for such losses.[1]

My father, born in August 1919 as a new Ireland was beginning, was named King in his memory, which was not perhaps the easiest inheritance for a Church of Ireland person in a country that had rejected the rule of a foreign monarch. Growing up as a young Protestant trying to fit into the Ireland of the 1920s, the first game he could remember was 'Fenians and Free Staters'. His name evidently caused him some discomfort, as when a new grandchild would be due to be born, he would quietly make an approach asking us not to name the child after him.

Robert, my brother, reflected on another aspect of the difficulties of remembering family who had died at war in the new Ireland: 'We were uncomfortable wearing the Poppy in remembrance, as Protestants in a mixed society, even though he gave his life for us. It's a dichotomy.' For many years, the names of the local soldiers of all religions who had died in the wars were read out by the Dean in our (Church of Ireland) cathedral church, St Edan's in Ferns, on Poppy Sunday; we didn't mention King Elmes, except in silent prayer and thought. Perhaps there was an unspoken sense of protection in this omission, a reluctance to expose his memory to the realities of an intolerant present that would not understand his reasons for going to war, whatever they were.

1 Email communication with Brian Bull, husband of Judy Bull, daughter of King's brother Samuel Elmes.

The extended family were all acutely aware of the long-reaching effects of his death – or rather the absence of his continued life – but knew little of his work in the army or the fuller circumstances of his death. There were, and are, so many unanswered questions. Why had he gone to war in the first place? Was it to serve the crown, or as a Wexford man to follow Redmond? Perhaps it was because as a doctor of conscription age he would not be employed by the Poor Law dispensary system, the entry-level job for newly qualified doctors? Given that he opted to join the London Regiment in Egypt in 1916, his motivation might have been adventure and travel, inspired by his uncle Robert Elmes, another family hero, who had served with the RAMC in the Crimea before returning to the more humdrum life of a dispensary doctor in Borris.

Historians tend to regard those investigating their own family history as being a smidgeon self-indulgent. But King's war story has strings that keep pulling me in: while the decade of centenaries has been an enabling force in filling gaps; renewed interest in the war has provided more information; and technology facilitated digital access to sources. It is a process that is still ongoing, slightly hampered by the apparent destruction of some records during the Second World War.

Happenstance has been one of my assistants. While working in the Royal College of Physicians in Ireland on other projects, RCPI archivists Robert Mills and Harriet Wheelock showed me the Thomas Percy Kirkpatrick index of Irish medical doctors.[2] A brown envelope contained some cuttings from the medical journals about his career and death, and more poignantly, a letter written by Thomas Elmes in a spidery hand in response to a request from Dr Kirkpatrick for more information about his son, promising to send on a picture, which did not arrive. A *British Medical Journal* cutting reported that the casualty list published on 16 October 1918 included the death of Captain King Elmes in action with the Royal Fusiliers of the City of London Regiment. Elmes had passed his medical finals in 1916, and was licensed to practise as a physician by the Royal College of Physicians of Ireland, and as a surgeon by the Royal College of Surgeons of Ireland. He immediately took a temporary commission in the RAMC, and had been promoted to captain after a year's service.[3] Cuttings from the *Evening Mail* and *Irish Times* supply the date of his death as 28 September 1918.[4]

A chance conversation about my grand-uncle with a colleague at Queen's University, Belfast, Tom Thorpe, revealed that he researches military group cohesion in the London Regiment during the Great War. He told me that the London Regiment was created as part of a territorial force in 1908, and had twenty-eight battalions. He describes the Queen's Westminster Rifles, the 2/16

2 For further details of the heritage centre at the Royal College of Physicians in Ireland see www.rcpi.ie/landing.php?locID=1.12.19. Kind thanks to Harriet Wheelock for providing copies of the file.   3 'Casualties in the war', *British Medical Journal* (Oct. 1918), 475–7. 4 *Irish Times*, 14 Oct. 1918; *Evening Mail*, 12 Oct. 1918.

13.1 Captain King Elmes taking a bath in the desert. Photograph courtesy of Susan Elmes.

battalion to which the RAMC assigned King in 1916, as being 'posh', a class corps affiliated to the Kings Royal Rifle Corps. As a rifle corps they wore black buttons rather than brass, were 'riflemen' rather than privates and referred to the bayonet as the 'sword'.[5] As Thorpe explained: 'Class corps battalions actively sought to protect their exclusivity by setting membership requirements which included in the Queen's Westminster Rifles and London Scottish an annual subscription of around £1 per year, that novitiates be public or grammar school educated and be recommended by a current member.' In addition, 'the London Scottish demanded initiates have Scottish nationality. These measures were designed to protect the social status of the battalions'. But Thorpe added that the introduction of conscription in 1916 lowered the social strata of recruits slightly.

Susan Elmes showed me photographs King had taken in Egypt and Palestine, mostly in Alexandria, which had been in the possession of her father, Euseby. They show little of actual war, other that the conditions of living in a tent in the

---

5 Email communication with military historian Tom Thorpe, Queen's University, Belfast, 18 Jan. 2016.

13.2 Captain King Elmes in Egypt. A typical pose with a chameleon.
Photograph courtesy of Susan Elmes.

desert and social engagement with the hospital medical staff. King's use of the camera reveals him as having quite a sense of humour, taking many self-portraits, with lizards on his head, sleeping in his tent, reading quietly, cooking in the outdoors and bathing in a canvas bath (figs 13.1, 13.2).

In The National Archives in Kew, I found the war diary of the 2/16, and was able to trace, to some extent, the final few months of uncle King's career. In June 1918 the unit was in Palestine, but was moved to Kantara for specialist training and to wait embarkation to Europe. On 16 June they boarded the HMT *Indarra* in Alexandria. The *Indarra* was 'unsuccessfully attacked' by a submarine in the Mediterranean on 21 June, and reached Taranto on the Italian coast of Apulia, that evening. From there, they were moved to France and thence to billets at Moulle. On 1 August they relieved the 2/14 Battalion on the front line at Locre (in modern Flanders). From then they served in several different periods at the front line, as in the final push forward, swapping with other units like the Sherwood Foresters and going back periodically for rest and training. On 28 September the 90th Brigade was ordered to advance, their final objective being a line running north–south about 1,500 yards east of Messines. The 2/16 sent forward fighting patrols under cover of artillery barrage to take their objectives, with most of the 2/16 remaining in the same position. On 29 September the 90 Brigade was ordered to advance to Comines. The 2/16 and 2/15 advanced and reached this objective by 14.30 hours, and the battalion remained overnight in the vicinity of Comines canal. On 30 September, the 2/14 London Regiment took over the line and the 2/16 withdrew. The diary notes that Captain K. Elmes, RAMC, was killed in action on 30 September, and that in total the unit lost 36 out of 751 men.[6]

Rifleman L.J. Rackham wrote to King's mother, Mary Ruth Elmes, on 2 October, explaining his connection to her son and the circumstances of his death at 7 p.m. on 28 September at Stinking Farm. He had known King since the young Wexford man had arrived in Egypt to join the battalion, and the small medical team under Captain Elmes' direct supervision had asked him to write on their behalf of his courage and self-sacrifice, his winning manner, and great care and sympathy for the sick and the wounded:

> You may perhaps bear with me whilst I outline the incidents which led to his death. He was on a reconnaissance scheme preparatory to the attack … when we were suddenly caught in a barrage of heavy fire. Captain Elmes laid at the bottom of a ditch for shelter, and one of the shells burst near and one of the best friends the regiment had was killed outright. At midnight two stretcher bearers volunteered to accompany me to the location where the tragedy occurred and we were able to bring his body to battalion headquarters near where he was afterwards buried by an Army Chaplain.[7]

King was buried on 29 September at Kandahar Farm. His possessions, apart from an electric torch the rifleman thought would be useful, were returned to his family. They included his army Red Cross armband.

I visited the battlefields of Flanders twice in 2014, as the war commemorations began. On the first trip in May, Irish Great War specialist guide Simon Louagie took me to the field where uncle King probably died, a vast newly sown cornfield that still revealed signs of the Iron Harvest, the military debris that pollutes farmland as the ongoing price that Flanders pays for playing host to war. Surrounded by the modern-day tranquility of that field, Simon talked me through the last days of the war and the vulnerability of the troops as they moved forward. I was struck by how different it must have been for uncle King and the thousands of others who died in the Great War, the silence replaced by the clangs and booms and shouts and screams, by the smells of human fear and suffering, of artillery smoke and gases, and by the expected unexpected.

Grief can visit us without warning in the present commemorations, even at a remove of almost 100 years. It visited me in that field, but more unexpectedly so

---

6 War diary of the 2/16 Battalion London Regiment (Queen's Westminster Rifles), June 1918–Oct. 1919, TNA, WO 95/2340/4.   7 Letter from Rifleman Packham to Mrs Elmes, Robinstown House, 2 Oct. 1918 (private collection).

in September in St George's in Ypres, an Anglican church built as a meeting place for visiting relatives of the war dead by the Ypres League, chaired by Field Marshal Sir John French. The church has a window dedicated to the memory of the RAMC; across from it stands the colours of the 2/16 battallion, the Queen's Westminster Rifles. Here was not only the end of King Elmes, but of his decommissioned unit. No doubt like King, whose name is carved by his own hand into barn eaves in Carlow, and by others onto commemorative plaques in Carlow and Wexford, his colleagues leave their names on other physical landscapes, and in the minds and hearts of the generations born since.[8]

8 I would like to thank Judy and Brian Bull, Margaret Doyle, archivist at Clongowes Wood College, Trevor Ellis, Susan Elmes, Simon Louagie, Sheila, Robert and George Milne, Tom Thorpe, Robert Mills and Harriet Wheelock of the Royal College of Physicians in Ireland Heritage Centre, and the staff at The National Archives in Kew for help with this research.

'The sons of South Hill and Mervue': T.E. Lawrence, Pierce Joyce and the Great War in the Middle East

DAVID MURPHY

During the Great War over 200,000 Irishmen served in the British forces. For many, the narrative of the Great War remains focused on the Western Front. Yet the Great War was a truly global conflict and thousands of Irish servicemen took part in campaigns in the Balkans, Africa, Mesopotamia, Egypt and Palestine. This paper will focus on two individuals: T.E. Lawrence and Pierce Joyce. In the case of Lawrence, he was unknowingly connected to a significant Irish gentry family, the Chapmans of South Hill and Killua. Lawrence would not learn of his Irish connections until 1919, following the death of his father. Joyce, born and raised in a gentry family in Galway, joined the British Army. The families of both men existed within the same social strata yet it remains unclear if Lawrence ever discussed his family connections with Joyce.

Many Irish scholars will be aware of Lawrence's link to Ireland through his father, Sir Thomas Robert Tighe Chapman, the 7th and last Baronet Chapman of Killua Castle, Clonmellon, Co. Westmeath. The Chapman family were members of the Anglo-Irish gentry and could trace their origins in Ireland back to the Elizabethan Plantation. John and William Chapman had travelled to Ireland in the late sixteenth century with Sir Walter Raleigh, to whom they were related. Captain Benjamin Chapman served with Oliver Cromwell during his campaign in Ireland in 1649.[1]

During the seventeenth and eighteenth centuries the Chapmans were awarded various grants of land for their services. The main family residence at Killua Castle was on land previously the property of the Knights Hospitaller of St John (fig. 14.1).[2] A Georgian house on the estate was begun around 1780, there were later additions, and a much larger castellated mansion was built in the Gothic Revival style. By 1950, however, this once-impressive house was in a ruinous condition, but recently it has been purchased and is currently under renovation to serve as a private home. The original estate was over 9,000 acres, but today only around 200 acres are associated with Killua Castle. The Chapman

---

1 Lawrence's family background is outlined in most major biographies. See Jeremy Wilson's *Lawrence of Arabia: the authorised biography* (London, 1989). See also John E. Mack, *The prince of our disorder* (London, 1978), and Lawrence James, *The golden warrior: the life and legend of Lawrence of Arabia* (London, 1990). 2 www.buildingsofireland.ie/niah/search.jsp? type=record&county=WM&regno=15306023 (accessed 30 Sept. 2012).

14.1 Killua Castle in Co. Westmeath. The ancestral home of the Chapman family.

family were extremely prominent in Ireland: three of Sir Thomas Chapman's ancestors had served as MPs for Westmeath and also held other county offices.[3]

The residence associated with Sir Thomas Chapman was not Killua Castle, however, but South Hill in Delvin. This was an impressive residence in its own right and stood on a large estate. Sources differ as to the date of its actual construction. It was originally the property of the Tighe family but had passed to the Chapmans, who were related to the Tighes through marriage. While it is often stated that the main phase of building took place around 1810, the house has a distinctly Georgian appearance. An architectural survey of 1993 noted plasterwork that has been attributed to the Danish stuccoist Thorvaldsen (1768–1844). It has also been suggested that the actual design was similar to other works of William Farrell, a prominent architect in Ireland in the early to mid-nineteenth century.[4]

3 http://www.historyofparliamentonline.org/volume/1820-1832/member/chapman-montagu-1808-1852 (accessed 30 Sept. 2012). 4 http://www.buildingsofireland.ie/niah/search.jsp?type=record&county=WM&regno=15401401 (accessed 30 Sept. 2012).

14.2 South Hill in Delvin, Co. Westmeath, 1899. The residence of Thomas Chapman and his family before he left to begin a new life with Sarah Lawrence (Irish Architectural Archive).

In 1873, Sir Thomas Chapman married Edith Sarah Hamilton and, once South Hill had been renovated, they used it as their main residence. They subsequently had four daughters – Eva Jane Louisa (b.1874), Rose Isabel (b.1878), Florence Livia (b.1880) and Mabel Cecele, sometimes spelled Cicele (b.1881).

Chapman's subsequent elopement with Sarah Lawrence is well-known and has been much written about. Having lived in various places, the couple settled in Oxford. They had five sons: Montague Robert (b.1885), Thomas Edward (b.1888), William George (b.1889), Frank (b.1893) and Arnold (b.1900). Throughout this period, the couple passed themselves off as the 'Lawrences', although there was no formal divorce from Edith.

The later life of Edith Chapman and her daughters, Lawrence's half-sisters, is less well known. While many details remain unclear, it is certain that the younger Chapman brother, Francis Vanisttart Chapman, took over the South Hill estate. It would seem that he allowed Mrs Chapman and her children to stay on at South Hill. Also, Thomas Chapman received an annual allowance based on the Irish estates. It would seem that some form of legal arrangement had been made to facilitate this, but the apparent disappearance of the Chapman family

14.3 Lawrence in Arab robes. Following his secondment to the Arab army, Lawrence began to wear Arab robes in order to blend in with the tribesmen (Imperial War Museum).

archives leaves much shrouded in mystery. The abandoned Chapman family divided their time between South Hill and a Dublin residence. Mrs Chapman died in October 1930.[5] South Hill finally passed from the Chapman family in 1952. Lawrence enthusiasts will be aware of the oft-reproduced period photograph of South Hill that appears in many of the biographies. Until recently this was thought to be the only nineteenth-century photograph of it. During the

5 *Irish Times*, 28 Oct. 1930.

course of research in 2010 the author was made aware of a file of photographs in the possession of the Irish Architectural Archive in Dublin. This file had been placed in the archive in the 1940s, apparently by a member of the Chapman family. One of those photographs is reproduced here (fig. 14.2).

During the course of the Arab Revolt of 1916–18, many British and French officers and men served in Arabia as part of the overall allied effort to aid the Hashemite cause. From a historical perspective the majority of these men have been largely overlooked. T.E. Lawrence has received so much public and historical attention that many other important players in the events of 1916–18 have been almost totally forgotten. One such figure is Lieutenant Colonel Pierce Charles Joyce. He played a highly important role in the revolt but has since been relegated to a footnote in the history of that campaign, despite the fact that Lawrence himself refers to him more than forty times in *Seven pillars of wisdom*. Yet this was not always the case. Joyce's contemporaries recognized that he had played a central role in the Middle East campaign. In 1936, General Harry Chauvel, the renowned Australian cavalry general, wrote some comments on *Seven pillars of wisdom*, remarking:

> Throughout the volume, it seems to me that Lt.-Col. Joyce has been kept in the background. He was in charge of the Hejaz mission, while Lawrence was only the liaison officer between Feisal and General Allenby. Joyce was the organizer of the only fighting force of any real value in the whole of the Arab Army and I always thought that he had more to do with the success of the Hejaz operations than any other British Officer.[6]

Considering the importance of Joyce's later role as commander of Operation Hedgehog, the British military mission to the Arabs, it seems strange that his career has received little scholarly attention, but then he, and major other characters, never became the focus of public attention in the way that Lawrence later did (fig. 14.3).

Pierce Charles Joyce was born on 23 June 1878 in Galway in the west of Ireland. His family were descended from Norman settlers who had established themselves in the Galway area by the fourteenth century. The original family name was 'Joyeuse', and they thrived as merchants and bankers in the county, basing themselves in Galway town. The family seat was the impressive Mervue House, Co. Galway, and the family owned land and property both in the county and the town. His father was Pierce John Joyce, JP and high sheriff of Galway town. His mother was born Selina Henrietta Mahon, daughter of Charles Mahon JP and DL of Co. Mayo. His only brother, Henry Ross Joyce, was born in 1881 but died the following year. He also had an elder sister, Henrietta

6 General Harry Chauvel to the director of the Australian Memorial, Canberra, 1 Jan. 1936 (St Antony's College, Oxford, Middle East Centre Archives, DS244-4).

Kathleen Joyce, who was born in 1876.[7] In many ways Joyce's family and early life could not have been more dissimilar to Lawrence's. Joyce was firmly rooted in the region and could trace his family back for centuries. While Lawrence also had links to an equally impressive Anglo-Irish family through his father, he was cut off from such connections and, indeed, was unaware of them for many years.

Also unlike Lawrence, Joyce's childhood was one of outdoor pursuits and sports. His grandfather, Pierce Joyce, was one of the founders of the Galway foxhunt in 1839, known locally as the 'Galway Blazers' and which still exists. Both grandfather and father had been instrumental in the founding of the Galway races in 1869, a meet that is still run to this day and which attracts a huge crowd from all over the world. He came from a family of renowned horsemen and would have hunted, fished and shot from an early age. By his early twenties Joyce stood at an impressive 6' 4". In addition to hunting and racing events, his parents were known for the lavish parties that they held at Mervue. Locally, the family were known as the 'Merry Joyces', a term that would later be attached to Joyce and his wife in the 1920s.[8]

Coming from this background, it is perhaps not surprising that Joyce chose the army for his career. This was a common career path for young men of the Anglo-Irish landed class. Many of the most prominent figures in the Victorian army had emerged from within Anglo-Irish society, including Field-Marshal Lord Wolseley, who had been born in Co. Dublin, and Field-Marshal Lord Roberts, whose family had historic links to Co. Waterford.

Having attended Beaumont College, Old Windsor, Joyce was commissioned as a 2nd lieutenant into the 1st Battalion of the Connaught Rangers in 1900. His battalion – originally the 88th (Connaught Rangers) Regiment of Foot – was one of several Irish regiments that had been formed in 1793 to counter the threat of Napoleon's invasion. The young 2nd Lt Joyce got his first taste of military service during the South African War of 1899–1902. His service there seems to have been fairly routine until he was caught in a Boer ambush on 31 May 1902 and wounded. This ambush occurred just six days before the end of hostilities. A rescue party that tried to recover Joyce and his sergeant was also ambushed, and they had to wait twenty-four hours before a mule-drawn ambulance wagon was brought up to evacuate them to the nearest hospital, which was half a day's journey away. Joyce was awarded both the Queen's and the King's South Africa medals and was promoted to full lieutenant.[9]

He served on home station with his battalion until 1907, when he applied for an appointment with the Egyptian Army. This was not an uncommon career choice for young officers during this period. Serving on secondment to the Egyptian Army, the commander (or sirdar) of which was also a British officer,

7 *Burke's landed gentry of Ireland* (1912), p. 358.   8 Ibid.   9 Ibid. See also H.F.N. Jourdain, *The Connaught Rangers* (London, 1924), vol. i, p. 4003. This history of the Connaught Rangers also contains a group photograph in which Joyce appears.

came with increased allowances and pay and also with promotion. Joyce was then a captain but was appointed to the local rank of bimbashi or major to command two companies of the 11th Sudanese. During this service he was stationed at Mongalla on the White Nile on the Sudanese–Ugandan border.[10] This service was not without incident: on one occasion in 1909 he was attacked by a rogue elephant. It would seem that Joyce thrived abroad, and Sir Reginald Wingate, governor-general of the Sudan and sirdar of the Egyptian Army, later stated that Joyce was 'one of the best officers he had in the old Gippy army'.[11] At the outbreak of the Great War Joyce was in Cairo with an appointment on the general staff. In 1915 he served as an intelligence officer during the disastrous Gallipoli campaign.

Lawrence's route into the military was quite different. On the outbreak of the war in 1914 he joined the Geographical Section of the General Staff (Intelligence) based in the War Office in London. By December 1914, however, Lawrence was in Cairo, where he joined the Intelligence Department. For the next two years his life was routine. Following the death of two of his brothers (Frank and William) in 1915, Lawrence became increasingly frustrated and sought a way to participate more fully in the war. The outbreak of a revolt among the Arabs in 1916 gave him such an opportunity; it also brought him in contact with Joyce.

It is impossible to cover the full extent of the Arab Revolt here, but it is sufficient to point out that Joyce, as commander of Operation Hedgehog, played a significant role in the campaign in the Middle East and cooperated with Lawrence throughout. Alongside his military duties Joyce found himself increasingly concerned with the political fallout caused by the revelation of details of both the Sykes–Picot Agreement and also the Balfour Declaration. Knowledge of both of these developments had reached the Arab army by November 1917 and caused widespread discontent, effectively stalling operations. The capture of Jerusalem in December 1917 and the Arab victory at Tafila in January 1918 did go some way to improving morale. Arab doubts remained, however, and Joyce emerged as the main handler of Arab leaders, in particular Feisal (fig. 14.4). In a report to Clayton he wrote: 'I had a very difficult time with Feisal for a few days. He is not a strong character and is much swayed by his surroundings.'[12]

In an effort to end Arab misgivings it was arranged that Feisal should meet the Zionist leader, Chaim Weizmann, in June 1918. Joyce acted as intermediary and interpreter and has left us the only eyewitness account of this meeting, which took place at Wahida on 4 June 1918. There has been some confusion in later writings about this meeting, some authors stating that Lawrence served as interpreter. This is perhaps due to the fact that Lawrence was present at later

10 It is interesting to note that Sir Arthur Conan Doyle penned a short story entitled 'The debut of Bimbashi Joyce'. 11 *The Ranger Magazine*, 73 (July 1965), Joyce obituary, pp 6–7. 12 Liddell Hart Centre for Military Archives, Joyce Papers, I/H77-78, Joyce to Dawnay, 27

14.4 Lt-Col. Pierce Charles Joyce. In this photograph, Joyce is wearing his Connaught Rangers uniform (Lowell Thomas Collection).

meetings between Feisal and Weizmann. But at the time of the meeting on 4 June, Lawrence was travelling towards Aqaba in order to board a ship bound for Suez. Joyce's own account makes it clear that he served as the mediator at this meeting, and he is also mentioned in Weizmann's own account, although oddly not as the interpreter. In his report to Clayton, Joyce noted that the meeting was 'cordial'. Both men laid out their positions – Feisal for an Arab kingdom based on Palestine, Weizmann for a Jewish settlement in Palestine. Joyce recorded that 'Dr Weizmann pointed out that the Jews do not propose setting up a Jewish government but would like to work under British protection with a view to colonizing and developing the country without in any way encroaching on anybody's legitimate interests.'[13]

Joyce noted that in response, Feisal 'declared that as an Arab he could not discuss the future of Palestine either as a Jewish colony or a country under

Sept. 1917.   **13** Weizmann-Feisal meeting file (Liddell Hart Centre for Military Archives, Joyce Papers, I/P).

British protection'. Despite the apparent contradictions in these standpoints, Joyce reported that the meeting had gone well, with some indications of under- standing and suggestions of future dialogue and support. It was the beginning of a conversation between these two figures that would continue over years.[14]

After two years of guerrilla warfare the officers of Hedgehog began to see their work bearing fruit during the late summer of 1918. The crucial railway station at Mudawwarah was finally taken in August, while Allenby's Megiddo offensive, which began on 19 September, was a success. The Turkish Army was finally collapsing, and throughout this phase the Arab northern army played a crucial role, continuing its raids in enemy rear areas and constantly threatening the Turkish left flank. Ma'an was vacated on 23 September, and in the hectic weeks that followed the Turkish Army was pushed gradually northwards. Throughout this phase Joyce was kept busy with the Arab northern army, and while Lawrence travelled with the irregular contingent, he commanded elements of the regular army. In the final phases of the war, the mobile force of armoured cars and lorried artillery made their presence felt. Supported by a flight of RAF Bristol fighters, they maintained the tempo of the offensive on the Turkish left flank and Arab elements reached Damascus on 1 October and Aleppo by 26 October. Faced with the collapse of its forces across this front, the Ottoman government sued for peace and an armistice came into effect on 31 October. The war in the Middle East was effectively over.

Like Lawrence, Joyce's war had really ended on reaching Damascus in October. A complicated political struggle was emerging as Feisal began his bid to become king of Syria. It would be easy to dismiss Joyce as a professional officer who had no real sympathy for Arab aspirations. Yet a memorandum survives that he wrote in 1919 while still in Syria. Like Lawrence, Joyce was alive to Arab aspirations, and in his memorandum he predicted that there would be problems if the Arabs are not given some level of independence in Palestine, Lebanon and Syria. He was wary of both French and Zionist influence in the region and stated that 'the Arabs argue, and with good reason, that having fought for the principles of freedom and independence, that it is the country's [Syria's] undisputed right to control their future.'[15] Like Lawrence's, his advice was not heeded. He later attended both the Versailles and Cairo conferences before returning to Egypt, where, in 1920, he was appointed as deputy assistant adjutant and quartermaster general of the Egyptian Army and as governor of Luxor. In 1921 he married Colin Murray, the daughter of General R.H. Murray. The couple had met and become engaged in Cairo, and Colin shared Joyce's passion for horses and dogs. She was also a woman of considerable property, owning an estate in Hampshire, and she would later inherit another property in

14 Ibid. See also Cecil Bloom, 'T.E. Lawrence and his attitude towards Zionism', *The Journal of the T.E. Lawrence Society*, 21:1 (2011–12), 54–80. 15 'Memorandum' of 1919 (Liddell Hart Centre for Military Archives, Joyce Papers, M/39).

Berkshire. It is unclear if Joyce brought his new bride to Ireland during this period. The War of Independence (1919–21) had reached a ceasefire in July 1921, but the country was still tense and the final stages of the war had seen much brutal violence.

Joyce's next posting was to Baghdad, where he served as military advisor to the government of King Feisal. Alongside wartime associates such as Jafar Pasha and Nuri Said, he was given the local rank of full colonel and set about raising, training and equipping the new Iraqi Army. He was to recruit officers (many of them former Ottoman officers) and men and train them to such a degree that British forces were able to withdraw, leaving the government of the country to the Iraqis. (Indeed, his experiences mirror those of many British officers during their recent service in Baghdad.) On a lighter level, both he and his wife became features of the Baghdad social scene and were regulars at soirées hosted by Gertrude Bell and at hunt meets. Joyce left Baghdad and went on the half-pay list in 1927. In 1932, he retired from the army altogether. For his service in the Middle East he was made a CBE and also awarded the French Legion d'Honneur and the Arabian Order of the Nahda, 2nd Class. After his retirement he divided his time between Galway and his wife's properties in England. He had been given an Arab thoroughbred by Feisal on leaving Iraq. He regularly showed it at the annual horseshow of the Royal Dublin Society, and both he and Colin would later become prominent breeders of Saluki hounds, effectively reintroducing the breed to Ireland.[16]

After the war, Joyce maintained a friendship with Lawrence, and an intermittent correspondence began that was to continue until Lawrence's death. The two men had been in touch while Lawrence was writing drafts of *Seven pillars of wisdom*, and Joyce had sat for a portrait that was to be included in the 1926 edition. The exact date at which Lawrence became aware of his Irish connections is still debated by Lawrence biographers and enthusiasts. Some state that he became aware of this in his early teens. What is certain is that he was fully aware of the facts following his father's death in 1919. In later letters he occasionally referred to these Irish connections. In 1928 Lawrence was serving (as Aircraftman Shaw) on the north-west frontier of India. He wrote to Joyce who was then in Galway:

> Dear Joyce,
> I am glad that your Seven Pillars did after all turn up. It is an inadequate thing, but possibly the best account of the Arab Revolt yet in print. Someday, someone will have to do a proper one. I'd have liked to have written a history; but I found that my judgement was too partisan. I do not

16 See B.P. Duggan, *Saluki: the desert hound and the English travelers who brought it to the west* (Jefferson, 2009); See also *Who was who, 1961–70*, p. 612. For further detail on British involvement in Iraq, see Charles Tripp, *A history of Iraq* (Cambridge, 2000); Peter Sluglett, *Britain in Iraq: contriving king and country* (London, 2007).

think that I would have been fair to the others. Do you know I'm glad, in some ways, that you are out of Irak. I'd have all of us stand a little bit aside, now, from the show. People learn by falling down, more than by being held up and Irak has (I fancy) passed the stage of infancy. I hope you will find something congenial to do instead, although Ireland cannot be a very good hunting ground just now. Galway sounds moist and pleasant (these Afghan hills are like Wadi Itm; and we are confined to the barbed wire, twenty-five RAF and 700 Indian irregulars – that's Miranshah) but I cannot come home till the summer of 1930. There is a film of 'Revolt' for the great B.P. [British public] to digest first. Even in 1930, it cannot be Galway for me, I'm afraid. We actually come from Killua, in Meath; but that side of the world is barred now.
Best of wishes,
Yours, T.E.S.
PS – Don't tell this. I hate having my real roots dragged up for inspection.[17]

It is an intriguing letter, one of a number that make reference to Ireland and the possibility of Lawrence visiting it, a journey he never did undertake. It raises an interesting question. It is highly likely that Joyce's parents knew Lawrence's father, Sir Thomas Chapman. They were of the same, small, social class and shared an interest in horses and hunting. Given the popularity of the social occasions at Mervue House, it is not inconceivable that Sir Thomas Chapman and his wife had attended such a gathering while in Galway for a hunt or race meet. Did Lawrence ever broach this subject with Joyce? Did he ask Joyce about the Irish side of his family, the half-sisters that were still living? It is a fascinating question but one that does not appear to have been addressed in their correspondence and now cannot be answered.

What of Lawrence's half-sisters, the Chapman daughters? In 1954, Rose and Florence were still alive, residing at 39 Northumberland Road in Dublin. That year Edith Kennington, wife of the artist Eric Kennington, went to Ireland to visit places associated with Lawrence. The Kenningtons and Lawrence had been good friends: Eric had created several studies of Lawrence, including a memorial bronze bust. He had also produced the illustrations for the original version of *Seven pillars of wisdom*. Edith's account of her visit outlines the poignant details of the Chapman daughters' later lives. Due to the family scandal they never married into 'polite' society. They had also been aware of the deaths of their half-brothers in 1915 and their father in 1919. They had followed the life and career of T.E. Lawrence, but had never made contact.[18]

17 Shaw (Lawrence) to Joyce, 14 June 1928 (Bodleian Library, Oxford, Lawrence Collection, MS Eng. d.3327, f242). The ancestral home of the Chapman family was Killua Castle in Co. Westmeath. His father, Sir Thomas Chapman, had resided at South Hill, Delvin, Co. Westmeath.   18 Edith Kennington's notes on her Irish visit, 1954 (Bodleian Library, Oxford,

In 1936, the year after Lawrence's death, Joyce announced his intention to write an account of the revolt and contacted former associates such as Colonel Cyril Wilson and Sir Reginald Wingate for access to their papers.[19] For whatever reason, he never continued with this project. Yet in April 1939 and July 1941 he recorded broadcasts for the BBC, the transcripts of which survive. They serve as an insight into his relationship with Lawrence, and at the bottom of the transcripts Joyce wrote: 'I have just given these few notes on my personal contact with Lawrence, that mass of contradictions. I shall never meet a greater character or more inspiring leader.'[20] In the 1950s, he and his wife sold Mervue House and another house at Yately, and they lived out their lives in quiet retirement at Firtrees, a house in Crowthorne, Berkshire. In 1963, he was contacted by scholars from Israel who were then cataloguing Chaim Weizmann's Papers for archiving.[21] In poor health in his later years, he still managed to send them some notes in answer to their queries. He died 1 February 1965.[22] His wife died three years later.

Like so many who served in Arabia during the Great War, Joyce has largely been forgotten, despite the fact that he played such a central role. His relationship with Lawrence would seem to have been close, at least during the desert campaign. But there is no evidence that the two men ever discussed their shared roots in Ireland. As Joyce has effectively left no legacy in the form of a history of the campaign, it is perhaps fitting to conclude with some words of Lawrence, who paid Joyce fitting tribute in a lyrical passage in *Seven pillars*:

> Joyce was a man in whom one could rest against the world: a serene, unchanging, comfortable spirit. His mind, like a pastoral landscape, had four corners to its view: cared for, friendly, limited, displayed. He had won golden opinion at Rabegh and Wejh, practising that very labour of building up an army and a base, which would be necessary at Akaba. Clayton-like, he was a good cartilage to set between opposing joints, but he had more laughter than Clayton, being broad and Irish and much over six feet in height. His nature was to be devoted to the nearest job without straining on his toes after longer horizons. Also, he was more patient than any recorded archangel, and only smiled that jolly smile of his whenever I came in with revolutionary schemes, and threw new ribbons of fancy about the neck of the wild thing he was slowly rearing.[23]

T.E. Lawrence collection, MS Eng. c.6752, fols 84–134).   **19** There is an exchange of letters between Sir Reginald Wingate and Colonel Cyril Wilson in Feb. 1936 on the subject of Joyce's proposed book and also making their papers available to him (Liddell Hart Centre for Military Archives, Joyce Papers, I/M).   **20** Transcript of P.C. Joyce's BBC broadcast of 14 July 1941 (Bodleian Library, Oxford, T.E. Lawrence collection, MS Eng. c.6752).   **21** Weizmann-Feisal meeting file.   **22** See Duggan, *Saluki*, pp 244–5.   **23** T.E. Lawrence, *Seven pillars of wisdom* (London, 1962, repr. 1988), p. 331.

'Like shooting snipe at Ballindoolin': William Upton Tyrrell and the Great War

CIARÁN REILLY

In early November 1918, with the war drawing to a close, William Upton Tyrrell (1896–1979), or Willie as he was affectionately called, informed his mother that she could soon begin collecting tar barrels for the bonfire to celebrate his return to Ballindoolin near Carbury in Co. Kildare (fig. 15.1). Throughout the war the young Tyrrell, a member of the Royal Irish Rifles, and later the Royal Flying Corps, had longed to return to Ballindoolin and now hoped to partake in the coming grouse-shooting season. However, with the war's end, his return to Ballindoolin was less celebrated than anticipated. For the Tyrrells, the intervening years had seen their local influence changed dramatically, and the world to which Willie returned was vastly changed. His involvement in the war would add to the growing resentment towards the family. Much of the local antipathy stemmed from the actions of his father, William J.H. Tyrrell (1851–1933) and his role as a land agent and JP in both Kildare and King's County (now Offaly) (fig. 15.4). At various times this antipathy had manifested itself in agrarian outrage and violence on the estate. Indeed, the Tyrrells had experienced these outrages as early as the 1860s when William's mother, Mary Ann, took the family to live in France for a period.[1] Moreover, by the 1880s the Tyrrell brothers, William J.H. and Garrett (1853–1912), the latter also a land agent, were regularly denounced from Land League platforms. It was during this time that William J.H. earned the sobriquet from local nationalists of 'Billy the Devil'.

The outbreak of war in 1914 did not impact upon the Tyrrells to any great extent, and it was hardly expected that the conflict would last long enough that their children would grow up to participate in it. However, having reached eighteen Willie was anxious to enlist and serve his country. For his father, Willie's service was a double-edged sword. On the one hand, as the most prominent public official and landowner in the area, Tyrrell was adamant that the family be seen to be contributing to the war effort. In nearby Edenderry, for example, over 300 men had enlisted by the time Willie saw active service in 1916.[2] However, for the family, his war service was fraught with worry. These fears were compounded by the losses that families of neighbouring country houses had already suffered in the early months of the conflict, most notably the deaths of their friends

---

1 Various correspondence of Mary Ann Tyrrell, 1863 (private possession).   2 See Catherine Watson, *Edenderry and the Great War, 1914–1918* (Naas, 2014).

15.1 Ballindoolin House, *c*.1912 (William Upton).

William and Sylvester Rait Kerr of Rathmoyle in November 1914 and May 1915 respectively. Over time, however, the family took immense pride in Willie's involvement. At Ballindoolin, photographs from the trenches and of Willie in military regalia adorned the house. His father regularly attended recruitment rallies and published his son's correspondence in local newspapers, even in those newspapers that had been hostile to the family during the Land League days. In later years, Willie's younger brother, Robert (Bobby) J.H. Tyrrell (1906–93), proudly recalled Willie's wartime experience: 'My brother [served] through the war and on one occasion was shelled for six days. They started with three officers and three hundred men. At the end, William Upton was the only officer alive with seventy-five men.'[3]

Willie received his commission in the Royal Irish Rifles from the Royal Military College Sandhurst in August 1915. He initially served with the Special Reserve in Dublin, and in March 1916, less than a month before the Easter Rising, there was considerable excitement at Ballindoolin when Willie received news that he would be sent to France (fig. 15.2). Following the call up to serve in France, accompanied by his father, Willie left Ballindoolin for Dublin, from where he set sail for France three days later. By now the family was actively

3 Copy of a letter, undated, written by Bobby Tyrrell (Ballindoolin Papers, OPW/Maynooth University Archive and Research Centre, uncatalogued). Unless otherwise stated all primary sources in this chapter are taken from the Ballindoolin Papers.

15.2 William Upton Tyrrell, pictured in 1916 having been commissioned into the Royal Irish Rifles (William Upton).

engaged in the war effort, so much so that Willie could boast that 'Daddy says if Garrett gets a commission there will be 12 of the family in the army.'[4] These family members included cousins in Canada who had enlisted there; Jasper Robert Joly Tyrrell (1876–1951) of Ballinderry House, Carbury, who served in the Indian Medical Service and reached the rank of major; and Edward William Mather of Brookville, near Edenderry, who was married to Jasper's sister.

The adjustment to life in the trenches was for Willie, like for so many others, extremely difficult. Within weeks of his arrival in France the glamour of war had faded. Writing to his father in June he remarked that 'this is the wettest day that I have ever seen in this country and the place is a foot deep in mud'.[5] He was also frequently frustrated by the long periods of stalemate, and even after he had joined the RAF he found that flying depended on the weather. Indeed, he often poked fun at the fact that his unit were 'fine-weather soldiers' who depended on cloud cover for carrying out raids. During what he called 'dud' days when there was no action, long hours were spent sleeping, eating, reading and writing, the last reflected in his voluminous wartime correspondence. Occasionally he even took the time to write to family members in French. These letters also reveal the casual nature of the conflict, which allowed men to take excursions into areas unaffected by the war. For example, on one occasion he informed his mother that 'as there was nothing doing we had a run down to Bologna'.[6]

These periods of inaction were to be rudely disturbed in early July when Willie was confronted with the horrors of the Somme. Back in Edenderry, the death toll at the Somme was quickly revealed and included Private George Nelson of the 9th Battalion, Royal Inniskilling Fusiliers. His father, Henry, was the clerk of the Edenderry petty sessions and a friend of the Tyrrells. Within days of Nelson's death, on 6 July, Willie Tyrrell was wounded 'in the chest but not seriously' and sent to London to convalesce.[7] The ease with which news and people travelled during the war was reflected in the fact that his father went to visit him in London, noting in his diary that he had 'stayed in the Grosvenor Hotel – an awful swindling hotel'.[8]

After spending a number of weeks in London, Willie returned to Ballindoolin for further recuperation, where he accompanied his father on estate agency business in the morning and spent the rest of the time hunting, shooting and attending parties at neighbouring country houses (fig. 15.3). In September he attended a two-day grouse shoot at Rathmoyle, the home of the Rait Kerr family near Rhode; his father noted that six guns had shot '95 grouse, 3 partridge and 1 hare'. No doubt what he had witnessed at the Somme was related to those in attendance at these gatherings, particularly to the Rait Kerrs, who had lost two

4 William Upton Tyrrell (hereafter WUT) to his mother, Elizabeth Tyrrell (hereafter ET), 4 Apr. 1916.   5 WUT to his father, William J.H. Tyrrell (hereafter WJHT), 6 June 1916. 6 WUT to ET, 14 Aug. 1917.   7 WUT to WJHT, 6 July 1916.   8 Diary of William J.H. Tyrrell, 14 July 1916.

15.3 William Upton Tyrrell shooting at Ballindoolin, 1916, while recovering from injuries sustained at the battle of the Somme (William Upton).

sons and had another two serving in France. There was a realization by all that Willie had been one of the lucky ones to have survived the carnage. Towards the end of October, after almost two months of shoots and hunts in the Kildare countryside, Willie was passed fit by a medical board in Dublin. Two days later, having visited his younger sister Victoria, or Minnie as she was affectionately called, in school at Bray, he rejoined his unit in Belfast. It was difficult for the family to part with Willie on this occasion, particularly when word filtered through that Edward William Mather had died of wounds received at the Somme. The death of Mather, who had recently married Harriet Tyrrell (1882– 1969), a cousin of William Upton, shook the Tyrrell household, William J.H. simply noting in his diary: 'Heard that Willie Mather had died of his wounds in France.'[9]

The family were obviously very proud of Willie's war service, and news from France and elsewhere was welcomed, which they subsequently published in the pages of the *Leinster Leader* and other local newspapers. They did so to encourage recruitment in Edenderry and its environs, which had slowed

9 Diary of William J.H. Tyrrell, 16 Oct. 1916.

15.4 William J.H. Tyrrell (1851–1933), land agent and justice of the peace (William Upton).

dramatically by 1916. Willie's sometimes humorous letters were used as a means of encouraging others to join the war effort. For the family, this daily correspondence also reassured them of his safety, and was especially welcome given the mounting death toll. They appreciated his news after he had joined the Royal Flying Corps (RFC); but although he tried to explain his role, it was difficult for them to understand aeroplanes.

The 1916 Easter Rising had a profound effect on the Tyrrell family, and their private correspondence and diaries provide a remarkable insight into the thoughts of both country-house owners and of Irishmen serving in the British Army at the time. On Easter Monday, the day the Rising commenced, there was no imminent threat, and although it was 'a very wet, stormy day in Edenderry', William J.H. Tyrrell went to fish at Kinnegad, where he caught 'six nice trout'.[10] Later that day his children Minnie and Bobby went to Edenderry and posted canvas shoes to Willie at the front. It was not until Tuesday that word of the Rising reached Ballindoolin, and later that night he visited the neighbouring Mather family at Brookville to enquire if there was any further news. Throughout the week information remained sketchy, and since no mail or trains arrived from Dublin, the Rising seemed far removed and there appeared little danger of local unrest. However, on Friday all that changed when Tyrrell noted in his diary that 'guns bombarding Dublin heard very plainly here at Ballindoolin'. On the following day Tyrrell attended the Edenderry petty sessions, but no business took place as martial law had been declared. According

10 Ibid., 24 Apr. 1916.

to Tyrrell there was a meeting of 'rebels' in Edenderry to promote a rising, but that he had 'taken precautions and the rebels went home quietly'. On Monday 1 May Tyrrell again walked to Edenderry to get news and was delighted to hear that the Dublin rebels had surrendered.

In France, Willie Tyrrell reacted angrily to the news that rebellion had broken out in Dublin. Writing to his mother, Willie exclaimed: 'Oh! If I could only get at those fellows now … if only I had been another month at home.' Hundreds of miles away, he was tormented by the constant rumours that circulated in the trenches and believed that 'it must have been a terrible business in Dublin'. Affirming the attitude of his comrades in France, Willie wrote: 'All the Irishmen here are frightfully mad with the scoundrels and want to get back to get a shot at them.'[11] He also feared for the safety of his family, perhaps because of the long-standing local tensions. Eventually, once the postal service resumed after the Rising, word from Ballindoolin confirmed that the family were not in danger; Willie 'simply shouted with joy'.[12] Having read in the French newspapers that the Rising had been crushed, he wrote ecstatically to his mother: 'I am very glad that the country is quiet around you and I hope it remains so.' His antipathy to the rebels was also made clear in his reference to one of the most notorious episodes of the Rising, which involved Captain J.C. Bowen-Colthurst of Bantry House, Co. Cork, who was responsible for the murder of the suffragist Francis Skeffington on 27 April at Portobello Barracks in Dublin. Tyrrell remarked: 'I hope the officer who ordered the execution of Skeffington will get off alright. I know him intimately but think his name has not been published.'[13] In further correspondence he related how rumours abounded in the trenches that the town of Edenderry had been overtaken by rebels and that the furniture factory, Alesburys, had been seized. Remarkably, this news had been given to him by an Edenderry native, Sergeant William Carroll (1881–1953), following a chance encounter in France. Carroll had been employed with another of the Tyrrell families at Clayton, near Carbury in Co. Kildare.[14]

In the wake of the Rising the Tyrrells received copies of oaths allegedly found on prisoners in Dublin that claimed that the 'Sinn Féiners' were intent on massacring all Protestants. The oaths read:

> I will wade knee deep in blood and do so as King James did and I further swear to owe no allegiance to any Protestant or heretic sovereign ruler …
> I will aid and assist with all my might and strength when called upon to massacre Protestants and out away heretics.[15]

The oath also called on those proclaiming it to have no dealings with judges or magistrates. In addition, a 'Sinn Féin hymn of hate', also said to have originated

11 WUT to WJHT, 28 Apr. 1916.   12 WUT to ET, 5 May 1916.   13 Ibid., 14 May 1916.
14 Ibid., 29 Apr. 1916.   15 'Copy of an oath found on prisoners in Dublin following the

15.5 William Upton Tyrrell on horseback (pictured right) in France, 1917 (William Upton).

during Easter Week, included the lines that the rebels would 'make the cowards yell, send them god of vengeance, to their place in hell'. These threats may have alarmed W.J.H. Tyrrell, a member of the Edenderry Orange Order who had served on the national executive. In addition, he was also a prominent member of the King's County branch of the Irish Unionist Alliance and in 1918 supported the 'Call to Unionists' issued by the Southern Unionist Alliance to reaffirm loyalty to the crown. Vehemently opposed to breaking the Union, as early as 1893 Tyrrell had attended Unionist demonstrations in London, and organized local meetings to denounce plans for Home Rule.[16] At his behest, as a mark of respect for those killed and injured on the Somme in 1916, there was no display or celebration of the annual 12 July commemoration in Edenderry. However, the changing nature of Irish society was very evident to the Tyrrells, and the continued rise of Sinn Féin was something that greatly troubled the family. This unease did not go unnoticed by Willie, who remarked in November 1917 that 'you all seem to be expecting a rebellion any day'.[17] Writing to his father that same month Willie claimed that the rebels were merely 'blackguards' but hoped that 'the military will keep them under their eye'.[18] In May of the following year he again related his fears about the upsurge in rebellious activity but was happy to hear that 'the military are in Edenderry' and that 'it would be a good thing if they took the market house'. Willie also used his correspondence

rebellion, May 1916'.   **16** See Ciarán Reilly, *Edenderry 1820–1920: popular politics and Downshire rule* (Dublin, 2007).   **17** WUT to ET, 10 Nov. 1917.   **18** WUT to WJHT, 11 Nov. 1917.

to reassure the family, and the wider community, that they had not suffered military setbacks, as 'the rebels' at Edenderry had claimed. As a result of the Sinn Féin agitation that followed, William Tyrrell, in his own words, did not 'venture out after dark'. Instead the family confined itself to Ballindoolin, which continued to receive visitors. Prior to the outbreak of the Great War, Ballindoolin had been very much a visiting house for the neighbouring gentry. In addition, the workers were entertained with 'magic lantern' displays and other amusements. By the end of the war only a tiny staff remained, including a cook, housemaid, gardener, yard man and house servant.

The sheer scale of death at the Somme and, indeed, the injuries he received had a lasting impact on Willie Tyrrell. In December 1917, he passed the spot where he had been on 1 July 1916, and although he did not say so directly, it was obvious that the Somme, where hundreds of thousands of men had been killed or wounded or had gone missing, had a profound effect on him. In an effort to block the reality of the situation, Willie continued to write anxiously for news of home. When he could take leave, he returned without delay to Ballindoolin. Although the family 'did not keep Christmas' in 1916 on account of his absence, by 28 December he had returned home for the shooting. To Minnie and Bobby he wrote frequently, enquiring about life at boarding school, and sending presents. In 1917, for example, he sent a football for Bobby, which, he was glad to hear, was 'a great success … it is the best game he could play'. He was also anxious that Bobby would learn how to ride, hoping that he would be soon able to take part in hunts. Willie was also particularly anxious that Minnie would continue to correspond with his fiancée, writing: 'I am glad you approve of Nellie, but knew it could not be otherwise'.[19] Willie frequently received packages of partridges, apples and clothes from family and friends.

In the summer of 1918, Willie Tyrrell transferred to the RFC and underwent training near Kent. After his first flight in an aeroplane, he wrote excitedly to his mother: 'little did you think a few years ago that I would take to the air' (fig. 15.6).[20] Such was his excitement that he wondered 'why on earth I did not go to flying corps long ago'. His initial duties included photographing enemy positions, which he noted was quite easy as they were flying at 4,500 ft and at 55–60 miles per hour. Although he initially reassured his father that he was not involved in military engagements, he soon was, and in September scored six victories, four kills and two 'out of controls', flying Bristol Fighters as an observer and gunner with 22 Squadron. In one of these engagements, his unit made a trip behind enemy lines where they shot at some 'Huns'. By this stage the demoralized German forces were retreating and showing little resistance. It was, Willie said, 'like shooting snipe at Ballindoolin'.[21] Although his commission

---

19 WUT to William J.H. Tyrell, 8 Dec. 1917; WUT to his sister, Victoria Tyrrell, 16 Sept. [1918?].   20 WUT to ET, 14 July 1918.   21 WUT to WJHT, 28 Sept. 1918.

15.6 William Upton Tyrrell pictured in the cockpit of a plane, September 1918.

into the RFC had reinvigorated the war-weary Willie Tyrrell, news of the Armistice was greeted with joy. He longed to return to Ballindoolin and to bring his fiancée there, telling his father: 'I just can't write a letter this evening the news is too astonishing to believe … did we actually fire our last shot today and did we chase our last Hun?'[22]

Back at Ballindoolin, during the War of Independence, 1919–21, the family became targets of local IRA battalions determined to settle old scores. Some of these 'old' grievances stemmed from the Land League days of the 1880s and the actions of his father as a land agent. In addition, the Tyrrells claimed that Willie's war service contributed to the intimidation that occurred throughout the War of Independence. Public opinion towards them changed dramatically following the Easter Rising. It was a similar fate for the neighbouring Beaumont Nesbitts at Tubberdaly House, near Rhode. Recalling his childhood, Frederick Beaumont Nesbitt (1893–1971) noted that he could not 'recall a single incident during my boyhood when hostility was shown either to myself or a member of my family at least not until the outbreak of Easter week 1916'.[23] On 28 July 1920, Ballindoolin House was surrounded and attacked by a party of forty-five armed men who had arrived in five cars and on a horse-drawn cart and numerous bicycles. The raiders shattered the windows with bullets and smashed the hall

22 WUT to WJHT, 10 Nov. 1918.   **23** 'Notes compiled by William J.H. Tyrell re. attacks on Ballindoolin, 1920–21'; memoir of Frederick Beaumont Nesbitt (Liddell Hart Centre for Military Archives, ref.).

door, but failed to get inside the house. William J.H. Tyrrell managed to shoot and wound two of the men. In the weeks that followed, the intimidation continued, large groups visiting Ballindoolin, where they would spend the night whistling on the lawn. In September Ballindoolin was one of several country houses raided for arms, and a number of sporting guns were taken. On 11 July 1921, the house was again attacked, this time with the intent of burning it down. The attempt failed, but the raiders managed to set alight the turf sheds, the fire from which burned for three days. All through the night the house was targeted and the 'glass was cut out of the windows over our heads'. None of the Tyrrells were injured in either attack but they were said to have been 'nerve wrecking experiences'.[24] Elizabeth Tyrrell, William's wife, suffered panic attacks and spent about six months abroad trying to recover. The attacks did not end with independence and on 15 December 1922, in the course of agency duties, William J.H. was again attacked on a farm and badly beaten. Tyrrell believed that only for the fact that his young son, Bobby, then aged sixteen, was with him he would have been even more seriously injured. On a number of occasions he was told that plans were being made to assassinate him and that Michael Foley, the Edenderry veteran of Easter Week, was the 'ringleader'.[25] Indeed, even the local Catholic priest, Revd Paul Murphy, warned him that he would be shot if he continued to act as a magistrate and land agent. Despite these constant threats to life and property, Tyrrell continued to operate the business until his death in 1933.

There were no burning tar barrels to welcome the returning Willie Tyrrell from the war in 1918. In December, en route to Bournemouth, he informed his father to go ahead with the winter shooting event and not to wait for him. This request came as a surprise to the family: throughout the war Tyrrell had longed for the grouse and pheasant shoots at Ballindoolin and on neighbouring estates. His youth had been spent traversing the countryside around the Kildare and King's County border with his favourite guns. During his time in the trenches he sarcastically remarked that 'somehow I rather think snipe would be hard to hit with 18 pounders'. He also longed for the old company of neighbours, with whom he had played tennis, croquet, cards and billiards. However, for his family and friends there would be no going back to that way of life. Indeed, Willie never returned permanently to Ireland. In April 1920, he married and rejoined the Royal Irish Rifles, where he served as a lieutenant in the 1st Battalion. In 1922, he applied for his service medals. War had taken its toll on him, and as late as 1929 there were concerns within the family about his financial troubles.[26] Despite this he later served in World War Two in India and the Far East, and died in Lincolnshire in 1979, aged eighty-three.

24 'Notes compiled relative to compensation following attacks on Ballindoolin House, 1921'.
25 Diary of William J.H. Tyrrell, 22 Jan. 1921.   26 WUT to WJHT, 29 Feb. 1929.

The Talbot family at war

DAWN WEBSTER

The earl of Shrewsbury's youngest son, the Hon. Alfred Talbot, lived with his wife and four children (Humphrey, Bridget, Geoffrey and Kathleen) at Little Gaddesden House in the village of Little Gaddesden, Hertfordshire, on the edge of the beautiful Ashridge estate. Their uncle, Adelbert Cust, 3rd Earl Brownlow, owned the enormous Gothic Revival Ashridge House as well as Belton House in Lincolnshire. Other aunts and uncles lived in stately homes and manor houses across England – Blickling Hall, Wilton House, Merton Hall, Ingestre Hall, Alton Towers and Kiplin Hall – and Curraghmore in Co. Waterford. These historic houses in rolling parklands were worlds away from the homes and shelters the Talbot siblings would occupy during the Great War. Bridget Talbot was the last owner of Kiplin Hall in Yorkshire's North Riding. She and her younger sister, Kathleen, kept many family letters and other items, and it is from these that we discover their wartime stories.

Bridget Talbot (1885–1971) was a spirited young woman of twenty-nine in the summer of 1914. She was interested in politics and already well travelled. Determined to be a part of what was coming, her preparations began before war was declared.[1] In July she attended a Red Cross course on home nursing and in August passed written and oral examinations at the end of an emergency course of instruction in first aid at Regent Street Polytechnic.[2] Bridget founded the Little Gaddesden cooperative allotment scheme in her home village to ensure that food would be produced locally in the event of a national shortage – a forerunner of the Dig for Victory campaign of World War Two.

By October 1914, Bridget was a member of the Committee for War Refugees at Alexandra Palace in London, one of the depots set up to house Belgian men, women and children who had fled to England following the German invasion in August. Copies of her lists of refugees who were sent on to Birmingham that month remain in Kiplin's archives.[3] We know less about her activities in 1915, apart from a letter dated 11 December thanking Bridget for her work with the Red Cross Voluntary Aid Detachment selection board,[4] which recruited young women volunteers to train as nursing assistants. London was far removed from the real action taking place on the Continent, but Bridget was about to become part of that action.

---

1 All references, unless otherwised stated, are taken from the Kiplin Archive [hereafter KA] on deposit at North Yorkshire County Record Office, Northallerton (ZBL items) and at Kiplin Hall.   2 KA, 1992.1027.32, scrapbook 32.   3 KA, ZBL B06-F05-D09.   4 KA, 1992.1027.32, scrapbook 32.

16.1 Bridget Talbot with Italian soldiers at a canteen just behind the Italian–Austrian Front in 1916 (© Kiplin Hall).

In January 1916, she travelled via Paris to the war zone on the Italian–Austrian Front, where her work was to continue until 1919. She joined a small team of English women led by Mrs Marie Watkins, who set up canteens and first aid stations at Cervignano and Cormons, near to the fighting. Funds to run the stations were provided by the Pro Italia Society in London, by other well-wishers and by Mrs Watkins' friends, while the volunteers paid their own expenses. Bridget and her co-workers received hundreds of thousands of wounded Italian soldiers from the mountain trenches, fed them and administered first aid before sending them on by train to the base hospitals (fig. 16.1). A letter to a friend written on 22 January, shortly after her arrival in Cormons, gives a remarkable insight into the conditions she faced:

> Please forgive this untidy scrawl, but I have so little time to write. It is extraordinary being up here so near the fighting – the guns make a terrific noise. An Austrian aeroplane dropped bombs nearby two days ago; one landed less than 15 yards off us, but luckily no-one was seriously hurt … We are in a very dangerous position here, as we have no dug-out and they always try and bomb the station. I suppose when some of us are killed they

will begin making one. Being British, it is beneath our dignity to ask for one! We have 'wounded' trains come up here with 200 or 300 men straight out of the trenches, mostly. They very often haven't had food for two or three days, and come down in the most awful state. We also make things for the Field Hospitals which are very poorly equipped.[5]

The letter continues on an entirely different note: 'We had a delightful evening yesterday … went to an Italian house and a Pernaza sergeant, a Roman opera singer, sang – a magnificent voice … It felt very strange: the opera singing going on and the guns booming away outside and the audience consisting of us and lots of Italian officers'.[6]

Bridget's diary records daily events and also her emotions: 'Rose at 5 in the pitch dark to do train of wounded. Felt very weird & warlike crawling down feeding men by the light of a lantern with the sun rising over the A[ustrian] hills' (5 February).[7] She soon learned more about the conditions endured by the Italian soldiers, as she recorded in a letter of 23 February:

> The weather has quite changed, and simply deluges of rain and snow today, and the roads knee deep in mud … We had some wretched men in this morning, their boots coming to bits and soaked through, and filthy after two months in the trenches, and the last bit in the front line, where most of their regiment had been cut to bits last week. There is one place where the English ambulances go where the trenches are on the edge of a precipice at the top of a snow mountain, and everything and everybody, including the wounded, have to be run up and down several thousand feet with a rope and basket.[8]

On 9 March, eight officers of the 1st Grenadiers invited the English ladies to dine. In his speech, Captain Pini thanked them for the honour of accepting the invitation and continued: 'I hope that they will remember this evening as one of the most joyful of our common military campaign – that is what we consider it – our charming and sympathetic companions of the war',[9] and then appointed them honorary officers of the regiment. Bridget wrote on the handwritten menu in pencil: 'Dinner given by the Roman Grenadiers … the night before the battle of Monte Santo – in a barn with candles in bottles. Only 1 officer came back alive.'[10] Five days later she recorded in her diary:

> After dinner we went out & watched the battle on Monte San Michele. The shells & shrapnel bursting continually & the Austrian incandescent searchlights flaring up. The 3 first peaks are Italian but neither side held

5 KA, 1992.1014.137.2.   6 Ibid.   7 KA, ZBL B09-F02-D01, p. 9.   8 KA, 1992.1014.137.6. 9 KA, 1992.1014.137.8.   10 KA, 2008.3.40.

the last point. Telephone messages kept on coming through. 'The Italians have reached the top.' 'The Austrians are advancing & counter-attacking.' 'If the Italians can hold for an hour they will be able to dig themselves in' & so on. Every now & then the firing stopped & then one knew they were charging with the bayonet. It was disgusting to stand there & almost hear them charging & not be in the thick of it oneself.[11]

The weather changed in mid-March and Bridget's letter of 17 March conjures up an idyllic image:

It has suddenly turned roasting hot here – too heavenly. Yesterday I went up to the hills and basked on a bank of hot smelling thyme in the roasting sun with bees and butterflies buzzing about and gurgling streams all round. Peach and almond trees all pink and the ground one solid mass of primroses, pink and blue bugloss, periwinkles, sweet smelling white and purple violets, anemones, cistus and other things I don't know the name of.[12]

The floral delight and the Italian spring represented a release from the strains of war.

Bridget also undertook work for the local hospitals, arranging for the delivery of the supplies of bedding and clothing sent from Britain, helping the nursing staff, talking to patients and rolling bandages. She sometimes travelled to the Villa Trento to help Countess Feodora Gleichen and her sister Mrs Nina Hollings with their work of developing x-rays to assist surgeons before they operated on the wounded, commenting on 21 April:

Countess Gleichen telephoned in despair for one of us to come and help … It is extraordinarily interesting work, but one feels very terrified of doing the wrong thing when developing, as the smallest mistake may mean spoiling the plate, and possibly losing the man's life … It is rather alarming doing it, as we only had a hurried lesson from the departing assistant … We have to go right up and develop in a car under fire.[13]

The death of her beloved younger brother, Geoffrey, on 29 June was a devastating blow. Bridget's diary ends shortly before this occurred, except for a torn sheet listing items of clothing that presumably she wished to take when travelling back to England for his funeral. There is a gap of several months in her surviving letters home.

In the summer of 1917, the British 7th Division was sent to Italy to help in the fight against Austria. Mrs Watkins' team transferred to work under the

11 KA, ZBL B09-F02-D01, p. 29.   12 KA, 1992.1014.137.10.   13 KA, 1992.1014.137.16.

16.2 Time for fun was much needed during the war. A smiling Bridget (centre) attends a horse show in September 1918 (© Kiplin Hall).

British Red Cross and Bridget ran canteens and recreation huts for the British battalions (fig. 16.2). She wrote to her younger sister, Kathleen, on 12 June:

> We had a terrific day yesterday, dealing out thousands of cigarettes to all the batteries from 9.30 to 6 when Gen. H. came down & gave us a very fierce lesson in storekeeping & accounts for 2 hours … to-day we hadn't counted the pen nibs in the boxes – a gt. crime. He is an extraordinary person for going into every detail & now I have to deal with about 6 or 7 army account books I am sure I shall make a hideous mess of it! It is satisfactory that there is no other canteen of any sort and the men are delighted.[14]

Bridget took part in the chaotic and frightening retreat from the front during the battle of Caporetto in late October 1917:

14 KA, 2013.6.149.

Some of the patients from the Hosp. had to walk 40 miles – two typhoid cases – & only had 2 sardines & a bit of chocolate. However they are none the worse. One man who had been through Mons said it was a cake walk compared to this! ... Knowing the roads I was able to get our motor along quite away from the crush till we got to the Tagliamento. Our big gun was only able to get over the bridge by the officer standing at the head of the bridge & shooting down the crowd. Several It[alian] officers have committed suicide & there is a gt. mystery over the fate of Capello. It is all too awful. V[illa] Trento nurses had to walk 20 & 30 miles in the pouring rain.[15]

But she was still in Italy a year later when the Austro-Hungarian Army was finally defeated, and she remained with the Red Cross until 1919. Bridget was awarded the Italian military medal for valour, the Croce al Merito di Guerra, and, in 1920, the OBE. However, this was not the end of her war work. In 1920 she went to Touzla camp near Constantinople, which housed 2,000 Russian war refugees, and later set up a cooperative farm colony for refugees in Asia Minor. Her letters and diary give a remarkable flavour of the danger and fun she experienced during the war.

Kathleen Talbot (1893–1958) was a shy twenty-year-old at the start of the war. Her mother had died in 1912 and her father in 1913, so her Talbot and de Grey aunts and uncles took her under their collective wings. In October 1914, Kathleen's aunt, the Hon. Mrs Francis Hodgson (née Odeyne de Grey), set up a British Red Cross Voluntary Aid Detachment (VAD) hospital with fifty beds in the Town Hall in Stratford-upon-Avon, Warwickshire, to receive wounded soldiers brought back from France. By March 1915, the doctors and VAD nurses had cared for 139 casualties and it was clear that larger premises were required. Odeyne and her husband, the Revd Francis Hodgson, offered their own home, Clopton House. Neighbours, townspeople and friends provided the finance to build three wards in its grounds and sent annual subscriptions to assist with the hospital running costs. The wards were named Douty, Gibbins and Wills after major donors.

Kathleen enrolled as a VAD in May 1915 and nursed at Clopton War Hospital under her aunt Odeyne, who was Commandant of the Stratford war hospitals from 1914 until 1919. Her cousin Avis Hodgson also nursed there. The girls were popular with their patients, many of whom sent notes back to Clopton after they had been transferred to convalescent homes or returned to France, often writing: 'wish I was back at Clopton'. Kathleen sent letters, food parcels and photographs to many of the 'boys' whom she had nursed and kept their letters to her: 'Everybody who writes to me from Clopton thanks me for the work I did whilst there, you all forget that chap with a hole in his thigh, who was in bed for seven

15 KA, 2013.6.159.

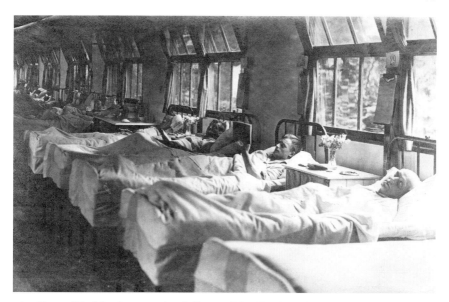

16.3 Douty Ward in the grounds of Clopton War Hospital, Stratford-upon-Avon, where Kathleen Talbot worked as a VAD nurse from May 1915 until January 1918 (© Jandy Spurway).

weeks & pretty helpless & yet never wanted for anything';[16] 'Dear Nurse, Just a line to let you know I am alright. I wrote this letter before I went into the trenches and could not get the letter away so I am sending it now for it is better late than never so cheer up and I hope you are in the best of health. Yours truly, Ginger'.[17] Some letters came from German prisoner-of-war camps: 'Dear Miss Talbot, I received your P.C. stating that you had sent me a parcel of eatables through the Red Cross Society, and I am pleased to say I received it on 20th this month. I am very grateful to you for the contents which arrived here in an excellent condition' (fig. 16.3).[18]

None of Kathleen's letters to her siblings in France and Italy survive, but we get a glimpse of what she was doing through their letters to her. She clearly spent a great deal of her free time and money sending parcels to Geoffrey, Bridget and Humphrey: 'Dearest K, Thank you very much for your letter – 2nd Nov. And for marrons glacés, truffles and foies gras – also a *Strand* magazine – You are wicked to keep on sending so many things – The socks will be most useful when they arrive as it is getting very cold in the air now';[19] 'My chocolate from K arrived & we thoroughly enjoyed it',[20] 'Thank you ever so much for the Fortnum & Mason things which arrived yesterday – biscuits, chocolates, sardines, turtle

16 Letter from W. Hearne, 4 Dec. 1915, KA, 2013.6.4. **17** Letter from A. Norton, n.d., KA, 2013.6.24. **18** Letter from E. Cooper, 21 Nov. 1915, KA, 2013.6.7. **19** Letter from Geoffrey Dunkirk, 6 Nov. 1915, KA, 2013.6.98. **20** Bridget Talbot diary, 27 Feb. 1918, KA, ZBL B09-F02-D01.

16.4 Geoffrey Talbot (centre) at Dunkirk aerodrome in France, 1915. He is wearing an extravagant fur coat for protection when flying an open-cockpit aircraft (© Kiplin Hall).

soup etc. All very good'.[21] She also sent magazines, books and board games to France for Humphrey's men and to Italy for Bridget's recreation huts.

In 1917, Kathleen was mentioned in despatches and promoted to Staff Nurse. But family letters show that, throughout the war, she wanted to nurse in France or Italy to be nearer to her brothers and sister. She finally transferred to Rouen

21 Letter from Humphrey Talbot, 25 June 1917, KA, 2013.6.85.

16.5 One of a number of aircraft crashes at Dunkirk aerodrome, 1915, from Geoffrey Talbot's photograph album (© Kiplin Hall).

in January 1918 and worked in several British Red Cross hospitals there until April 1919.

Geoffrey Talbot (1888–1916) was working for the East India Railway Company when war was declared. Not wanting to miss the action, he returned to England and by summer 1915 was training as a pilot with the rank of flight sub-lieutenant in the Royal Naval Air Service (fig. 16.4). His letters give remarkably light-hearted accounts of flights and fog and crash-landings, which must have been far from reassuring for his sisters. Flight was in its infancy and extremely dangerous. The lightweight wood-framed Avro and Caudron aircraft that Geoffrey flew were fragile and parachutes were not provided. The average life expectancy of RNAS pilots was just a few weeks or months, with many casualties occurring during training. Geoffrey received frequent praise from his commanding officer, who described him as 'a keen officer and a good aeroplane pilot'.[22] His uncle, Major General the Hon. Sir Reginald Talbot, wrote to Kathleen on 25 September 1915: 'I was able to run down to Dover to see Geoffrey fly. He does it beautifully and I felt very proud of him and I am sure he will distinguish himself if he gets the chance. He is as keen as mustard'.[23]

In October 1915, Geoffrey was transferred to Dunkirk with Fighting Squadron 'A' Group, No. 1 Wing, RNAS. Soon after he reported an accident to his sister Kathleen: '19.10.1915 – I managed to smash a machine yesterday – my

22 Certificate of instruction, 28 Aug. 1916, KA, ZBL B04-F02-D07.   **23** KA, 2013.6.119.

engine gave out and I came down plosh on Dunkerque beach and turned upside down! No damage to myself, but spoilt the look of machine absolutely' (fig. 16.5).[24] The officers lived remarkably well, with champagne, cigarettes and excellent food, which Geoffrey recorded in an album of photographs taken while he was stationed there. He also photographed a number of crashed aircraft.[25]

In 1916 Geoffrey was based at Dover, where there was plenty of activity from enemy aircraft and zeppelins. 'Gt air raid over Zeebruge & last Sunday over Dover. Geoff had nasty smash when chasing a German plane but luckily was not badly hurt. His machine crashed into one of the Dover forts & some barbed wire entanglements'.[26] He was not the only pilot to have a lucky escape: 'Do you remember Viney? He started off in another machine a day or two before, smashed up at Brooklands and then, just as he was starting from Chingford in the other machine he was to bring back, smashed that and turned upside down! Very bad luck – however he wasn't hurt'.[27] But some of Geoffrey's friends were not so lucky, as Geoffrey told Kathleen:

> Burlington Hotel, Dover, 2nd March 1916
> Yes, it was very sad about poor (?) Rosher. It happened about half a mile from the aerodrome and I am inclined to think something went wrong with him and not the machine, although it is very difficult to tell. They buried him here today. I am glad I didn't actually see it happen, although I was there immediately afterwards. He must have been killed instantaneously.[28]

His frustration with constantly failing aircraft and guns is often expressed: 'I wish they would give us good machines to fly as then we might have a chance to get a Hun – The one I was on had failed 4 times in 3 days just before it failed with me. The result is we can't catch them and people say we are no use'.[29] In April, Geoffrey was delighted to be promoted to flight lieutenant, but the crashes continued: 'I had another smash yesterday & turned upside down so am feeling rather as if I had been rolled down a hill in a barrel to-day! It was my fault & not the machine's on this occasion as I bounced when landing & she turned right over'.[30]

Geoffrey was clearly an excellent pilot, as he flew for a year while many others survived only a short time. He was killed when he crashed at Dover on 29 June. The official record says the 'aeroplane was caught by a gust of wind, side-slipped, and was wrecked'.[31] A letter from an eyewitness to his uncle describes how Geoffrey was caught in air currents above Fort Burgoyne where thousands of

24 Letter to Kathleen Talbot, KA, 2013.6.94.   25 KA, 1992.1027.39.   26 Bridget Talbot diary, 29 Mar. 1916, KA, ZBL B09-F02-D01, p. 33.   27 Letter to Kathleen Talbot, 11 Feb. 1916, KA, 2013. 6.101.   28 KA, 2013. 6.102.   29 Letter to Kathleen Talbot, 21 Mar. 1916, KA, 2013.6.104.   30 Letter to Reginal Talbot, 2 Apr. 1916, KA, 2008.3.30.   31 KA, ZBL B04-F02-D02; death notice in *Morning Post*, 7 July 1916.

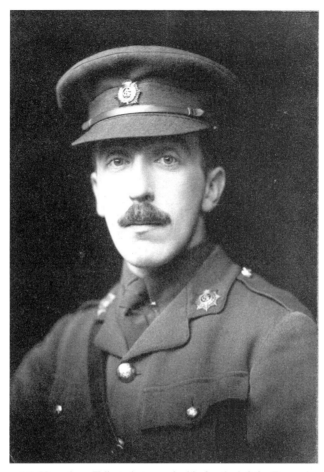

16.6 Humphrey Talbot photographed before he left for France in
January 1917 (© Kiplin Hall).

men were drilling and, to save many lives, he heroically sacrificed his own by
crash-landing outside the fort.[32] Bridget kept precious mementoes of Geoffrey
– his letters, battered silver cigarette case, RNAS cap badges and pilot's log
book. The final log-book entry is for 18 June, when he took off on a reconnaissance flight but had to turn back because of a faulty gun. He notes that he
'Bent axle on landing owing to striking ridge'.[33]

Geoffrey's family was one of so many devastated by the loss of a loved one.
Friends sent messages of sympathy to Kathleen:

32 KA, 2008.3.36.   **33** KA, 2008.3.33.

Hall's Croft, Stratford-on-Avon, 9 July 1916
Thank you so much for your letter this morning. It was good of you to write and I was very glad to hear from you just how it happened. You must be very, very proud of him – it gives one joy to hear of such unflinching courage – and I know it must comfort your brave heart.[34]

Military service for Humphrey Talbot (1883–1944) followed that of his sisters and younger brother (fig. 16.6). Like Geoffrey, he was working in India at the outbreak of war and remained there until late 1916. In January 1917, he embarked for France as a lieutenant in the Army Service Corps. It was less glamorous than flying, but its soldiers were frequently under enemy fire and faced constant danger as they delivered munitions and essential supplies to troops at the front. Humphrey's letters to Kathleen during 1917 give a flavour of his time there:

We left the base about 10 days ago and made our journey up here in 4 days stopping at various places en route. The roads very bad at first with deep snow but we gradually left it behind. Here I am billeted with a lady with a furious temper. She allows me to sleep but not to have meals so for 2 or 3 days Crawford and I have been eating under a tarpaulin rigged up in the street and doing our own cooking … We went to take stores up to the battery position the same night we arrived in the district. It is close to the line … The other af[ternoon] I took 62 men to have baths which they were very grateful for.[35]

And two days later, on 27 February, he wrote to tell her that 'I was out all last night carting shells to the battery which is a long way from here and close to the trenches. We have to take the gas masks and steel helmets when we go up there – rather weird doing it all in the dark.'[36]

Like everyone else, Humphrey was becoming weary of the war. On 31 March 1917 he wrote: 'The Boche has been more lively lately round here & has been shelling several of the villages we pass through and also dropping shells near our Battery. I wish the beastly war would get on & get finished, but it seems likely to go on for ages yet and probably starvation all round will end it rather than actual fighting'.[37] But there was the possibility that Kathleen might transfer to a hospital in France: 'It would be very nice if you could manage to get out here and be somewhere near. There are plenty of Casualty Clearing Stations about and a Hospital on the most approved lines in a village about 2 miles away', he told her on 25 April.[38] A month earlier he had mentioned there was even a chance that a recently bereaved uncle might travel to France: 'I wonder what we can invent to

34 KA, 2013.6.127.   35 KA, 2013.6.40.   36 KA, 2013.6.41.   37 KA, 2013.6.46.   38 KA, 2013.6.51.

interest Uncle Addy … he would find a trip out here very interesting & he could probably manage to see all that is possible'.[39] Humphrey felt that the front in France had an appeal as a tourist destination.

Writing on 24 July, he was grateful for Kathleen's parcels: 'The books and papers all go on to the men who very much appreciate them. They too practically get no amusement except a game of cards or a game they play with halfpennies on the principle of knucklebones'.[40] Five days later on 29 July he added: 'Very many thanks for a parcel from F[ortnum] and Mason wh[ich] also arrived tonight. I am going to have a whitebait supper! That ready-mixed cocoa is an excellent idea and very useful out here. I shall become quite fat with all the things you have sent out'.[41]

The story of the Talbot family comes full circle with the last known photograph of the three surviving siblings together.[42] It was taken in 1930 during Queen Mary's visit to Swakeleys, an Elizabethan house in Middlesex that Humphrey bought to save from developers. The Great War had changed all their lives, and the world of country houses, forever.

39 KA, 2013.6.46.   40 KA, 2013.6.69.   41 KA, 2013.6.71.   42 KA, 1992.1027.43, scrap-book 43, p. 1.

Index

by Eve Power